Edexcel GCSE (9–1)

Business

Helen Coupland-Smith   Andrew Redfern   Catherine Richards   Ian Rowbory   Julie Smith

Pearson

Published by Pearson Education Limited, 80 Strand, London, WC2R 0RL.

www.pearsonschoolsandfecolleges.co.uk

Copies of official specifications for all Edexcel qualifications may be found on the website: www.edexcel.com

Text © Pearson Education.
Typeset by Tech-Set Ltd
Illustrations by Tech-Set Ltd
Original illustrations © Pearson Education
Designed by Colin Tilley Loughrey
Cover photo: © Getty|Hero Images © Getty|Carlina Teteris © Getty|Andy Smith © Getty|andresr
© Getty|Squaredpixels © Getty|Plume Creative © Alamy|JOHN KELLERMAN © Alamy|Ammentorp
Photography © Shutterstock|alphaspirit © Shutterstock|ESB Essentials © Shutterstock|mavo
© Shutterstock|Eugene Partyzan © Shutterstock|Savanevich Viktar © Shutterstock|Uber Images
© Shutterstock|blvdone © Getty|Micheal Blann

First published 2017

19 18 17 16
10 9 8 7 6 5 4 3 2 1

The rights of Helen Coupland-Smith, Andrew Redfern, Catherine Richards, Ian Rowbory and Julie Smith to be
identified as authors of this work has been asserted by them in accordance with the Copyright, Designs and
Patents Act 1988.

British Library Cataloguing in Publication Data
A catalogue record for this book is available from the British Library

ISBN 978 1 29217 984 1

Printed and bound in the UK by Bell & Bain Ltd, Glasgow

Acknowledgements
For image and text acknowledgements please see page 296.

A note from the publisher
In order to ensure that this resource offers high-quality support for the associated Pearson qualification, it
has been through a review process by the awarding body. This process confirms that this resource fully covers
the teaching and learning content of the specification or part of a specification at which it is aimed. It also
confirms that it demonstrates an appropriate balance between the development of subject skills, knowledge
and understanding, in addition to preparation for assessment.

Endorsement does not cover any guidance on assessment activities or processes (e.g. practice questions or
advice on how to answer assessment questions), included in the resource nor does it prescribe any particular
approach to the teaching or delivery of a related course.

While the publishers have made every attempt to ensure that advice on the qualification and its assessment
is accurate, the official specification and associated assessment guidance materials are the only authoritative
source of information and should always be referred to for definitive guidance.

Pearson examiners have not contributed to any sections in this resource relevant to examination papers for
which they have responsibility.

Examiners will not use endorsed resources as a source of material for any assessment set by Pearson.

Endorsement of a resource does not mean that the resource is required to achieve this Pearson qualification,
nor does it mean that it is the only suitable material available to support the qualification, and any resource
lists produced by the awarding body shall include this and other appropriate resources.

Contents

Welcome to Edexcel GCSE (9–1) Business
Developing Enterprising Minds

Congratulations on choosing to study Edexcel GCSE Business. This exciting and challenging course will introduce you to the dynamic world of business. It covers a broad range of topics that are designed to provide you with the knowledge and understanding that underpin modern business. You will learn how entrepreneurs turn simple ideas into profitable businesses, as well as how companies operate and make important business decisions on a local, national and global scale. Above all, the course will encourage you to become enterprising and think creatively and commercially in order to solve problems, and explore what is takes to be successful in business today.

The course is divided into two themes.

Theme 1: Investigating small business

In Theme 1 you will study five topics covering:

- enterprise
- spotting a business opportunity
- putting an idea into practice
- how to make a business effective
- external influences on business.

By learning about these areas you will gain an understanding of the core concepts, issues and skills that are involved in starting and running a small business. You will examine these in relation mainly to local and national businesses in the UK.

Theme 2: Building a business

In Theme 2 you will look at five more topics which focus on making decisions in the areas of:

- growing a business
- marketing
- operations
- finance
- human resources.

You will build on what you have learnt in Theme 1, by examining these topics in relation to developing businesses. You will also explore the interdependent nature of business through the relationships between these different business areas. The context for these topics will be presented through both national, as well as global, businesses.

How you will be assessed

Your assessment will consist of two separate written exams. Paper 1 covers Theme 1: Investigating small business, and Paper 2 covers content from Theme 2: Building a Business. Each paper is worth 50% of the qualification final mark.

How to use this book

Each of the 10 topics from the course is covered in a chapter of this book. Each topic guides you through the content of the course in a practical and engaging way, making it clear what you will cover, and providing useful activities and questions to help you practise what you have learned. Each topic is introduced through a case study, so that you can begin to understand the content as it applies in the real world. At the end of each topic you will find two pages of exam practice that will help you reflect on what you have learnt and to prepare for the exams.

Features of the book

This student book contains a number of different features that are designed to both support and challenge you. You will get the most from this book if you use each feature as part of your study; they will help your explore the topics in your course in different ways, reflect and on what you've learnt as well as extend your understanding. They will also help you develop the knowledge and skills that will make you feel confident for the exams.

Topic overview – at the start of each topic an outline of what is covered in that topic is provided.

Topic opener case study and questions – the case study will introduce you to the key themes of the topic you will be studying; providing an example that relates directly to the content. The case study is then followed by a set of questions that are designed to get you thinking.

Your learning – at the beginning of each topic a summary is given that outlines exactly what you are going to learn.

Topic overview

This topic introduces the dynamic nature of business by considering how and why business ideas come about. It explores the impact of risk and reward on business activity and then goes on to investigate the role of entrepreneurship.

Case study

Whisk

Nick Holzherr is the co-founder of Whisk, a food app. Holzherr was a runner-up on the BBC television programme *The Apprentice*, and Whisk is his third start-up.

Whisk helps users to find and bookmark recipes. It is also integrated with supermarkets such as Asda, Tesco and Waitrose, meaning that users can buy the right food for the recipe they have chosen and have it delivered, all from within the app. The app also learns about users' preferences and makes recipe suggestions. The app is free for anyone to download and use. Food retailers pay to advertise within the app and the integrated supermarkets pay Whisk a fee whenever a user purchases from their store through the app.

One of Holzherr's previous start-ups was a coffee shop business, but the high-street coffee industry is very competitive. This meant that the business's profit margins were very small, and expanding the business was difficult because every time that Holzherr wanted to open a new outlet he had to raise more money.

Between its launch in 2013 and 2016, Whisk grew from a start-up run by its two founders to a business run by a team of 10 employees. It has already set up partnerships with the American online grocery store, Peapod, and the Australian supermarket, Woolworths.

Activity ?

1 What does Whisk offer its customers?
2 What difficulties did Holzherr face when setting up a coffee shop business?
3 What are the advantages of setting up an app-based business?

Your learning

In this topic you will learn about:

- customer needs – identifying and understanding customer needs
- market research – the purpose, methods and the use of data in market research
- market segmentation – how businesses use market segmentation to target customers
- the competitive environment – understanding the strengths and weaknesses of competitors, and the impact of competition on businesses.

Introduction

Case study – each sub-topic is introduced through a short case study, which are similar to the topic opener case studies.

Key term

Focus group: a group of people who discuss their views on a product, service, advertisement or idea, either face-to-face or online.

Key terms – there are certain terms that you will need to know and be able to explain. Key words that are explained within the main text are in **bold** to emphasise their importance. They are explained in the nearby Key terms boxes.

Exam–style question

Explain **one** reason why businesses are likely to have different aims and objectives.

(3 marks)

Exam-style question – these questions match the style of questions that you are likely to find in the written exams. You should find a broad range of question types are used throughout the book. Answering these questions will give you useful practice as you go through your course.

Did you know?

Digital or mobile wallets are a new technology designed to make it easier for customers to pay for goods and services

Did you know? - this features includes interesting facts and figures about business.

Maths tip

If you are not sure how to approach a percentage calculation, work through a simple percentage calculation that you know the answer to – for example, 5 per cent of £100 = £5. Be sure that you understand how you came to this correct answer and then apply these steps to the calculation you are working on.

Maths tip – this short tip will help when you are carrying out a mathematical task. It might include ideas on what to remember as well as tips on how to approach maths questions you may finding challenging.

Link it up

You will learn more about the marketing mix in Topic 1.4 *Making the business effective*.

Link it up – this provides a reference to where you may have covered similar content elsewhere in the course, or highlight that you will be looking at the content again at another point. This will help you to understand how the content of each topic relates to the course as a whole.

Activity – throughout you will find a range of suggestions for different activities. You may be asked to work individually or in groups to complete a task which relates to the content that you are studying.

Checkpoint – this feature is designed to allow you to assess your learning at key points. The **'strengthen'** questions help you to check your knowledge and understanding of what you have been studying, while the **'challenge'** questions are an opportunity to extend your learning.

Preparing for your exam

At the end of each topic is a dedicated exam preparation section. This section provides tips and guidance for success in your written exams. You'll find examples of a range of different question types that reflect the type of questions you may have to answer in both your exams. Sample answers to each question are also provided, together with notes and explanations about the quality of the answers shown. This will really help you build your understanding of how to write stronger answers.

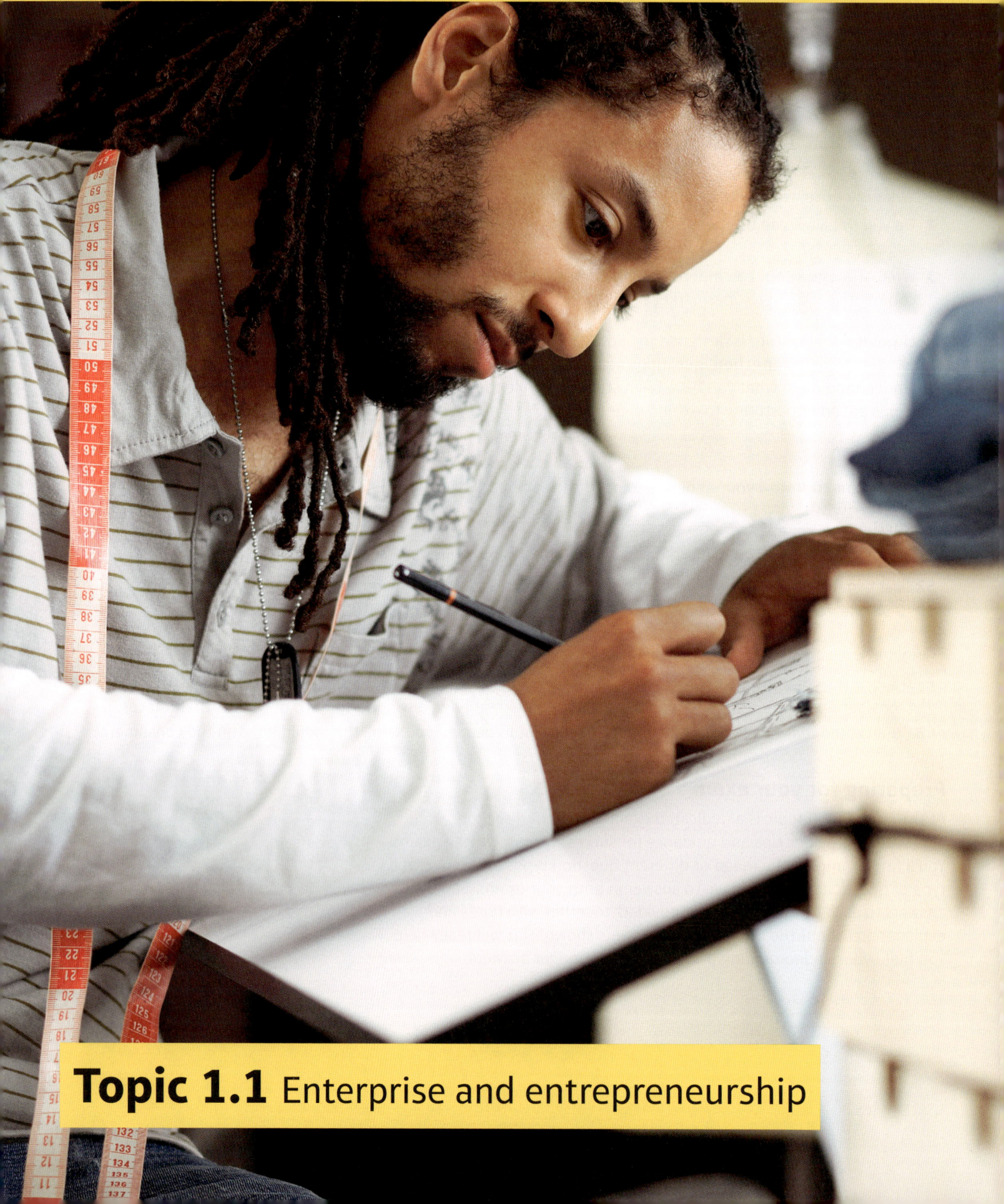

Topic overview

This topic introduces the dynamic nature of business by considering how and why business ideas come about. It explores the impact of risk and reward on business activity and then goes on to investigate the role of entrepreneurship.

Case study

Farfetch

Farfetch is an international fashion website that sells products from more than 400 fashion boutiques based around the world. It was started in 2008 by José Neves, a Portuguese entrepreneur based in London. Farfetch helps small independent fashion brands and boutiques sell their clothing to a global audience. Using Farfetch's platform allows these retailers to keep their own independent identities while boosting their position in the market.

In 2016, Farfetch's website received more than 10 million hits a month. The small retailers who sell through it could not hope to attract so many potential customers on their own. Neves claims that Farfetch aims to help these 'little guys' to compete with much larger fashion companies, using technology entrepreneurship to allow small businesses to succeed.

In 2015, Farfetch's sales grew by 70 per cent, rising to more than US $500 million that year, and the company bought a London boutique called Browns. The business is now a global operation, hosting different versions of its website in several languages and employing people around the world, in cities such as Lisbon, London, Tokyo, Hong Kong, Moscow and Shanghai.

Neves attributes some of his entrepreneurial success to the example set by his grandfather, who ran his own shoe factory. However, he thinks that the main reason for Farfetch's success is that the company lives by its own values and fulfils its aim to make its customers happy.

Activity ?

1 What service does Farfetch provide for independent fashion boutiques?
2 What do you think the word 'entrepreneur' means? Write your own definition or list some of the qualities you think an entrepreneur needs to have.
3 Why do you think Neves would consider making customers happy to be a major reason for Farfetch's success?

Your learning

In this topic you will learn about:
- the dynamic nature of business – why and how new business ideas come about
- risk and reward – the impact of risk and reward on business activity
- the role of business enterprise – the purpose of business activity and the role of entrepreneurship.

Theme 1: Investigating small business

The dynamic nature of business

Activity ?

Discuss the reasons why Ego failed.

Key terms

Enterprise: entrepreneurial activity (can also mean a business or company).

Entrepreneur: someone who creates a business, taking on financial risks with the aim of making a profit from the business.

Consumer: someone who buys and uses goods and services.

Obsolete: out of date or not used anymore.

Case study

Ego

Ego was a successful video and DVD rental business in Newtown, Powys. It survived local competition but the rise of online film-streaming services led to falling demand and it closed in 2016.

The world of **enterprise** is dynamic and ever-changing. This allows **entrepreneurs** to spot business opportunities and encourages them to develop new business ideas.

Why new business ideas come about

New business ideas usually arise because of changes in society and **consumer** trends. Entrepreneurs look at these changes and identify business opportunities based on their observations. These changes include:

- advances in technology, such as the introduction of fast and reliable broadband internet
- changes in what consumers want, such as increased interest in gluten-free and dairy-free foods
- products and services becoming **obsolete**, such as VHS videotapes.

Activity ?

Working in pairs, complete the following tasks.

1 Research different definitions of the word 'entrepreneur'. Compare the definitions that you have found and decide which one you think is best or most accurate.

2 On your own, write down eight qualities that you think an entrepreneur has to have in order to succeed. It might help you to think about well-known successful entrepreneurs. Compare your list with your partner's list. Have you listed the same qualities?

Changes in technology

Technology is constantly developing and this can have a huge impact on what consumers want and need. For example, in 2005, very few people had a smartphone, but within 10 years many consumers were using their smartphone to access the internet. This affected many businesses, because they needed to make sure that their websites could be looked at using a smartphone.

Businesses have to be flexible and must innovate in order to respond to continuous change. Coming up with new business ideas, new products and new processes can allow entrepreneurs and businesses to remain up to date in a world of rapidly changing technology. Examples of the ways in which changes in technology can provide business opportunities are:

- making expensive technology affordable
- **e-commerce** and mobile commerce (**m-commerce**)
- **social media**.

Making expensive technology affordable

Changes in technology not only provide opportunities for entrepreneurs to start their own businesses, they can also trigger new entrepreneurial ideas, new businesses and new products or services. This is often because previously expensive technologies become cheaper to use and produce, and as a result they can be used more affordably in a company's products and services.

One example of this is the advance of three-dimensional (3D) printing. Although 3D printing has been used in some industries and processes since the 1980s, it was very expensive. As a result, it was usually only used to model the first version of a new product. However, the cost of the technology has fallen since its initial introduction, which means that it can now be used in the production process to reduce manufacturing costs. 3D printing can now be used to create products such as medical devices, consumer electronics and parts for home appliances. For example, some hearing aid manufacturers intend to use 3D printing to produce all of their hearing aids in the near future. 3D printing makes it easier than ever to make a whole range of products without needing to buy expensive equipment, which reduces costs for businesses wanting to get into manufacturing.

E-commerce and m-commerce

Using the internet for buying and selling products and services is called e-commerce. In 1995, when widespread use of the internet was just taking off, an American called Jeff Bezos identified a business opportunity for an online bookshop. That business opportunity led to the creation of Amazon, the online retailer.

Thanks to e-commerce, a small business operating out of an entrepreneur's garage or home office can trade with customers all over the world. Payment systems such as PayPal and Sage Pay allow businesses to take online payments without having to create their own **payment platforms**. Some small businesses even trade over the internet using the platforms provided by larger businesses, such as Amazon or eBay. In many industries, the internet defines the way in which consumers interact with businesses.

The rise of e-commerce means that the barriers to starting up a small business have decreased, as entrepreneurs do not have to rent physical premises before they can begin trading. Instead, they can bring their new business ideas straight to the **marketplace**.

Many consumers now access the internet through mobile devices, such as smartphones and tablets. Using mobile devices to buy and sell products is

> **Key terms**
>
> **E-commerce:** using the internet to carry out business transactions.
>
> **M-commerce:** using mobile technologies, such as smartphones and tablets, to carry out business transactions.
>
> **Social media:** websites that allow users to interact with other users, by sharing text-based messages, pictures or links to online content.

> **Key terms**
>
> **Payment platforms:** enable businesses to take online payments from customers. They are usually free for the customer to use, but take a small amount of commission from the seller.
>
> **Marketplace:** the activities involved in buying and selling particular types of goods or services, in competition with other companies.

Theme 1: Investigating small business

known as m-commerce. The development of m-commerce has also helped to generate new business ideas. For example, Orderella is a business that only exists thanks to customers' use of smartphones. An Orderella user can use the business's smartphone app to order food and drink from the restaurant or bar they are in, rather than having to queue.

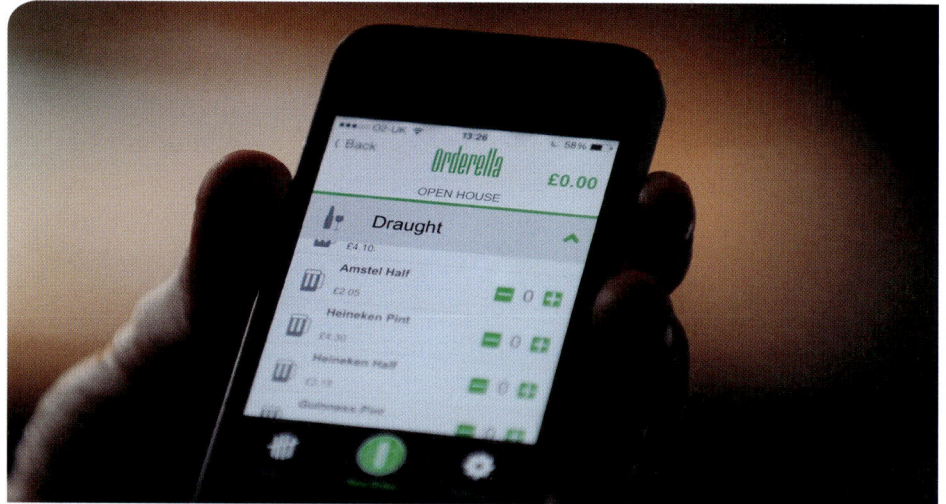

The Orderella app allows customers to avoid queues and pay at restaurants using their smartphones

Case study

Deliveroo

Deliveroo is a business that delivers food from good quality restaurants to people's houses. An American called Will Shu was inspired to start the business when he moved to London and found that it was almost impossible to get good quality food delivered. Customers order their meal through the Deliveroo app, and delivery takes an average of 30 minutes. In the first 2 years after Deliveroo launched, over 50,000 people used the service, with 80 per cent of customers using the service again.

Social media

Social media platforms allow people to interact instantly with other people all around the world. The popularity of social media has not only transformed personal relationships, but also relationships with businesses. Social media can be used as a relatively inexpensive way to promote businesses and to interact with existing and potential customers, as well as encouraging customers to talk to one another about the business's products or services.

Examples of social media platforms include Facebook, Twitter, YouTube, LinkedIn and Pinterest. These can all be used by large and small businesses alike to attract customers. For example, a business may set up a page on Facebook and offer special offers to people who 'like' the page. This then allows the business to communicate easily with these customers and encourage them to buy their products.

Social media platforms can be used to reduce the work involved in marketing. They enable businesses to utilise customers as a means of promoting products and services, such as when they share a company's Facebook posts, retweet tweets on Twitter or upload photographs of purchased products onto Instagram. This can have a huge impact on small businesses in particular, which may not have any dedicated marketing staff.

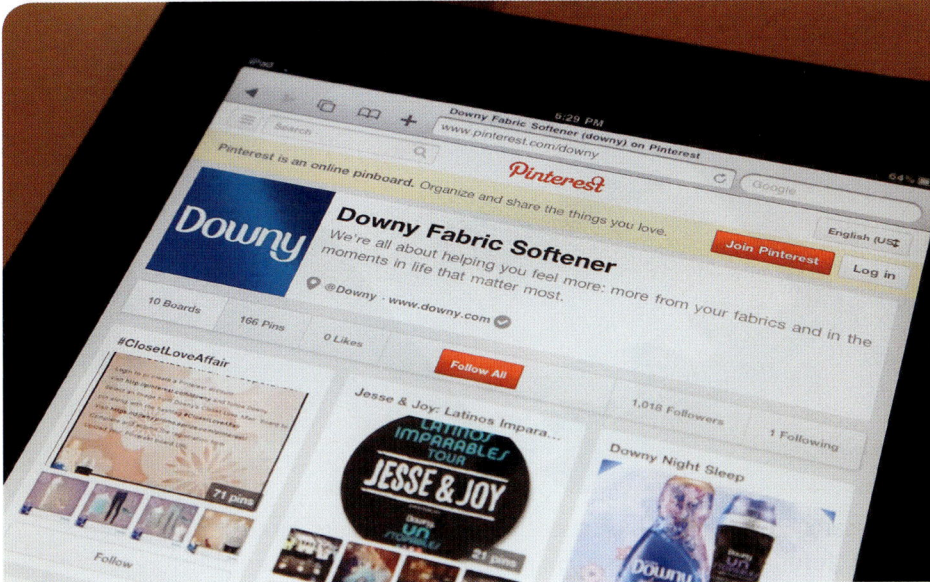

Social media is an inexpensive way to promote a business and keep new and existing customers talking about the business

Activity ?

Many consumers use online reviews and opinions expressed on social media to help them make decisions about their online purchases.

In small groups or pairs, discuss the following questions.

1 Do you think your purchasing decisions are more influenced by the opinions of friends and people on social media or by advertising?

2 What impact do you think this trend might have on a business?

Write up your findings in bullet points on flipchart paper to present to the rest of the group.

Changes in what consumers want

Another reason why entrepreneurs come up with new business ideas is that consumers' wants and needs also move on over time. As you can see in the Deliveroo case study, changes in lifestyle and technology have an impact on what consumers want, and entrepreneurs create businesses to satisfy these new demands.

Businesses need to listen to their customers in order to understand what they are looking for and to see how customers' wants and needs are changing. This allows businesses to keep up with changing trends, retaining

Theme 1: Investigating small business

Link it up

Market research is covered in more detail in Topic 1.2 *Spotting a business opportunity*.

their existing customers and attracting new ones. Businesses can do this by asking customers to fill out feedback questionnaires or surveys, by engaging with customers on social media or by using online review services such as Trustpilot and Reevoo.

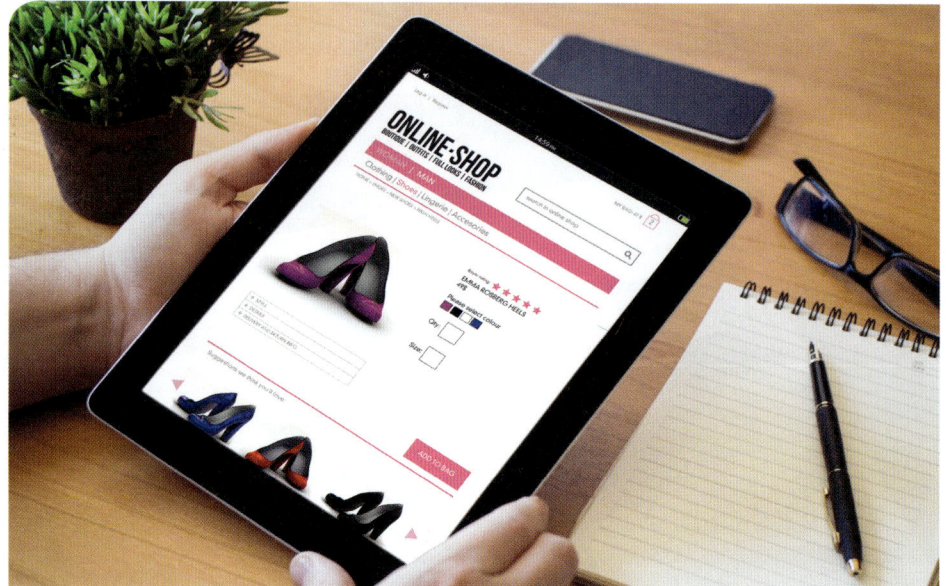

Online technologies allow businesses to track customers' interests and suggest ideas for future purchases based on products they have looked at before

Businesses can find out their customers' interests by trialling new products. These trials can be used as marketing opportunities, such as the Doritos' 'A or B' campaign in 2016. As a result, Doritos not only identified what customers were looking for, but also reconnected with existing customers and raised awareness of the brand among potential customers.

Finally, businesses can use **data** to identify customers' wants and needs. For example, Amazon can recommend a product to an existing customer by analysing the data that it has gathered about that customer, such as their previous purchases, as well as data that it has gathered about similar customers. This detailed information can help businesses to make their customers' shopping experience easier.

Data can also help businesses to rethink the way in which they design, produce and market their products and services. For example, **demographic** data may show that the average income in a country has increased. This may encourage businesses selling luxury items to start operating in that country.

Key terms

Data: information, particularly statistics, that can be collected and analysed.

Demographic: relating to the population, such as average age, average income and so on.

Exam tip

Try to link the method you identify to a reason for how this will help develop a new business idea.

Exam-style question

Outline **one** way in which a business like Walker's might identify a new business idea. **(2 marks)**

Products and services becoming obsolete

Most products have a limited lifespan and, at some point, will no longer be sold. This lifespan is known as the product life cycle. The product life cycle describes the sales of a product over time – at its launch and throughout its lifespan until its decline.

Technology is one reason why products can become out of date or obsolete. Advances in technology mean that older technologies are replaced, and this can create new business ideas. The music industry is a good example of this. Audio cassettes played using cassette players like the Sony Walkman were gradually replaced by CDs throughout the 1990s, which meant that cassettes and the devices used to play them became obsolete.

Sometimes, products can recover from becoming obsolete. For example, vinyl records were once considered obsolete, having been replaced by cassettes, CDs and digital downloads, but sales of vinyl have increased in recent years.

A product can also become obsolete due to changes in fashion or taste. For example, sales of wooden flooring have increased in recent years while sales of carpet have declined. Tea has become less popular while sales of coffee have risen.

Link it up

You will learn about the product life cycle in detail in the 'Product' section in Topic 2.2 *Making marketing decisions.*

Did you know?

Some businesses and brands can have very long lifespans. Cadbury has been in existence since 1824, with Fox's Biscuits launching 30 years later. The Kit Kat was first sold in 1935, while Lyle's Golden Syrup dates back to 1883.

Activity ?

What products or services do you think may become obsolete in the next 5 or 10 years?

Exam tip

Identify one reason and then develop your response further to explain your answer.

Exam-style question

Explain **one** reason why an enterprise needs to listen to its customers.

(3 marks)

How new business ideas come about

Case study

Success on a plate
In 2008, soon after graduating from university, Griff Holland met Ed Brown at a business networking event in Bristol. They identified a gap in the market for a lunchtime takeaway that sold healthy, sustainably-sourced delicious food. Out of their planning came 'Friska', a successful fast-food business with a difference. Friska's strapline is 'feel good food'.

There are two ways in which entrepreneurs usually come up with new business ideas.

They may:
- adapt an existing product or service to keep up with changes in consumer trends
- create a completely original product or service to satisfy a new or previously unknown customer trend.

Activity ?

Many enterprises adapt their products for different markets. In pairs, discuss some of the possible reasons why a business might want to adapt its product.

Adapting existing products and services

Adaptation is the process of modifying an existing product or service so that it is suitable for different customers or markets. It can be seen as a less risky business option than launching a brand new product. One form of adaptation is when a product is physically changed or modified to appeal to different customers or cultures. For example, a restaurant may change its menus and serve a wider range of foods as customers' tastes change.

An example of adaptation for cultural reasons is the way that UK-based website Hitched.co.uk, a source of information for planning a wedding, had to evolve when it launched sister websites abroad. Based on the success of the UK version started by Surrey businessman Dean Yardley in 1997, Hitched.co.uk launched similar websites in Australia, Canada, South Africa and Ireland in 2010 and 2011. However, differing cultural attitudes to weddings in these countries required a re-think of some of the site's elements, which include search facilities to help find local venues, as well as articles on changing wedding trends.

For example, in Ireland, particularly in rural areas, brides usually rely on personal and family recommendations when selecting wedding venues and suppliers much more than they would in the UK. This meant that the Irish version of the site, Hitched.ie, focused more on wedding planning tools than on venues.

Some innovations are, in fact, clever adaptations of existing products. For example, burgers have long been a staple food in the UK. But some small businesses have recognised that in 21st-century Britain there is now, potentially, a much wider market for burgers than simply satisfying fans of the traditional beef burger.

In response to the growing demand for meat-free products, vegan food manufacturer Fry Family Food was formed by Northants couple Wally and Debbie Fry. Like many small food-based businesses, the Frys started Fry Family Food in their own family kitchen. It was not the first company to produce vegan burgers, but it did introduce an Asian Spiced Burger to the market to appeal to those who like their burgers spicy, as well as meat-free. Contrastingly, a new halal burger restaurant called Burger&Co aims to cater for a completely different type of burger eater. The opening of Burger&Co in Newport, Wales in early 2017, reflects the growing opportunities for businesses to adapt ideas for cultural reasons.

Other types of adaptation include:

- adapting the promotion strategy of a particular product or service
- changing a product's brand name
- responding to new fashions, for example by offering different coloured products.

Sometimes, just a subtle change to the marketing or packaging is all it takes to sell an already successful product into a new market. A small distributor

Activity ?

Working individually or in pairs, identify two existing products that you think could be combined to make a new product.

Did you know?

Creative thinking is a skill that can be developed with practice. It is about solving problems and refusing to take no for an answer. The most creative people ignore what is widely accepted and focus on things that seem unconventional.

of telecoms accessories based just outside London, Frequency Telecom, was looking for products suitable for the Norwegian market.

Its research showed that Norwegian customers were interested in sustainable products that do not use a lot of plastic packaging. Frequency Telecom used this information to sell Thinksound earphones, which were already selling well in the UK and US, successfully in Norway. Minimal packaging was supported by a marketing campaign that emphasised the environmentally friendly nature of both the product, which uses wood and metal to replace plastic, and its casing.

Case study

Easiphones

The mobile phone provider Easiphones, based in Bath, supplies a niche market with specially adapted handsets. Recognising that some people can find smartphones daunting and difficult to use, Easiphones offers a range of simplified mobile phones designed to be more user-friendly for elderly people and customers with disabilities, who just want to make and receive calls or send texts. Its phones feature large keypads with bigger buttons, loudspeakers, large fonts, extra-large displays and louder ringers, all aimed at people who do not want to bother with touchscreens and advanced features they will never use.

To add to the appeal for its niche customer base, a few emergency features have been added, such as an SOS button that links to a 24-hour call centre. Customers can also have the phone numbers of relatives pre-programmed into their phones for them.

Deciding whether to adapt

Adapted products will not always succeed. Even if they do succeed, they may not do well enough to make the adaptation process worthwhile. Businesses have to balance customer and market needs with the cost of development and the likely return they will get for investment in the adaptation process. However, product adaptation can be worthwhile. For example, some businesses may find that customising existing products can cut development costs and makes it quicker for them to launch 'new' products adapted from existing products.

Some businesses might not have a choice: they might need to make significant adaptations to their main products if their customers begin to change. For example, if a restaurant sees its main customer base change from couples to young families, it might need to change its menu, its prices and the look and feel of the restaurant in order to become a family-friendly restaurant.

Activity ?

In pairs or small groups, research three companies that have adapted existing products. Your chosen examples could be food and drink, home electrical items such as refrigerators and televisions, or cars. Present your examples to the rest of the group.

Exam tip

Identify one reason and then develop your response further to explain your answer.

Exam-style question

Explain **one** reason why a business might adapt one of its existing products. **(3 marks)**

Theme 1: Investigating small business

Link it up

You will learn more about spotting business opportunities and filling gaps in the market in Topic 1.2 *Spotting a business opportunity*.

Original ideas

It can be very challenging for an entrepreneur or business to come up with a completely original business idea. Changes in technology have encouraged original ideas in the development of new consumer products, especially when the original idea is a new angle on an existing product. For example, the cyclone technology used in Dyson vacuum cleaners was revolutionary when it was first introduced. This innovative design was an improvement upon existing products that did not satisfy customers' needs.

However, entrepreneurs do not usually focus on coming up with a unique idea that no one has ever heard of. Instead, they usually focus on answering the following questions.

- How can I improve on this product or service?
- Can I do this better or differently than existing businesses?
- Is there a gap in the market that I can fill?

Exam tip

You need to be able to demonstrate your knowledge and understanding of business concepts and issues, using appropriate terminology. Make sure that you finish the answer with a well-reasoned conclusion.

Exam-style question

Sammy left college and had set up his own business running a successful sports equipment shop aimed at sports clubs. He tried to develop a unique business idea which he hoped would make his fortune. He thought about designing clothing aimed at university students and a battery charger which would be powered by the kinetic energy of the wearer.

Evaluate whether it is more important for an entrepreneur to meet customers' needs than to develop something unique and original.

(12 marks)

Checkpoint

Now it is time to review your understanding of the dynamic nature of business.

Strengthen

S1 Describe a reason why a business might decide to change a brand name.

S2 Describe what is meant by the phrase 'product adaptation'.

S3 Why might a fast-food restaurant offer different products in different countries? List as many reasons as you can think of.

Challenge

C1 Why do businesses take social factors into account when considering business ideas?

C2 Choose a well-known British business and identify one of its products that you think could be adapted for a new market. Write a proposal of no more than 250 words identifying the product, the adaptation and the new market.

C3 Outline the potential advantages and disadvantages of your business proposal.

Risk and reward

Case study

CubeSocial

Linda Cheung gave up a high-flying role in banking to set up a marketing business called CubeSocial, based in Basingstoke. Having seen her father run his own business, she knew all about risk.

She says: 'My inner business sense tells me that risk is not a negative thing. Nor is it necessarily a positive thing, but more a challenge. Risk and reward have to be seen as a balance. I knew that I could forego earning an income for a period of time, and our focus during start-up was on seeing connections, joining the dots and identifying the opportunities more than the risk. It is about seeing the glass as half full.'

Activity ?

1 Do you think that entrepreneurs can avoid taking risks? What are the reasons for your answer?

2 In pairs or small groups, research an example of a risk taken by a successful entrepreneur. What do you think you could learn from their example?

3 What potential rewards would motivate you to start your own business?

Being an entrepreneur involves **risks**. When an entrepreneur launches a new business, they risk losing the money that they have invested in the set-up of that business. However, if the business succeeds, then they will receive **financial reward** for their risk. The most successful entrepreneurs spend time studying others' successes, analysing others' methods and strategies, and considering how these can be applied to their own business.

When starting a business or exploring new business ideas, it is impossible to completely avoid taking risks. Risks can be minimised by being informed by plenty of evidence, such as **market research** and **revenue forecasts**. However, a calculated or well-informed risk is still a risk. For a small business, even a small crisis could lead to the failure of the business, so an entrepreneur needs to estimate the potential impact of a crisis and calculate the likelihood that such a crisis might actually happen.

Risks

There are a number of risks associated with starting up a business. The main risks that an entrepreneur takes when they start up a business are:

- business failure
- financial loss
- lack of security.

Key terms

Risk: the possibility that an enterprise will have lower than anticipated profits or experience a loss.

Financial reward: the money that an entrepreneur or investor receives when a business succeeds.

Market research: the process of gathering information about the market and customers' needs and wants in order to help inform business decisions, including product design and marketing.

Revenue forecast: a prediction of future revenue based on expected sales; this is either a judgement or based on previous sales patterns.

Link it up

You will learn more about market research in the 'Market research' section of Topic 1.4 *Making the business effective*, and more about minimising risks in the 'Business plans' section of Topic 1.4 *Making the business effective*.

Business failure

There are many reasons why businesses fail. One major cause is a business having a problem with its **cash flow**. Even a successful business can face serious financial problems if its customers are slow in paying their bills. This can mean that the business does not have enough cash in its bank account to buy essential supplies or pay its employees' wages, and can lead to the business having to borrow money. Cash-flow problems can cause even profitable businesses to fail.

Unexpected costs can also have an impact on cash flow and on a business's success. For example, if a key employee leaves, the business must find a replacement and this can often cost many thousands of pounds. This cost is not only due to having to spend money on recruitment but also because the new employee will not be working as efficiently when they first start.

Another reason for business failure might be an unexpected drop in **sales revenue**. This could happen because of something that the business has done or failed to do, such as running out of raw materials. However, this can also happen for reasons outside the business's control, such as:

- recession – the sales revenue of a luxury goods business might drop suddenly at the beginning of a recession, as people stop spending their money on non-essentials
- behaviour of suppliers – the sales revenue of a local tile shop could be affected by the closure of a factory that makes most of the tiles that the shop sells
- competition – the sales revenue of a local independent petrol station could suffer if a nearby supermarket cuts its fuel price.

Key terms

Cash flow: the amount of money coming in and going out of the business and the timing of this movement.

Sales revenue: the amount of money that comes in from a business's sales.

The sales revenue of tourism-based businesses in a seaside resort could fall if the weather is particularly bad during the summer

14

In the case of the independent petrol station, the business only has two options. The business could respond by cutting its own prices, resulting in a drop in revenue, or it could leave its prices unchanged, resulting in a drop in sales. Either option could lead to business failure.

Activity ?

Find a partner and a pair of dice. Each of you should take one die.

Imagine that you are starting the activity with £15. Rolling a die costs £5, but you do not have to roll. If you roll a six, you get £100. If you roll a three or a four, you will lose a further £5. If you roll any other number, you do not gain or lose anything.

Now, take it in turns to roll (or decide not to roll) your die three times. Record the choices that you make each turn, as well as the result of the throw and whether you gained or lost money.

After you have finished, think about whether you are someone who is prepared to take risks or play safe. What impact do you think this might have if you were an entrepreneur?

Financial loss

There is a risk of financial loss when starting a business. An entrepreneur could lose the money that they have **invested** in their **start-up**, but they may also damage their reputation and this could have an impact on being able to raise finance for other start-ups in the future. Often, financial loss is caused by an error or oversight during the business planning stage.

One example of financial loss has been experienced by Watsons of Perth, a homeware outlet and a fixture of the Scottish city's high street since 1900. The store closed down in December 2016, having struggled to meet changing customer tastes. They were also unable to afford the business rates that had been increased to £40,000 a year. Watsons had seen a fall in demand for the quality ranges it made its name on, which had seen its income fall. Taking into account the reduction in its takings, coupled with the high business rates, its owners decided that its city centre location was no longer affordable.

Different types of risk can lead to financial loss. These include:

- competitive risks – the risk that a business's competitor might do better than the business, such as by spending more on marketing and attracting more sales
- technical risks – the risk that a product or service might not work as intended, such as a faulty charger which increased the risk of fire or electric shocks for users and resulted in the prosecution of a retailer in Wales, which was fined £190,000
- financial risks – the risk that a business does not have the right amount of investment, such as not having enough money to launch a product in a way that attracts customers' attention.

Key terms

Investment: putting money into a business with the intention of making a profit.

Start-up: a new business, usually with only a small number of employees – perhaps only one.

Link it up

You will learn more about starting a company in Topic 2.1 *Growing the business*.

Lack of security

Launching their own business means that an entrepreneur does not have the security of working for someone else. This may mean that they do not have a regular wage, sick pay or a pension run by their employer. Self-employment can give people the opportunity to develop their own ideas and control their own future, but it often does not offer job security.

Starting up a business may also mean financial insecurity. Many entrepreneurs use their own savings to fund their start-up, leaving them with no savings. If their savings are not enough, they will also need to borrow money or find people who are willing to invest in the business. This is why it is important for entrepreneurs to work out how long it will take before the business starts to make a profit, because this knowledge can help to make them less financially insecure.

The lack of security can also have an impact on an entrepreneur's health. They have to make all of the business's decisions for themselves, and this can cause a lot of stress.

Key term

Intuition: knowing something instinctively or understanding something easily without conscious thought.

Activity ?

Do you think that an entrepreneur should research a business idea thoroughly or trust their intuition? What are the advantages and disadvantages of each approach?

Activity ?

1 Choose two different industries (for example, fashion and engineering) and research some of the industry awards available to businesses in those industries.
2 Why do you think entrepreneurs value receiving industry awards?

Intuition

Many entrepreneurs say that they make critical decisions intuitively rather than by analysing fact-based business data. **Intuition**, which some call a 'gut feeling' or a 'hunch', is good for seeing the big picture. It produces judgements that are connected to our feelings, rather than our analytical minds. And, most usefully for entrepreneurs, it is quick.

Rewards

What motivates an entrepreneur to set up a business? They might feel rewarded by the thrill of founding a business that succeeds and produces goods that people want to buy, or they might be driven by making a profit. They may even simply like working for themselves and having the independence to make their own decisions.

Business success

Many entrepreneurs are motivated by the satisfaction of building a business from nothing or of thinking up an idea that no one has ever thought of before. Some particularly like the fact that their enterprise provides jobs for their employees, while others enjoy providing a product or service that customers really love. Many entrepreneurs value receiving industry awards, such as a Great Taste Award for businesses in the food and drink industry.

Profit

Entrepreneurs make a choice to invest in and run their own business and to take the risk of financial failure. They do this with the intention of making a profit from the business when it succeeds, but many successful entrepreneurs say that they had no idea whether their business would succeed. Setting up a business is rarely a quick route to financial success. Even the most successful business start-ups suffer setbacks, and most successful entrepreneurs require a great deal of skill and hard work in order to succeed.

Authors are a good example of self-employed entrepreneurs who take risks, and whose worth depends on their creativity and their ability to sell their idea. J.K. Rowling was an unemployed single parent when she first came up with the idea for her books. Writing a book requires a large investment of time before the possibility of any financial return, and this was a risk for her. The first *Harry Potter* novel was rejected by 12 publishers, but the series has now sold nearly 500 million copies.

Exam-style question

Explain **one** reward of starting up a business. **(3 marks)**

Exam tip

If you are asked for **one** of something, only give and explain one thing. Writing about more will not get you any extra marks and will leave you less time to answer other questions.

Independence

Many entrepreneurs are motivated by having the opportunity of working for themselves rather than working for someone else. This comes with its risks, as you have seen, but most entrepreneurs consider the rewards of running their own business to be greater than working for someone else, even when they make mistakes.

Entrepreneurs often think that having the independence to make your own decisions is the key benefit of starting up a business. Being independent means that entrepreneurs are more likely to take risks and try out new things that they think might work, rather than stick to things that are more conventional or expected.

Did you know?

In 1975, Bill Gates took a risk and dropped out of university to co-found the computing company Microsoft. The company succeeded and Gates became one of the richest entrepreneurs in the world. In 2016, he was worth US $90 billion. However, other entrepreneurs, such as Jeff Bezos, finished their education before launching their business start-up.

Activity

Research an entrepreneur of your choice, focusing on:

a their main idea

b any risks that they took

c whether they were successful

d whether they had to overcome any difficulties.

Now present your findings to the rest of the group and discuss whether you think your chosen entrepreneur is a good role model for other entrepreneurs.

Checkpoint

Now it is time to review your understanding of risks and rewards.

Strengthen

S1 List three of the main risks and three of the main rewards of setting up a new company.

S2 Describe a reason why cash flow is important to a business.

S3 Explain one reason why sales revenue could be lower than expected.

Challenge

C1 Do you think that experiencing failure can help an entrepreneur? Try to find an example of an entrepreneur who has failed and then gone on to succeed.

C2 Produce a poster or leaflet for an entrepreneurship event in your local area. The leaflet should be aimed at people thinking about starting up their own business, and should explain the risks and rewards of being an entrepreneur. If you can, use examples of local businesses.

The role of business enterprise

Case study

Center Parcs

Center Parcs is a European business that operates a number of holiday 'villages' in countryside locations around the UK. The business decided to enter the market for residential business conferences, so it built a suitable venue at Woburn Forest Center Parcs, which is close to London.

Many hotels put on residential conferences, but the countryside setting of Center Parcs is unusual as it allows participants to take part in outdoor activities. The village also contains a luxury spa and a tropical rainforest-style indoor swimming pool.

Activity   ?

In pairs, discuss the selling points of Center Parcs as a conference venue. To do this, you may need to research other conference venues to get an idea of the competition. Now decide whether you think Center Parcs offers selling points that cannot be found elsewhere.

Key term

Stakeholder: anyone who has an interest in the activities of a business, such as its workers, its suppliers, its directors, the local community and the government.

Business enterprise is the entrepreneurial activity undertaken by entrepreneurs or businesses, either by setting up or expanding a business.

There are many different opinions on the role of business enterprise. Some people think that the main aim of most businesses is to make as much profit as possible, and they try to achieve this by providing goods and services that consumers want or need. In order to produce these goods and services, businesses have to employ people. These employees then spend their income on other businesses' goods and services. Businesses can then reinvest their profits into their business activities and grow, hiring more employees and producing more products and services for consumers to purchase.

On the other hand, some people believe that businesses should behave in certain ways towards their **stakeholders**. They argue that businesses have social responsibilities and that the enterprise must be conducted **ethically**, such as not selling alcohol to young people or reducing the environmental impact of a business's products and services.

Between 2000 and 2015, the number of businesses in the UK increased by 55 per cent. In 2014 alone, 351,000 new businesses were started.

Type of business	Number of businesses (1,000s)	People employed (1,000s)	Revenue (£ millions)
Micro (1-9 employees)	1069	4010	436
Small (10-49 employees)	204	3967	543
Medium (50-249 employees)	33	3183	538
Large (250+ employees)	7	10260	1956
Total			

Table 1.1.1 The number of private sector businesses in the UK

Source: BIS Business Population Estimates 2015

Activity ?

1 Add up the numbers in each column to work out the total number of businesses in the UK, the total number of people employed by all of those businesses and the revenue of all of those businesses.

2 Work out the number of each type of business as a percentage of the total number of businesses that you have just calculated.

Maths tip

A percentage is a way of expressing an amount of something by stating it as a proportion of the total. 'Per cent' means 'per 100', so a percentage is always 'out of 100'. For example, 10 per cent means '10 per 100', or 10/100. You could say that 10p is 10 per cent of £1.

If you asked 25 people whether they wanted to set up their own business and 12 people said yes, you could express this as a fraction (12/25) and then convert it to a percentage.

You can check that this makes sense, because half (or 50 per cent) of 25 is 12.5.

The purpose of business activity

Business activities have three main purposes:

- to produce goods or services
- to meet customer needs
- to add value.

Key term

Ethics: moral principles or standards that guide the behaviour of a person or business.

Link it up

You will learn more about ethics in business in Topic 2.1 *Growing the business*.

Producing goods or services

One purpose of business activity is to make goods and services that satisfy consumers' wants and needs. The rise in the standard of living in many countries is due to entrepreneurial activity and competition between companies. The profit made is reinvested by businesses, leading to further growth. In this way, business enterprise has an important role to play in society by creating jobs and wealth.

Meeting customer needs

Another purpose of business activity is to meet customer needs by offering them products and services that they want. A business will not succeed if it does not understand customers and meet their needs.

In order to understand customers' needs, a business needs to develop a relationship with them. A positive relationship allows a business to learn from customers by getting feedback, and the business can use this information to improve existing products and services or develop new products and services.

The needs of customers are not just the needs that are satisfied by the product itself. Customers' needs also include factors such as:

- fast delivery
- reasonable, competitive prices
- friendly and helpful customer service
- prompt answers to their enquiries
- enough stock in a shop so that they can buy a product there and then
- a website that is easy to navigate and use.

If a business meets the needs of its customers, its customers will be happy. This will make them more likely to buy again from the business and to recommend the business to friends and relatives.

> **Exam-style question** ⬤
>
> Discuss the impacts on a business of failing to meet customers' needs.
>
> **(6 marks)**

Link it up

You will learn more about meeting customers' needs in the section 'Customer needs' in Topic 1.2 *Spotting a business opportunity*.

Adding value

Added value is the increase in a product's value as a result of a business producing that product. For example, the price of a car is higher than the cost of making it. The difference between the final price and the cost of production is the value that has been added. The amount of added value depends on the price that a customer pays. For example, a celebrity chef is able to charge substantially more for a meal made from certain ingredients than a local cafe would be able to charge. The service that is provided by the celebrity chef adds a lot of value. A business that successfully adds value should be able to operate profitably.

Value can be added to a product in a number of ways, including its:

- branding
- convenience
- quality and design
- **unique selling points (USPs)**.

Branding

Branding is a key factor in adding value and can be just as important for small businesses as it is for big businesses. Branding is not just a business's logo or strapline: it is also a way of defining the business, its aims and its **values** in a way that can be communicated to consumers. The award-winning, employee-owned Childbase Partnership is a leading childcare and education provider, rated 'Extraordinary' by Best Companies. It has been a Sunday Times 'top UK workplace' for over a decade. 'Delivering childcare excellence since 1989' is a commitment to the best local provider and employer in 43 day nurseries throughout the south of England, giving each and every child and employee exceptional care and opportunities.

How important is it for a business to get its message across to customers?

> **Key terms**
>
> **Unique selling point (USP):** something that makes a product stand out from its competitors.
>
> **Values:** standards of behaviour or moral principles.
>
> **Loyalty:** wanting to always support something or someone.
>
> **Market share:** the proportion of sales in a market that are taken by one business.

When customers can connect emotionally to a brand or feel that they share the same values and beliefs as a brand, they are more likely to buy that brand's products.

Branding can also create a lot of customer **loyalty**. Think about the goods or products that you buy. Do you tend to buy a particular brand of clothing, sports equipment or even tomato ketchup? If you do, you are 'brand loyal'. Customer loyalty is very important to businesses and can even protect a business that sells higher-priced goods when competitors offer promotional discounts to increase their **market share**.

Convenience

Another method that businesses use to add value to their products is by making them convenient. This includes excellent customer service, having products that are easy to pay for and products that are available.

Providing a great customer experience adds value to the product and also encourages customers to be brand loyal, rather than going to a competitor. For example, a local garage that cleans your car as a standard part of a full service may receive more repeat custom than a garage that does not. Similarly, friendly staff in a cafe or restaurant can add value by making diners feel welcome, encouraging them to return.

Another way in which businesses can add value to their products is by making them easy to pay for. This is particularly true of online retailers, which often allow customers to save their payment details so that the checkout process is quicker. Small online businesses are able to use the same technologies as larger companies. Real Foods, an online organic fruit and vegetable business, keep a history of orders for each customer which acts as a shopping list for the next time a customer wants to order, therefore saving time.

Being available is a third way of adding value. For example, a small newsagent may offer longer opening hours on Sundays, meaning that it is open for business at times when larger competitors, such as supermarkets, are closed. This could attract the custom of people in their local area.

Quality and design

'Quality' is a word often used in marketing, but simply saying that a brand represents quality is not enough. Instead, a business needs to demonstrate the quality of its products or services and show customers that they can depend on its brand.

It is important to build a reputation for quality, as this can add a great deal of value to a company's products. For example, a fish and chip shop could use better quality, healthier oil to fry its products, meaning that customers receive a better meal and experience. This should attract repeat business. If returning customers then receive the same quality of meal again, they will feel reassured that the food will always taste good and so choose that fish and chip shop rather than its competitors.

Design is another important factor in adding value to a product or service. This may be the design of the product, the design of the marketing or the design of the website through which customers purchase a service. A well-designed product or website not only looks professional, but it also communicates the business's values and can encourage consumers to buy from that business.

In many industries, if a product looks attractive then people are more likely to pay a higher price. For example, Linn is a small British company that manufactures high quality music systems. They have a reputation for the quality and design of their products, which are more expensive than other manufacturers' products.

In other industries, unusual or innovative designs may be used to improve a product and attract consumer attention. For example, the innovative design of the Dyson vacuum cleaner allowed it to be marketed as a new and improved form of vacuum cleaner. It did not look or function like existing products, and this attracted a great deal of attention when it was first launched in the 1990s.

Unique selling points (USPs)

A USP is something unique that differentiates a product or service from its rivals and should be promoted in order to encourage consumers to buy that product or service. Potential USPs include:

- price – for example, the cheapest product of that kind in the market
- quality – for example, the best quality product in the market
- being first to market – for example, the first product of its kind or the first to incorporate a new feature.

Activity ?

In small groups, discuss and write down the unique selling points of your school. What are the features or qualities that make it special? Why do you think students should choose it? Now suggest some improvements that the school could make in order to offer more USPs.

The role of entrepreneurship

As you have already seen, some people think that entrepreneurship has an important role to play in the society and **economy** of a country. Now you will think about the role of the individual entrepreneur. An entrepreneur is not only someone who has an idea for a new business and tries to make it a success. An entrepreneur also has to:

- organise resources
- make business decisions
- take risks.

Key term

Economy: the system by which a country's money and goods are produced and used.

Organising resources

Activity ?

1 Think of a new start-up business – for example, a chocolate-maker. Then close this book and list all of the resources that you think the entrepreneur would need to organise.

2 How do you think this list of resources might change as the business grows? Are there any resources that you think the entrepreneur might not have to continue to organise, or are there more resources that would need to be added to your list?

One of the responsibilities of an entrepreneur is organising the resources required to set up and run their new business. A key resource for a new business is finance. The entrepreneur has to raise enough money to set up the business, covering the costs of their premises, equipment, raw materials and staff. As the business grows, they then have to think ahead and identify ways in which they can raise enough money to cover any future expansion. Another key resource of any business is its staff. An entrepreneur cannot succeed only on the strength of their business idea. They also have to be able to motivate, lead and manage people.

Making business decisions

When an entrepreneur sets up a business and commits to working for themselves, they become responsible for making all their own business decisions. This is a huge responsibility, especially if the business employs people who depend on its success for their wages. This means that the entrepreneur has to focus on demonstrating a new concept before they develop a product. They need to have a long-term vision of how they think the product and business will develop and succeed, but they must be able to focus on each small short-term stage of the process as well. This should enable them to make good business decisions.

An entrepreneur also has to be capable of solving a customer problem, rather than simply coming up with something that they want to do. They have to know their market well in order to know what problems their customers have and to understand how they can solve these problems.

Exam tip

Plan your answer by writing down the things that an entrepreneur does when starting up a business, then consider how important these things may be to the success of a business.

Exam-style question

Discuss the importance of an entrepreneur in the success of a start-up business. **(6 marks)**

Taking risks

As you have seen in the 'Risk and reward' section of this topic, there are many risks associated with becoming an entrepreneur and setting up a new business. These risks cannot be avoided, so an entrepreneur has to be capable of taking risks. Some of the risks they will have to take will be financial risks while others will be key business decisions, such as coming up with a unique or innovative strategy that no one else has thought of before.

However, an entrepreneur can minimise the risks that they have to take. They can do this by having a good knowledge of the market and gathering evidence, such as market research.

Checkpoint

Now it is time to review your understanding of the role of business enterprise.

Strengthen

S1 Using a real-life example, describe how branding can be used to add value.

S2 Identify and explain one purpose of business activity.

S3 Describe the role of an entrepreneur.

Challenge

C1 Why is it important for a business to have a unique selling point?

C2 Do you agree with the outline of the role of an entrepreneur on pages 24–25? Do you think that any key qualities are missing from this list?

C3 Read the statement: 'Starting a business is the best thing that an individual can do for their local community'. Decide whether you agree or disagree with this statement. Justify your opinion.

1.1 Enterprise and entrepreneurship

1. Which **two** of the following would be examples of adapting a product for a fast-food restaurant?   *(2 marks)*

   Select **two** answers:

   A Advertising a special offer ☐

   B Changing its opening hours ☐

   C Changing the brand name of one of its products ☐

   D Training its staff to serve customers more quickly ☐

   E Changing a recipe to cater for religious diets ☐

2. Explain **one** method by which a business could add value to its product or service.   *(3 marks)*

Student answer

One method a business could use to add value is branding. Branding tells you what the business is like. It builds an image for a product so consumers are engaged and want to buy more.

Verdict

The student made a good start by identifying a relevant example, branding. They then developed the point by showing how branding adds value.

Read the following extract carefully, then answer Question 3.

> Cultivate is a gardening and horticulture enterprise based in Newtown in Mid Wales. It is a social enterprise, providing goods and services to tackle social problems. Cultivate's profits are reinvested in the business and the local community.
>
> Cultivate's original mission was to turn food waste into compost, and it soon got an opportunity to collect food waste from all over Mid Wales. The enterprise now focuses on educating people about good nutrition and it intends to expand by improving its promotion and attracting more local producers.
>
> The enterprise runs its own nursery where organic vegetables are grown and there are allotments for local community use. It also runs a shop, selling organic vegetables and locally-produced organic food and drink. Their growers are also paid fairly for their organic produce.

3. (a) Outline **one** method of promotion that would be appropriate for Cultivate to adopt. **(2 marks)**

Student answer

Cultivate could use a loyalty card system where a card is stamped every time £10 is spent and after so many stamps a customer could get something such as a small bag of potatoes or something similar.

Verdict

The student has identified a relevant method of promotion, loyalty cards, and developed this through an example of how this method could be used.

(b) Explain **one** reason why an enterprise needs to listen to its customers. **(3 marks)**

Student answer

Enterprises need to listen to their customers to understand how customer needs are changing. Most products have a limited lifespan and so will not always be sold, because they are no longer needed by consumers. For example, the availability of digital music has made sales of CDs decline.

Verdict

The student has identified one reason why an enterprise needs to listen to its customers, and has backed this up with a clear explanation.

(c) Evaluate whether Cultivate is likely to be a success. You should use the information provided as well as your knowledge of business. **(12 marks)**

Student answer

If Cultivate were a traditional business, success could be measured by increased sales and profit. However Cultivate have other aims, such as educating people about good food and encouraging people to grow food on allotments. They also want to pay a fair price to their suppliers. This means that success for them might be not making a loss and doing well in promoting nutrition and providing jobs for suppliers.

One thing on their side is that organic food is increasingly popular. However, organic food is selling more in supermarkets and they could outcompete Cultivate on price.

Cultivate could focus on locally produced products that supermarkets are unlikely to sell. They also need to stock a wide range of organic products, which, again, supermarkets might not do. They need to keep costs under control and ensure they do not run out of popular items. They need to drop products that do not sell. They also need to market their shop in the local press and perhaps have market stalls.

If they keep costs under control and promote the fact that the food is locally produced then they can build on the success referred to in the passage.

Verdict

This student has started well by stating what 'success' might mean for Cultivate, rather than thinking about success generally. They then suggest some of the obstacles that the business might face and also how it could overcome them. This answer also shows a recognition that the business's success is not just based on selling enough organic products but also on controlling costs.

Topic overview

This topic explores how new and small businesses spot opportunities by understanding customer needs and using market research. It also examines the importance of understanding the competition.

Case study

Whisk

Nick Holzherr is the co-founder of Whisk, a food app. Holzherr was a runner-up on the BBC television programme *The Apprentice*, and Whisk is his third start-up.

Whisk helps users to find and bookmark recipes. It is also integrated with supermarkets such as Asda, Tesco and Waitrose, meaning that users can buy the right food for the recipe they have chosen and have it delivered, all from within the app. The app also learns about users' preferences and makes recipe suggestions. The app is free for anyone to download and use. Food retailers pay to advertise within the app and the integrated supermarkets pay Whisk a fee whenever a user purchases from their store through the app.

One of Holzherr's previous start-ups was a coffee shop business, but the high-street coffee industry is very competitive. This meant that the business's profit margins were very small, and expanding the business was difficult because every time that Holzherr wanted to open a new outlet he had to raise more money.

Between its launch in 2013 and 2016, Whisk grew from a start-up run by its two founders to a business run by a team of 10 employees. It has already set up partnerships with the American online grocery store, Peapod, and the Australian supermarket, Woolworths.

Activity

1 What does Whisk offer its customers?
2 What difficulties did Holzherr face when setting up a coffee shop business?
3 What are the advantages of setting up an app-based business?

Your learning

In this topic you will learn about:

- customer needs – identifying and understanding customer needs
- market research – the purpose, methods and the use of data in market research
- market segmentation – how businesses use market segmentation to target customers
- the competitive environment – understanding the strengths and weaknesses of competitors, and the impact of competition on businesses.

Customer needs

JustPark

JustPark is an online marketplace for car parking spaces, where people can rent out a car parking space to JustPark users. This allows people to make money from an unused parking space and allows drivers to pay less to park their car: JustPark's short-term parking is up to 70 per cent cheaper than pay-and-display. The business was founded by Anthony Eskinazi in 2006 after he struggled to find parking near a sports stadium. It launched as a website and is now also available through iPhone and Android apps. In 2015, JustPark came first in the Grow category of Richard Branson's VOOM competition.

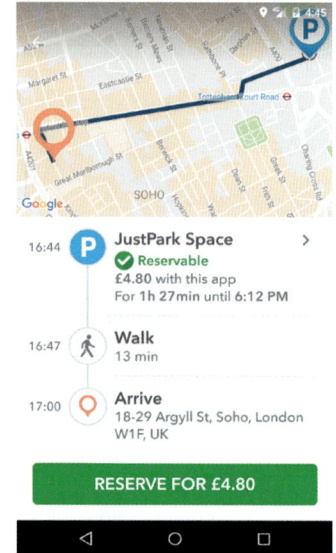

Did you know?

Many businesses like JustPark raise money through crowdfunding. Crowdfunding is the process of raising small amounts of money from a large number of people, usually on the internet.

Activity

1 What is the attraction of JustPark for customers?

2 How did Eskinazi identify his business opportunity?

3 What do you think is meant by the term 'the sharing economy'? Do some research to find out what it means and identify three examples of businesses in the sharing economy.

The most important thing that an entrepreneur has to do is be able to spot a business opportunity. They do this by identifying a need for a particular product or service.

Personal experience is an important way in which opportunities can be spotted. Every entrepreneur is also a customer and will have ideas about what they need or would like. For example, if someone with a dietary requirement, such as vegan or gluten free, finds it difficult to find nice-tasting food that meets their needs at their local supermarket, they may have identified a business opportunity. They could start to create meals for themselves, then for others, and then may be able to develop this into a thriving company.

Some business opportunities can also be identified if an entrepreneur sees a way of making something possible that seems impossible. Proposing a solution that nobody else has thought of will put a business ahead of any competitors. The JustPark case study shows how Eskinazi not only identified an opportunity through his own personal experience but also proposed a solution that had not previously been suggested.

Activity ?

Think of a business idea that you could launch right now. Consider your skills and the resources available to you. How could you use them to help you? Do you need any additional resources? How would you do this?

Now write up your idea as a business proposal as though you were going to pitch it to someone else. In your write-up, you should:

a explain what your idea is

b outline the resources that you would need to start

c justify why you think that this business idea could be successful.

Identifying and understanding customer needs

There are four main customer needs that a business must consider:

- price
- quality
- choice
- **convenience**.

An entrepreneur needs to think about these needs when proposing a business idea and launching a new business. Older and more established businesses also need to consider customer needs and ensure that they are meeting them.

Price

Customers will be influenced by price, especially by low prices. You can see this in the example of JustPark, which charges less than other parking providers and therefore attracts customers. Normally, businesses find that lowering their prices will increase their sales. For example, supermarkets use low prices to attract customers, publicising low-priced products and comparing their prices with their competitors' prices. Sometimes they will even sell products for less than their value in order to attract customers – products priced like this are called loss-leaders.

When launching a new product or service, it is important to research potential customers' opinions about pricing. The price that customers are willing to pay will depend on the value that they place on the product. This value can change depending on circumstances. For example, a customer might be willing to pay more for an ice-cold drink on a sunny day or for an umbrella when it is raining.

Exam-style question

Explain **one** customer need that a business must consider. **(2 marks)**

Key term

Convenience: a product or service's ability to fit in well with a customer's lifestyle or routine, the ease with which it can be used and/or its easy-to-reach location.

Exam tip

This question has only asked you for **one** need. Do not give more than one because this will not help you to achieve any more marks.

Quality

Quality is a key customer need. Customers assess 'quality' as a product's suitability or 'fitness for purpose', and a customer's opinion will depend on their expectations. For example, someone who spends £5 on a meal at a fast-food restaurant will have lower expectations of their chosen product's quality than someone who pays £50 for a meal at a gourmet restaurant. However, the fast-food customer still has expectations that their meal will be tasty. If the fast-food restaurant burns its burgers, it will not meet these expectations and the customer will assess the quality as poor. A customer assesses a product's quality based not only on the amount that they spend, but also their expectations of the product and whether the product meets their expectations.

Quality is also linked to customer service, as this is a key element of a customer's assessment of quality. A successful business will identify its customers' needs and train its staff well to ensure that customers' expectations are met every time that a customer buys a product or service. The quality of customer service is determined by the business's ability to meet its customers' expectations.

Choice

When buying products, customers like to have a choice because different customers have different tastes and needs. For example, an independent convenience store will stock several brands of baked beans, allowing customers to choose between the supermarket's own brand, low-price value brands and higher-priced market leader brands such as Heinz. Similarly, a fast-food restaurant will provide a variety of choices on its menu, such as beef, chicken and vegetarian choices served in a variety of ways (for example, in a burger bun, wrap or panini).

Choice can also help customers make buying decisions. Thanks to the internet and e-commerce, customers have far more information about products and services than ever before, which means that the choices available to customers can seem overwhelming. To help customers make buying decisions, a business with a lot of brands or products could make a point of showing how the different brands or products represent very distinct choices. For example, a toothpaste manufacturer may offer:

- a brand for people with sensitive teeth
- a brand for children
- a premium 'dentist-recommended' brand
- a standard mint-flavoured brand
- a brand that comes in different flavours.

This sort of product differentiation makes it easier for a customer to choose which of a number of products is most suitable for them. A business should aim to make customers feel confident about making a buying decision.

Convenience

Convenience is an important factor in determining how customers make decisions about what to buy and what services to use. For example, JustPark's service is convenient for customers to use: parking locations are often closer to the driver's destination than pay-and-display parking, and the booking process is made convenient through a smartphone app. Customers usually have a preference for convenient goods and services.

In 1927, an American called Joe Thompson set up a small shop selling eggs, milk and bread. The shop opened early in the morning and closed late in the evening, even at weekends, unlike other shops at the time. Gradually, Thompson started to sell more items and rebranded the shop, 7-Eleven, in reference to its opening hours (7 a.m. to 11 p.m.). By 2016, 7-Eleven had become the world's largest convenience store franchise in the world, with more than 56,000 stores worldwide.

Sometimes, customers' need for convenience can help a business to reduce its costs. For example, Palmair, owned by Bournemouth-based Peter Bath, is the smallest airline in the UK, with only one plane. It found it could reduce its costs by encouraging travellers to print their boarding passes at home and go straight to their departure gate, rather than by employing enough members at the airport to give customers their boarding passes. This allowed the airline to reduce its staff wage bill and encouraged its customers to feel that the process is more convenient, even though the airline is actually saving money by encouraging the customers to do the work instead.

Exam-style question

Read the case study on page 30 again.

Evaluate whether JustPark could be considered a success. You should use the information provided in the case study as well as your knowledge of business. **(12 marks)**

Exam tip

Remember to give a balanced answer looking at more than one viewpoint.

Meeting customer needs

A business's success is largely down to meeting its customers' needs. Meeting customer needs will ensure that customers are happy with the quality of the product or service that they purchase. This is likely to encourage repeat custom and generate customer loyalty, leading to increased sales. Satisfied and loyal customers are also more likely to recommend a product or service to others.

Customer need	Example of meeting customer need
Price	Offering products at a competitive price.
Quality	Training and encouraging staff to provide a very friendly and helpful service.
Choice	Keeping a wide variety of products in stock for customers to choose between.
Convenience	Offering same-day or next-day delivery.

Table 1.2.1 Customer needs and examples of how needs could be met

Theme 1: Investigating small business

If a business can meet the needs and expectations of its customers, it is likely to succeed

Activity ?

Choose five businesses from which you buy products or services. These could be physical shops on the high street or internet retailers. Now, using a scale from one to five with one being the worst and five being the best, rate each business on its:

a price

b convenience

c quality

d choice.

Do not forget to consider customer service as part of your assessment, and think about whether the business meets your customer needs.

Once you have assessed the businesses, add up the score for each of the four criteria, with a maximum possible score of 20. For the business with the highest score, write a brief summary of why you think it won. For the business with the lowest score, list at least three ways in which it could improve its score.

The importance of identifying and understanding customers and their needs

It is very important that a business knows who its customers are and what they want. A business could launch a brilliant new product or service, but the idea is likely to fail if the business has not understood and provided what its customers actually want. The idea will not generate enough sales, because customers will not buy a product or service that does not meet their needs.

As a consequence of this, the product or service may be withdrawn and the business may fail completely.

Customers make buying decisions based on a number of needs and behaviours, such as:

- family needs
- financial needs
- emotional needs
- brand loyalty.

These needs and behaviours can have a huge impact on the success or failure of a product or service. For example, if a business launches a new product that is too expensive for its intended market; the product will not generate enough sales. Similarly, if a supermarket stops selling a particular well-known brand of soft drink, customers who are loyal to that brand may start shopping at a rival supermarket in order to buy that brand of drink.

Activity ?

Choose a business whose products you buy (for example, a clothing company or a soft drinks manufacturer) and then answer the following questions.

1 Do you feel that the business understands your needs?
2 Does this have an impact on how you feel about that business or its brand?
3 Do you think you would continue to buy from the business if you did not think that it understood your needs?

Now discuss your thoughts about the business or brand with a partner. Have you chosen similar businesses? Compare your answers to see any similarities or differences.

Checkpoint

Now it is time to review your understanding of customer needs.

Strengthen

S1 List the four main customer needs that businesses have to meet.
S2 How do entrepreneurs spot a business opportunity?
S3 How important is customer service as part of meeting customers' needs?

Challenge

C1 Using a real-life example, describe how the convenience of a product or service can help a business to meet customer needs.
C2 What do you think would happen to a business that does not care about meeting its customers' needs? What impact would this have on the success of that business?

Market research

Hook Research

Market research helps small businesses understand and familiarise themselves with the competition and get to know what people are prepared to pay for products or services.

Debbie Bray from Hook Research says market research is vital because it will enable a small business to ensure that it invests in the right sectors and the right products. She explains: 'If you've got the name wrong, or maybe the ingredients list wrong that can have fundamental impacts later on.'

Key terms

Viable: able to work properly or successfully.

Market research: the process of gathering information about the market and customers' needs and wants in order to help inform business decisions, including product design and marketing.

Activity ?

Research an advertising campaign by a local business in your area. Describe the campaign and decide whether you think it could be successful.

After an entrepreneur has identified a possible business opportunity, they have to be able to test whether their business idea is **viable** by carrying out **market research**. Market research can also be used by established businesses in order to test new business or product ideas and to find out how satisfied their customers are with their existing products.

The purpose of market research

Market research is used to gather accurate information about three key influences on a business's success: the market, the needs of potential or existing customers and any competitors the business may have. This knowledge and understanding of the market and customers is vital if a business is going to succeed. In particular, it can help an entrepreneur to decide whether their business idea is viable before investing their money and time in a new business.

Key influence	Questions answered by market research
Market	• Who is currently buying the product or service?
	• How many people are interested in buying it?
	• Why might some people not want to buy it?
	• What is the right price to charge for it?
Competitors	• Who is/are the main competitor/s?
	• What is their market share?
Customers	• What are customers' lifestyles?
	• Does the product or service fit in with their lifestyles?
	• Why would they buy it?
	• Where would they buy it?
	• What need are customers trying to satisfy when they buy it?
	• What is the best brand image for it?
	• What is the main benefit that it offers customers?
	• What improvements could be made to products or services to improve customer satisfaction?

Table 1.2.2 Important questions that can be answered using market research

Methods of market research

There are two main types of market research: primary research and secondary research.

Primary research

Primary research is new research that is carried out to answer specific issues and questions. It usually involves surveying consumers' opinions by asking them questions through questionnaires, **focus groups**, interviews and observations. Surveys ask people questions in order to measure their opinions or experiences and can do this in a number of ways. For example, a survey could be conducted:

- online, using online questionnaires and online focus groups
- in person or face-to-face, using interviews and focus groups
- over the telephone or through the post.

Questionnaires

A questionnaire is a set of questions with a choice of answers. Questionnaires need to be carefully planned in order to provide useful feedback. A business using a questionnaire needs to have a clear set of objectives that the questionnaire will help them achieve, as this will help them to identify what sort of information they need to obtain from consumers.

Following this, the business has to identify the type of customer that they would like to question. This may include thinking about the customers':

- age group
- income bracket or social group
- home town or region
- gender.

Theme 1: Investigating small business

The business then needs to decide how the survey is going to be carried out and consider how this may affect the questions in the questionnaire. For example, if the questionnaire is going to be conducted as part of a face-to-face survey rather than an email or online survey, it is easier to help a respondent if they misunderstand the question. However, it is important that all questions are clear and easy to understand and answer, no matter which method is being used.

Have you completed any online surveys? Can you think of any changes you would make to improve your experience?

There are three main types of question, as shown in Table 1.2.3.

Type of question	Description	Example
Multiple-choice question (MCQ)	Choose from a number of provided options.	Which of the following financial products do you currently have? **A** Current account **B** Mortgage **C** Savings account **D** Credit card **E** Home insurance
Yes/no	Give an answer that is either yes or no.	Do you currently own a home? • Yes • No
Sliding scale	Use a scale to give a product or service a score. Frequently used scales are 1–5, 1–10, or 'very bad'–'very good'.	How would you rate the service provided by your current bank? • Very unsatisfactory • Unsatisfactory • Satisfactory • Very satisfactory • Not sure

Table 1.2.3 Types of question used in questionnaires

Activity **?**

1 Your local sports centre is considering replacing its current vending machines with ones that sell healthier products. You have been asked to create a questionnaire to find out:

   a what people currently buy from vending machines

   b how often customers make purchases

   c what customers think about the idea of switching to healthy drinks and snacks

   d what products should be stocked in the new vending machines.

   In your questionnaire, use multiple-choice questions, yes/no questions and sliding scale questions.

2 Swap your finished questionnaire with someone else in your class and review it. Remember to give constructive criticism that will help them to improve their questionnaire.

3 Once your questionnaire has been reviewed, use the feedback to help you revise the questions that you have asked.

Focus groups

A focus group is a group of people who are asked about their views, opinions, beliefs and attitudes towards a product, service, advertisement or idea. Questionnaire-based surveys are good for collecting information, but a focus group can be used to help a business understand its customers' opinions more deeply.

Usually, a focus group is a group of about 10 people led through an open discussion by a skilled interviewer. Focus group sessions usually last for about 90 minutes and the questions are decided in advance, though the discussion is allowed to flow freely.

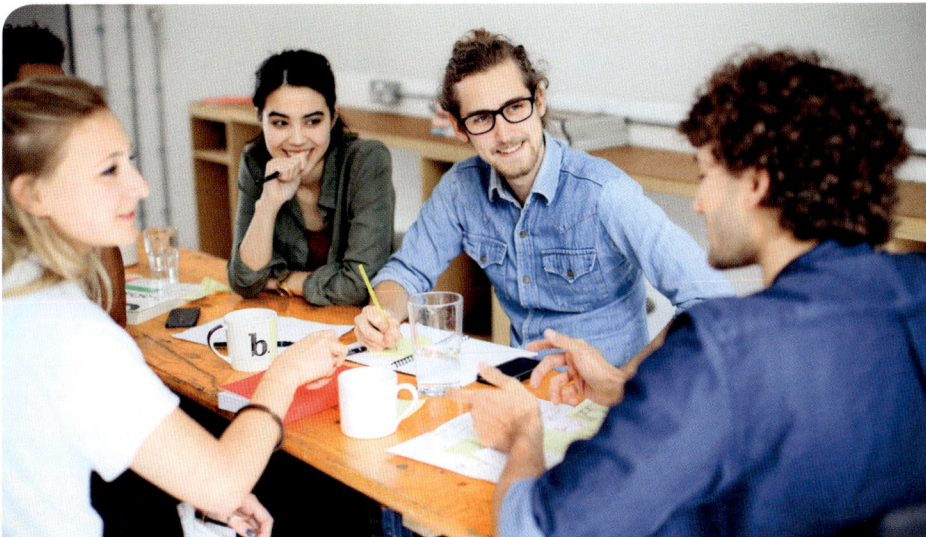

Carrying out market research in a focus group should provide a wide range of subjects from different backgrounds and age groups

Theme 1: Investigating small business

The group needs to be large enough to generate a discussion, but not so large that people are missed out or feel that they cannot contribute. Participants should feel comfortable in the group but they should not know each other, and it is important to choose participants from the intended **target market**. Participants are normally paid to join in.

Market research cannot be based on just one focus group because one group of people may not accurately represent the opinions of the wider population. The interviewer leading the session needs to make sure that the group is not dominated by one or two participants. They also need to be careful that the way they ask the question does not prompt participants to give a particular answer.

The growth of the internet means that focus groups can be held online. This can significantly reduce the cost of holding focus groups and allows participants to be brought together from all over the world. As more products and services become global, hosting online focus groups can make the **sample** more representative.

Case study

Focus groups

A car manufacturer asked a market research company to run some online focus groups. This formed part of an investigation into the attitudes of members of **Generation Y** towards different car brands. Each of the 15 participants was sent a disposable digital camera and were asked to take photographs of their cars and other items that were important parts of their lifestyle. During the focus group discussion, participants explained their photographs to the others. The results could then be compared with the attitudes of older generations.

Activity ?

1   State a possible advantage and a possible disadvantage of hosting focus groups online.
2   What do you think the car manufacturer was trying to achieve through this market research?
3   Take a photograph of an item that is an important part of your lifestyle. Share your photograph with a partner, then take it in turns to discuss why you chose your particular item. What do you think this information could tell a market researcher?

Interviews

In-depth interviews can be conducted by telephone, face-to-face or, increasingly, online. The questions asked in an interview can be open questions, leading to long, detailed responses with a lot of explanation. These questions are designed to produce responses that will help a market researcher to identify trends and find out customers' opinions. The interviewer needs to be very skilful in order to create a positive relationship with the interviewee and make them feel that they can be honest with the interviewer.

Face-to-face interviews can take place in people's homes, a hired meeting room, on the street or at a particular event such as a football match or a conference. The cost of hiring a room, paying for interviewer or interviewees' travel can be expensive. In comparison, telephone and online interviews are more cost-effective and can help to save time, as a lot of interviewees can be contacted one after another.

Exam-style question

Discuss the advantages to a business of using primary research.

(6 marks)

Observations

Observation means watching how customers behave naturally, when they do not think they are being watched. It is a very effective way of gathering primary **data**. Observations can be carried out in person or by using appropriate technology, such as CCTV cameras or webcams. For example, the manager of a shop could film a particular display and study customers' reactions to a particular product, layout or advertisement. Other examples of situations in which observation could be used include:

- understanding people's reactions to different packaging designs
- measuring how long it takes someone to make a purchase decision in a shop
- understanding how people actually use a product and whether they encounter any problems.

Activity **?**

Find a vending machine and observe it from a distance. Note how long it takes people to choose and buy an item, as well as their gender and their approximate age. You should also note whether they had any problems, such as difficulty in paying or not getting the item they wanted.

Write up your observations and suggest improvements for the vending machine company based on your observations.

An advantage of using observation as a research tool is that the customer behaves relatively naturally, according to their own feelings or thoughts, because they are unaware that they are being observed. This means that the research is less likely to be **biased**. In comparison, someone who is being interviewed or filling out a questionnaire may give an answer that they think the interviewer wants to hear, rather than an answer based on their own thoughts and feelings.

A disadvantage of using observation in market research is that it is time-consuming. Observations can also be inconclusive, meaning that they do not provide a definite answer, and do not give the researcher many clues about a person's wider attitudes or opinions.

Research **ethics** is a particularly important factor when planning an observation. Research must be conducted in an ethical manner and must respect the people being studied. If the researcher is looking at particular

Exam tip

When discussing the advantages, you should refer to the impact of primary research and the benefits that will be gained by undertaking this method of research.

Key terms

Data: information, particularly statistics, that can be collected and analysed.

Biased: unbalanced or inclined to agree with a particular judgement or idea rather than presenting the evidence fairly.

Ethics: moral principles or standards that guide the behaviour of a person or business.

Theme 1: Investigating small business

Activity ?

1 How reliable do you think observation is as a method of market research?

2 Think of three examples where you think that observation would be a useful market research technique to use.

Key terms

Source: a place, person or thing, such as a book or report, that can provide information to be used in research.

Chamber of Commerce: a local association that promotes the interests of businesses in a county or region.

individuals' specific behaviour, they will probably need to ask those individuals for consent before they are observed. However, if the research is looking into the general or public behaviour of a number of participants, they may be able to proceed without consent as long as the research will not use any individuals' personal information.

Case study

DJS Research

DJS Research is a market research company based in Stockport that carries out observations for market research. It observes people's behaviour to help businesses make their shop layouts more effective, for example, or to count the number of people using particular rides at theme parks.

Secondary research

Secondary research is research using existing **sources** of information that has previously been researched, often by other people or for other purposes, including published research reports, scientific reports produced by industry bodies or government, consumer surveys and the internet. This information can be sourced internally or externally.

Internally-sourced information

Internally-sourced information is the data, statistics and research that a business has accumulated in the past. For example, small stores can use sales information from their tills to gather information about what items are selling and when they are bought. This helps them to understand their customer needs and provide information for reordering stock quickly.

Externally-sourced information

Externally-sourced information is information published by people or organisations that are not related to the business. Sources include government agencies, industry and trade associations, trades unions, **Chambers of Commerce** and media sources such as newspapers.

One key source of information in the UK is the Office for National Statistics (ONS). The ONS is a government agency that gathers and analyses data about people in the UK. This includes:

- social trends – social and economic data collected by government departments and other organisations, which is used to create an overview of modern British society and how it changes

- regional trends – a range of statistics (demographic, social, industrial and economic) about life in the different regions of the UK.

Other government departments also publish data that can be used in secondary research. For example, the Department for International Trade provides information and advice for businesses that are researching the possibility of exporting their products or services to other countries.

Commercial sources of information are usually market research companies such as Mintel and Kantar Media. Businesses have to pay a fee to use their services. These market research companies publish studies and data that can help businesses to plan for the future.

Trade associations can be valuable sources of information used in secondary research. In the UK, there are more than 1,600 trade associations. One example is the British Hospitality Association (BHA), which provides information and advice to hotels, clubs, restaurants, and leisure and hospitality outlets. The BHA publishes regular reports about the tourism and hospitality industry, such as the industry's employment figures and financial highlights.

Educational institutions, such as universities and colleges, are also useful external sources of information. Universities in particular produce a lot of research data.

The use of data in market research

Market research is based on data **analysis**. This data analysis reveals useful information from a set, or sets, of data in order to come to a conclusion that can provide insights into a business's customers, market or competitors. Often, market research produces large quantities of data that must be summarised and presented in order to communicate the most important features and conclusions.

There are two different types of data that can be used.

- **Qualitative data** is descriptive data that cannot be measured in numbers.
- **Quantitative data** is numerical data.

It is important to realise that it is not an 'either-or' situation, as both qualitative and quantitative data can be gathered at the same time. For example, a business that is conducting a customer satisfaction survey might first carry out some qualitative research through interviews or focus groups in order to find out what sort of questions they should ask in a questionnaire that will provide quantitative data.

Qualitative data

Qualitative data is gathered by finding out what people think and why they think that way in order to understand people's habits or preferences. It often focuses on getting people to talk about their opinions, so the questions used to gather qualitative data are 'open' questions, meaning that people need to give a long explanation, rather than a simple 'yes' or 'no'. This means that focus groups and face-to-face interviews are a good method of collecting qualitative data. These qualitative data-gathering methods are useful when gathering feedback on new product ideas or new marketing campaigns in order to understand customers' reactions.

> **Key terms**
>
> **Trade association:** organisation founded and funded by businesses that operate in a specific industry.
>
> **Analysis:** the process of looking at data to identify patterns or trends.

Case study

Shazia Khan

Shazia Khan is a chef who owns a successful restaurant. Following excellent customer feedback, she created a sauce that home cooks could use as a 'finishing sauce'. She asked some customers to use the sauce at home and video themselves using it. Shazia noticed that people ignored her instructions and used it as a stir fry sauce instead. She tried it and realised it tasted much better that way, so she changed the instructions.

Activity ?

1 Why do you think that Shazia Khan wanted to see real-life experience of using the sauce?

2 What do you think are the advantages of this sort of qualitative data? Can you think of any disadvantages?

Uses of qualitative data

Businesses can use qualitative data-gathering techniques to find out customers' views on:

- products and services – for example, to check whether customers like a proposed new recipe
- design and packaging – for example, to find out which colour of packaging is more appealing to customers
- advertising and marketing messages – for example, to find out whether customers have seen a recent advert and whether it encouraged them to buy the product
- price changes – for example, to find out whether putting up a product's price would stop a customer from buying that product.

Using qualitative data has its advantages and disadvantages, as shown in Table 1.2.4

Advantages	Disadvantages
Provides depth and detail, giving a detailed picture of why customers behave in a particular way.	A relatively small sample of people is surveyed, so the results may be biased.
Helps a business to listen to what their customers want, rather than jumping to conclusions.	Responses are very subjective, meaning that they are based on one person's opinions and beliefs.
	Results can depend on the skills of the interviewer – for example, making sure that they do not 'lead' the interviewees' answers.

Table 1.2.4 Advantages and disadvantages of qualitative research

Exam tip

Do not write down everything you know about qualitative research – focus on the benefits of qualitative research for creating a marketing campaign.

Exam-style question

Discuss the benefits to a business of using qualitative research to design a marketing campaign.

(6 marks)

Quantitative data

Quantitative data is gathered by asking people for information about their habits and lifestyles in a structured way using a tool such as a questionnaire. To get reliable quantitative data, it is important to survey people in large numbers to make sure that the results are based on a representative sample of the population.

Gathering quantitative data is a quicker process than using qualitative data methods

The questions used to gather quantitative data are 'closed' questions, meaning that they can only be answered with a simple 'yes' or 'no' rather than with a long explained answer. For example, the question, 'Do you buy a newspaper?' is a closed question. By asking lots of people the same closed questions, a business can build a clear picture of what customers want and how they behave.

Quantitative data is most often gathered using questionnaires. These can be conducted in person, over the telephone, by post or email, or online. Because it can sometimes be difficult to get people to fill out questionnaires, businesses often offer participants an **incentive**, such as vouchers or the chance to be entered into a prize draw. Face-to-face interviews can also work well if the customer needs to have a product demonstrated or explained before giving feedback.

> **Key term**
>
> **Incentive:** something such as a payment or gift that encourages someone to do something.

Theme 1: Investigating small business

Uses of quantitative data

Quantitative data can be used to answer a number of questions that a business might need to ask.

- Is there a market for this product or service?
- To what extent are consumers aware of our products or services?
- How many people are interested in buying our products or services?
- What type of people are our most loyal customers?
- What are our customers' buying habits?

Businesses often use quantitative data to find out about and compare different groups of their customers. A business using quantitative data in this way has to ensure that it surveys enough people in each customer group so that it can build up a clear picture of the characteristics of each group. This data can then be used to help the business to direct their marketing at each group in the most effective way for that group.

Quantitative data is usually used to generate statistics. The results will be expressed in numerical form, for example:

- 40 per cent of 11–15-year-olds buy three chocolate bars a week
- 60 per cent of 1-week holidays were taken in the UK
- 35 per cent of people have not been to a cinema in the past year.

If quantitative data is gathered regularly using the same survey technique, a business can monitor how customers' opinions change and how its new products, services or marketing campaigns are received by customers. It is important that the survey technique is kept as similar as possible each time it is used so that comparisons can be made between new results and previous results.

Case study

Birds of a Feather

Birds of a Feather is a cafe and delicatessen in a large town. Its owners noticed that the type of customer varied depending on the time of day and wanted to find out more about this. They asked customers to fill in a questionnaire in return for an extra stamp on their coffee loyalty card.

The owners discovered that there were several distinct customer groups:

- people on their way to work picking up an early coffee and something for lunch
- commuters buying breakfast on their way to the railway station or bus stop
- parents meeting friends for coffee
- ethical shoppers purchasing Fair Trade products
- shoppers who liked that the cafe sells organic products
- students coming in after college.

Using this information, the owners took the following steps:

- opened earlier to catch the commuters
- provided a larger breakfast menu
- started a book club to target the parents
- advertised Fair Trade and organic products in the window
- introduced live music by local bands in the early evenings for the students.

Activity ?

1 Based on the results, what questions do you think Birds of a Feather would have asked in their questionnaire?

2 The owners of Birds of a Feather have asked you to carry out some further market research by holding some focus groups. Create five short lists of questions that you would ask each of the different groups. Remember to ask open questions in order to encourage discussion during the focus group.

The role of social media in collecting market research data

Market research can be expensive and time-consuming. However, many businesses have started to use social media as a cheaper way of understanding their customers. Using social media in market research has other advantages, allowing businesses to:

- deepen their understanding of their market
- identify popular trends
- improve their products and marketing
- save time conducting market research.

Did you know?

Businesses can use free or paid-for tools to gather and analyse information on social media platforms. This is often a lot cheaper than using techniques such as focus groups and questionnaires.

Understanding the market

A business can set up a Facebook page in order to communicate with its target audience. This allows a business to see what interests its customers and potential customers, as well as what they like and dislike. Competitors' pages can also give a business information about its rivals' activities and their customers' satisfaction levels.

Identifying trends

Social media platforms such as Twitter and Facebook allow businesses to analyse market trends. For example, a business can look at the latest posts and popular search terms or hashtags in order to understand what customers are talking about at that moment. By setting up automated searches relating to a brand or particular term, the business can also receive an instant notification when customers, clients or competitors mention the brand name or term.

Improving products and marketing

Because social media platforms allow people to talk to one another, a business can see how customers talk to one another about its products or services. The business can then start to use that language in its marketing. Another advantage of observing customers' discussions and joining in with the discussions, rather than asking questions, is that it can lead a business to discover insights that might not have emerged using traditional market research methods.

Saving time

One of the attractions of using social media for market research is that it can provide results within minutes rather than over months. In addition, the majority of people with internet access use social media. This means that social media can provide much larger samples than other sources of data. The fact that social media platforms are casual places that are easy to access can also encourage participation and honest feedback. This improves the chances that a business will be able to gather useful and accurate data.

Case study

The Red Lyon

The Red Lyon is a rural pub and restaurant in a small village outside the city of Nottingham. Its owners wanted to attract more customers so they looked at what local people were saying on Twitter, Facebook and TripAdvisor. This research suggested that people in their area were unhappy with the quality of Chinese and Thai takeaway food, and were dissatisfied with the opening hours of restaurants and takeaways.

The owners of The Red Lyon decided to:

- specialise in Chinese, Thai and Malaysian cuisine by taking on an experienced chef
- change the pub's opening hours to 11 a.m.–11 p.m. with full menu availability
- make their pub family-friendly by installing play equipment in the garden
- add a takeaway menu to appeal to local people
- spend time developing their Facebook page to target this takeaway market and interact with customers
- use Twitter to advertise special offers.

The Red Lyon is now so popular that people travel to eat there and locals now use it as their local pub.

Activity ?

1 Identify the different types of customer that purchase from The Red Lyon.

2 How honest do you think customers are when leaving reviews on Facebook or TripAdvisor?

The importance of the reliability of market research data

When a business uses market research results to make decisions, it has to be confident that those results are accurate. All market research, no matter how well it is planned and controlled, can have the potential to be wrong. For example, election opinion polls can produce inaccurate results, as they did before the 2015 general election, when most polls wrongly predicted that the Labour Party would win in a majority of constituencies.

In market research, most errors can be traced to problems with the way in which the data was gathered, particularly relating to **validity** and reliability.

- Validity is a measure of how good the design and methods of research are and suggests whether the findings of the research can be trusted. For example, research conducted by a researcher who asks leading questions is not valid, as the participants' answers may be swayed by the way in which the researcher has asked the questions.

- Reliability is an indication of whether the research results from a sample are representative of a wider group or the population as a whole. For example, research based on a sample of people from just one social or ethnic group will not be reliable if it is used to make generalisations about the whole British population.

Key term

Valid: having a solid or accurate basis of facts.

Activity

1 What mistakes did Arthur Lewis make in his use of market research?

2 What questions should have been asked as part of the taste tests?

Case study

Substitute coleslaw

Arthur Lewis ran a successful deli aimed at the lunchtime market in London. He wanted his food to be healthier and experimented with a low-calorie coleslaw. He conducted 100 blind taste tests and found that more than 80 per cent of participants preferred the low-calorie version. Arthur stopped making the original coleslaw. However, he got a lot of complaints from customers looking for the original coleslaw and his sales of coleslaw fell dramatically. He realised that people liked the original more than he had taken account of and that participants in the taste tests had not realised that he planned to replace the original with the healthy option. He quickly reversed his decision.

Exam-style question

Discuss the benefits of market research to a manufacturer launching a product. **(6 marks)**

Exam tip

Underlining the key words or terms in the question may help you to plan your answer. Key words in this question include 'market research' and 'launching'.

Checkpoint

Now it is time to review your understanding of market research.

Strengthen

S1 Describe the purpose of market research.
S2 List three external sources for secondary research.
S3 Describe the differences between primary and secondary research.

Challenge

C1 Using a real-life example, describe why it is important to use data that is reliable and valid.
C2 Write a short blog post for a market research company to explain the advantages and disadvantages of observation as a method of conducting research.

Market segmentation

Case study

Essential Trading

Essential Trading is a worker co-operative, based in Bristol, which manufactures and distributes sustainable wholefoods, ecological household products and cruelty-free body care items. It stocks more than 5,000 lines, including convenience foods, raw ingredients, vegan and vegetarian products, speciality foods and products that are free from dairy and gluten. A business like this would segment its market into customers who need their products for dietary reasons, those who are vegan or vegetarian and customers who have a particularly ecological focus.

Activity ?

1 How has Essential Trading divided up its customers?
2 What do you think is the benefit to a business of dividing its customers into different groups?

Market **segmentation** is the process of dividing a target market into smaller categories by grouping together consumers with a particular need or interest. Identifying market segments is one of the most important parts of a business's marketing strategy. This is because a business needs to know who its intended customers are in order to aim its products or services at those target customers.

Using market segmentation to target customers

The specialist boutique clothes business is a good example of how segmentation can be carried out. A high-street boutique could segment its market by age – for example professional women aged 30–55, young high earners and teenagers – or it could segment by buying behaviour, for example women buying everyday items, those who like classic items and customers looking for more expensive clothing for a special occasion.

Identifying market segments

Market segments that businesses use to help them market effectively to their target customers include:

- location
- **demographics**
- behaviour
- lifestyle
- income
- age.

Key terms

Segmentation: the process of breaking something up into smaller parts.

Demographics: relating to the structure of a population.

Location

A business may choose to divide its market into groups based on where they live. This is known as geographic segmentation. It uses the type of home or the area in which a consumer lives as a predictor of their purchasing behaviour, including the types of products and brands they might purchase. One system for breaking up a market in this way is the ACORN (A Classification of Residential Neighbourhoods) system. It classifies homes rather than individuals as a basis for segmentation.

Demographics

Demographic segmentation divides the market by factors such as sex or family type. Segmenting a market based on sex is common for many products. For example, manufacturers of toiletries do not often advertise their moisturisers in a unisex way: these products are usually aimed either at men or at women.

Another factor in demographic segmentation is called the family life cycle. This defines the different types of person, couples or families in the population. For example, using the family life cycle, one person could move through the following classifications throughout their life:

- young single person living alone
- young couple with no children
- family with young children
- family with teenage children
- older couple with no children at home
- retired couple.

Dividing a market into different groups based on their current stage of the family life cycle can help a business understand the way in which its customers' choice of products or services will change throughout their life.

Activity ?

Working in pairs or small groups, think about your local area and the people who live in it. Can you think of any products or services that might or might not be targeted at your local area? Why do you think this?

Exam tip

If you are asked to define a term, you do not need to explain it in detail. Just give one sentence about what the term means and then move on to the next question.

Exam-style question

Define the term 'market segmentation'. **(1 mark)**

Behaviour

Behavioural segmentation divides the population based on people's behaviour. For example, people behave differently around special occasions, such as birthdays or Valentine's Day, and this will influence what they will buy. A greetings card business will target customers who are approaching occasions such as religious festivals and exam results day.

Impulse buying is another behavioural impact on market segmentation. Psychologists suggest that unconscious thoughts can drive people to buy things, and businesses can use this as a marketing ploy to encourage consumers to buy products or services that they do not necessarily need. Reasons for impulse buying include:

- getting satisfaction from buying something nice without considering the cost
- deciding to save money by buying immediately in order to take advantage of a sale, two-for-one offer or discounted price.

Theme 1: Investigating small business

Did you know?

Small businesses now use loyalty cards, having learned from their larger rivals that the cards provide a valuable source of data about customers. They can also provide data on which to base tempting offers targeted at individuals, getting them to come back again and again.

Some businesses, such as supermarkets and coffee shops, offer loyalty cards as a way of influencing consumer behaviour. They reward repeat customers by giving them benefits such as discounts and vouchers for products that they usually buy. In exchange for these benefits, customers give the business their permission to collect data about them, such as when they shop, what products they buy and how often they buy those products. Research has shown that 92 per cent of shoppers who have loyalty cards use them at least once a month, but 30 per cent forget to take their loyalty cards with them some of the time.

Activity ?

In pairs or small groups, discuss the reasons why a small business might choose to use a loyalty card system.

Lifestyle

The term 'lifestyle' refers to the way in which customers live their lives. Customers can be sorted into groups defined by the things they like to do in their spare time. A business can use this information to connect with its customers' interests, and this can help a business to build a relationship with that customer. A customer that buys a product because of lifestyle-based marketing is likely to be brand loyal because they see the product and the brand as part of who they are rather than something that they buy.

First Flight is a hot air balloon company, based in Bristol, that segments its market based on lifestyle. Its Champagne balloon flights in the local area are offered to its highest income customers.

Exam tip

If you are asked to discuss, try to use real examples. This will help you to frame an answer and to explain that answer as clearly as possible.

Exam-style question

Discuss the ways in which a small business could segment its market.

(6 marks)

Income

A business can also segment customers by their income, which is the amount of money that they earn. For example, a car manufacturer may sell differently priced cars to different income segments. A young person on a relatively low income might buy a small hatchback, whereas a family with children might buy a more expensive people carrier.

Income segmentation is used by luxury brands in particular. Because luxury products are expensive, there is no point in advertising them to customers who cannot afford them. This sort of income segmentation will help a business to choose where to advertise its products. For example, a luxury watch manufacturer may choose to advertise in newspapers and magazines that are bought by people who work in high-paying industries such as finance.

Age

Customers' needs and wants change as they get older. A product bought by people in their 20s may not appeal to people in their 60s. This means that a business may want to segment its customers depending on their age and offer different products for different age groups. Alternatively, a business might choose to launch a new product to target a particular age group. For example, globally, the number of people aged 65 and over is increasing, so a business may want to target this growing market segment.

Market mapping to identify gaps in the market and competitors

Market mapping is the process of creating a diagram, known as a market map, that identifies all products in a market and maps them against two of their features (for example, price and quality). After a business has identified an appropriate segment of the market that it can target, it needs to create a market map. Figure 1.2.1 shows an example of a market map.

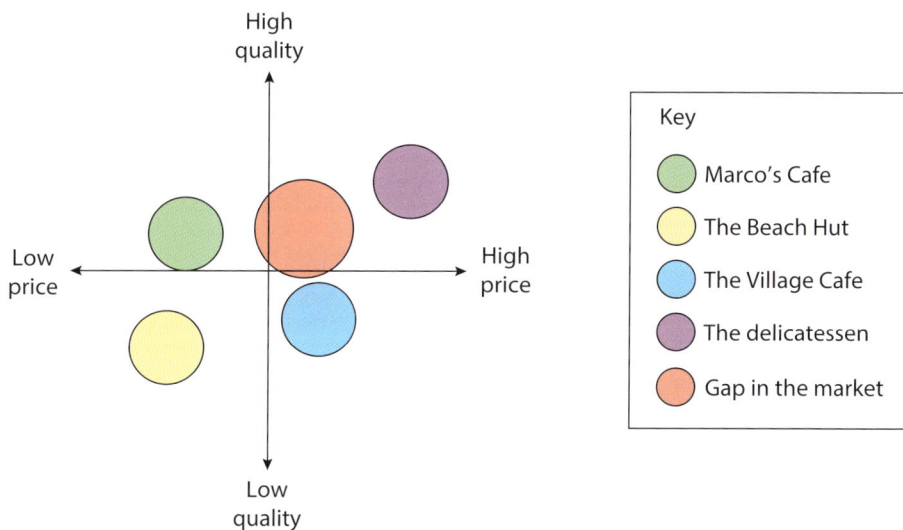

Figure 1.2.1 A market map showing fast-food outlets in a town

A market map allows a business to:
- see all the products or services in the market
- identify its competitors
- spot any gaps in the market.

The features used as the **axes** on a market map can vary. They can include price, quality, luxury and age.

However, even if a market map suggests that there is a gap in the market, it does not necessarily mean that there is demand for a product or service to fill that gap. There might be a reason why consumers do not want to buy a product that would fill the gap, so a business should only use a market map as the starting point for its market research. Market mapping is an attractive technique to use because a market map looks clear and straightforward. However, market maps are subjective, meaning that they are based on opinion rather than fact.

Key term

Axes: the reference lines on a graph.

Activity ?

Using the features of quality (high/low) and price (high/low), create a market map showing the following confectionery products:

a MARS® Bar

b TWIX®

c Ferrero Rocher

d Thorntons chocolate bar

e Cadbury Dairy Milk

f Galaxy®

g Kit Kat

h Toblerone

i Lindt EXCELLENCE.

Once you have created your marketing map, compare it with someone else's map. Have you both placed the products in the same places on the scale or have you made different decisions?

Checkpoint

Now it is time to review your understanding of market segmentation.

Strengthen

S1 Describe what is meant by market segmentation.

S2 List two different ways in which a business can segment its market.

S3 Explain how market mapping can be used to identify a gap in the market.

Challenge

C1 Discuss the weaknesses of using market mapping. How could these weaknesses have an impact on a business's decision-making?

C2 Choose a product (for example, a bicycle or a magazine). Create a market map showing the available brands of that product on the price/quality scale.

The competitive environment

Case study

Grocery retail

According to figures produced by the government, there are 26,873 independent grocery stores in the UK which is 26 per cent of all UK grocery stores. They take £7.5 billion a year in income, which is 6 per cent of the value of all grocery stores. The competitive environment for independents is challenging, as large supermarket chains have moved into their market by opening local convenience stores with lower prices.

Most businesses have competitors, so it is important for businesses to understand the nature of the competition if they are going to succeed.

There are two different types of competitors: direct and indirect competitors.

- **Direct competitors** are businesses that sell the same type of product or service. For example, McDonald's and Burger King are direct competitors.
- **Indirect competitors** are businesses that do not sell the same product or service but still find themselves in competition with one another. For example, someone planning to travel from the UK to France can choose to take a ferry, an airline flight, a train or a coach, or even choose to drive themselves using the Channel Tunnel. All of these businesses are in indirect competition with one another.

Understanding the competitive environment

In a highly competitive environment, a business must know its target market very well. It must be able to sell the right product in the right place and at the right price, and promote the product in the right way. These factors (product, place, price and promotion) are known as the marketing mix. It is also important for a business to know and understand its competitors' marketing mixes.

Competition is strong if there are lots of competitors in an industry and there is little difference between the products that they offer, because this enables customers to shop around for the best deals. In comparison, if there are very few businesses in an industry, those businesses have a lot more power over factors such as price, because customers do not have as many alternatives to choose from and cannot shop around for really good deals.

The competitiveness of an industry also depends on the barriers to entry – that is, anything that makes it harder to start a business in that industry. For example, if the cost of starting a new business is relatively low, such as in designing and creating smartphone apps, that industry will be competitive, because more new businesses can come along and enter the market. In comparison, if the cost of starting up a new business is high, such as in dairy farming, the threat of new entrants is lower and so the industry is not as competitive.

Strengths and weaknesses of competitors

If a business is to compete successfully, it needs to know the strengths and weaknesses of competitors. This knowledge will help the business to improve its own performance and outperform its rivals on their weak points.

Key competitor strengths and weaknesses include:

- Price: for example, a sandwich business charges higher prices than its nearest competitor. The competitor's lower price is a competitor strength.
- Quality: for example, the sandwich business finds that its lower-priced competitor makes lower-quality sandwiches. The quality of that competitor's sandwiches is a competitor weakness.

Activity ?

In groups, discuss the following questions.

1 What is a price war?

2 Do you think a small business could survive the competition from a large business?

3 What strategies could an independent petrol station use to stay competitive if a large supermarket drops its petrol prices?

Link it up

You will learn more about the marketing mix in Topic 1.4 *Making the business effective.*

- Location: for example, another of the sandwich business's competitors is located near the railway station, meaning that its location is convenient for commuters buying lunch on their way to work. That competitor's location is a competitor strength.
- Product range: for example, the sandwich business finds that a competitor makes a wider variety of sandwiches than it does. That competitor's wider product range is a competitor strength.
- Customer service: for example, the sandwich business finds that a competitor takes a long time to serve customers and employs staff who are rude to customers. That competitor's customer service is a competitor weakness.

Activity ?

Look at the information given in Table 1.2.5 about a number of pasta sauces.

Brand	Product description	Price (£)
A	• Leading brand name • Well-advertised on television for the last 20 years • Well-known and widely recognised brand	1.20
B	• Imported from Italy • An authentic Italian sauce	1.50
C	• A reasonably well-known brand (less famous than Brand A) on special offer	1.00
D	• An unknown discount brand	0.80
E	• A supermarket's own label sauce	0.90
F	• A handmade sauce produced and sold in a local delicatessen	1.70

Table 1.2.5 Comparisons between different brands of pasta sauce

1 Decide which pasta sauce you would choose to buy and explain your reasons why.

2 Find out how your choice compares with others' decisions and how important the product's price was in people's decision-making.

3 Look at the product you would choose to buy. What are its competitors' strengths and weaknesses?

SWOT analysis

One method of analysing a business's strengths and weaknesses is to complete a **SWOT analysis**. SWOT stands for **S**trengths, **W**eaknesses, **O**pportunities and **T**hreats. SWOT analysis involves identifying the strengths and weaknesses of a business, as well as any opportunities it might be able to take advantage of or threats that it might face. A business can complete a SWOT analysis on itself as well as for its competitors.

Key term

SWOT analysis: a study undertaken by a business to identify the strengths and weaknesses, opportunities and threats.

Using a SWOT analysis to understand its competitors can help a business to:

- identify the **strengths** of competitors and learn about what they do well
- review competitors' **weaknesses**, such as the loss of market share or clients
- investigate the **opportunities** that exist for it and its competitors, such as the dissatisfied customers of a rival
- find out what **threats** are posed by competitors, such as a good reputation for customer service.

The findings of a SWOT analysis can be applied to many parts of a business. For example, it may lead a business to update its marketing, start developing a new type of product or change its prices.

The impact of competition on business decision-making

Businesses are strongly affected by competition. For example, the price that a business charges is limited by the extent of the competition. If there is a lot of competition, having higher prices than competitors will have an impact on a business's sales. Look again at the case study about supermarkets on page 54, which shows that the grocery market is very sensitive to price changes.

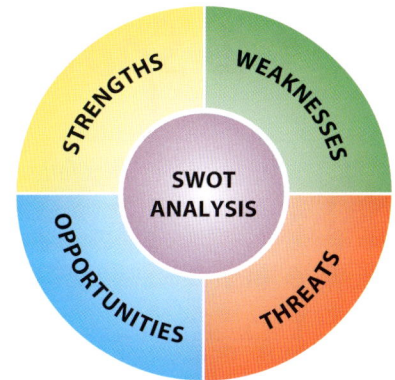

Figure 1.2.2 A SWOT analysis matrix.

Exam tip

When you have finished writing your answer, reread the question to double check that you have definitely answered it.

Exam-style question

Explain **one** reason why it is important for a business to know the strengths of its competitors. **(3 marks)**

Competition can make businesses more likely to innovate or think of new product ideas, in order to get ahead of competitors. It can also make them try to keep costs under control, in order to make a profit even if their prices have to remain low. The services sector is a competitive industry. In 2015, small businesses saw their sales fall by 38 per cent and many had to reduce staff numbers. (Source: smallbusiness.co.uk)

Checkpoint

Now it is time to review your understanding of the competitive environment.

Strengthen

S1 Describe the difference between direct and indirect competitors.
S2 List two reasons why it is important for businesses to understand their competitors?
S3 Give one example of location as a strength and one example of location as a weakness.

Challenge

C1 Choose a business whose products or services you buy. Complete a SWOT analysis for the business, considering its strengths and weaknesses and then identifying any opportunities or threats that it faces.
C2 What could make an industry uncompetitive? What impact do you think this would have on the consumer?

1.2 Spotting a business opportunity

1. Which **one** of the following is an example of secondary research? (1 mark)

   A Questionnaires ☐   B Statistics published by the government ☐

   C Interviews ☐   D Focus groups ☐

   E Observing customer behaviour ☐

2. a) Explain **one** method that a business could use to undertake qualitative market research. (3 marks)

Student answer

One method is using focus groups. This is a group of about 8–15 people and an interviewer asks the questions. It is important that more than one focus group takes place and the questions are the same for each group. These days online focus groups are being used more.

Verdict

This is a good answer. However, the student could have explained why holding more than one focus group and asking the same questions is important, rather than just saying that it is important.

   b) Explain **one** advantage of using social media for market research. (3 marks)

Student answer

One advantage of social media for market research is that a business can talk directly with customers. This means that information is up to date and should be more honest. It means that by joining in a discussion more information can be collected and compared to other types of market research.

Verdict

This answer starts well as it is first identifying an advantage. It then develops the advantage.

Read the following extract carefully, then answer Question 3.

Nadiya runs a street food business in Manchester. She makes South East Asian food which she sells in three different locations: a regular lunchtime pitch in Manchester, markets in local towns and local sporting events.

There are a lot of fast-food vans operating at lunchtime. When she was setting up her business, Nadiya did some market research to find out what people wanted to buy. She offers a cheap range for people in a hurry, a range of alternative 'healthy' products such as salads and a higher-priced range of 'gourmet' meals.

Nadiya drives through another area of Manchester, where there are a lot of offices. She has seen that there is a fish and chip shop and a corner shop, but thinks that they might not offer much variety.

3. (a) Discuss the likely benefits of Nadiya carrying out market research. **(6 marks)**

Student answer

The benefits of market research for Nadiya will be that it will tell her if people in that area are likely to buy her food. She could ask customers what they would like. This would tell her which ranges she should try to sell in that area, like the cheap option or the high-priced option, or if they would actually like a different range. Although market research could cost her money, or if she did it herself it could take up a lot of her time, the market research will help her see if the expansion could succeed.

Verdict

This answer is OK. The student explains the benefit of market research and gives a reason why Nadiya might want to do it. However, they could improve their answer by using business terminology and saying what sort of market research would be beneficial.

(b) Outline **one** way in which Nadiya uses market segmentation. **(3 marks)**

Student answer

Market segmentation means splitting up customers into groups and Nadiya used market segmentation to offer different meals to different customers because not all customers want the same thing. This means that Nadiya can sell to customers who want a cheap lunch as well as people who want to spend a bit more money on their lunch so Nadiya has more customers and more sales.

Verdict

This is a good answer. The student outlines how Nadiya specifically has used market segmentation (offering different meals to different customers), using information from the extract to make their point.

Nadiya is considering whether or not to do some market research before expanding into the new area that she has identified.

(c) Justify whether or not Nadiya should undertake market research before expanding. **(9 marks)**

Student answer

Nadiya should do market research because it will tell her if people in that area would buy food. Market research means asking people who might be customers what they would like. This would tell her which ranges she should try to sell in that area, like the cheap option or the high-priced option, or if they would actually like a different range.

However, market research could cost her money especially if she uses a company to do it. Or it could take up a lot of her time. But the business is successful so she could probably afford to do it.

Overall, I think that Nadiya should do market research because it will help her see if the expansion will do well.

Verdict

This answer is OK. The student explains what market research is and gives a reason why Nadiya might want to do it. They also give some advantages and disadvantages to Nadiya of undertaking market research and come to a conclusion. However, they could improve their answer by using business terminology and analysing the advantages and disadvantages in more detail.

Topic overview

This topic focuses on making a business idea happen. You will examine how a business identifies aims and objectives and calculate key financial aspects of putting a business idea into practice.

Case study

Toucan Wholefoods

Sally Eveleigh wanted to run her own business so that she could combine her passion for healthy lifestyles with her family commitments. Sally took over an existing shop called Toucan Wholefoods, just as the UK was recovering from recession. She worked out how much money she needed to take each day in sales to cover the costs of the business and eventually the business began to show a profit. Sally then calculated that she could afford to take a bank loan to move the business into its current premises on the ground floor of a three-storey building.

After the move, Sally could think about her future business objectives. She expanded the business onto the first floor of the building, but knew that this would be a risk as it would increase the business's running costs. Unfortunately, not enough customers were attracted up the stairs to the first floor and the shop was not making enough sales to cover the costs of using both the ground and first floors. This led Sally to decide to use her passion for healthy eating and open a cafe on the first floor, relocating the shop to the ground floor instead.

The cafe offers a healthy vegetarian menu and displays art by local artists for sale. Sally also expanded onto the second floor of the building, where she runs treatment rooms for alternative therapies. The business has become a success, although Sally continues to look for new opportunities to move the business forward, such as launching an e-commerce site where she can sell products and services online.

Activity ?

In groups, discuss the following questions.

1 Why did Sally want to run her own business?
2 How did Sally ensure that the business had enough money to pay its bills?
3 How important is it for an entrepreneur to have clear objectives when starting up and expanding a business?

Your learning

In this topic you will learn about:

- business aims and objectives – what business aims and objectives are, business aims and objectives when starting up, and why aims and objectives differ between businesses
- business revenues, costs and profits – the concept and calculation of key financial aspects of running a business and the interpretation of break-even diagrams
- cash and cash flow – the importance of cash to a business and the calculation and interpretation of cash flow forecasts
- sources of business finance – sources of finance for a start-up or established small business.

Business aims and objectives

Pompy's Cycles

Pompy's Cycles is a cycle shop in Somerset, founded by Grant Portsmouth in 1992. From the very beginning, the business's aim was to be family run, supplying the local community and tourists to the area. The business stocks a variety of bicycles, cycling clothing and bicycle-related equipment. Pompy's is the local official dealer for a number of leading bicycle brands. It also advertises cycling events, cycle groups and routes around the local area.

Key term

Market share: the proportion of sales in a market that are taken by one business.

Activity

In pairs, discuss the following questions.
1 What do you think a business objective is?
2 What do you think the objectives of Pompy's Cycles are? How might these objectives relate to the success of the business?
3 Can you think of any other objectives that the business could adopt in order to meet its aim?

Defining business aims and objectives

All businesses have aims and objectives. A business aim is what a business wants to achieve. You could think about an aim as being a business's goal or ambition. A business objective is how the business will achieve its aim or aims. Each objective will focus on a particular area of the business, and a business is likely to have several objectives at one time. Objectives should always be linked to measurable targets that a business can set and revisit in order to find out how well it is doing during a given week, month or year.

The ultimate goal of any business is to meet its aims and objectives. However, once they have been met, it is important that the business sets new aims and objectives in order to continue to improve and grow.

Aims and objectives for start-ups

A start-up business is likely to have a range of aims and objectives that can be divided into the following categories:

- **financial** – such as survival, profit, sales, **market share** and financial security
- **non-financial** – such as social concerns, personal satisfaction, challenge, independence and control.

Did you know?

A financial backer will want to see a start-up business's aims and objectives before choosing to invest. It is a good idea to include these in the business plan and any presentations that will be given to potential investors.

Financial aims and objectives

Start-up businesses in most industries are likely to have similar financial aims and objectives. When starting up, businesses are likely to have an aim as to where they would like to be at specific points in the future, such as at the end of the first, third and fifth years of operation. In order to be fulfilled, the business's aim needs to be broken down into ways in which the aim will be achieved. These are the business's objectives.

All start-up businesses will have an initial objective of survival, and this is likely to be linked to an objective concerning the business's financial security. A business may focus on achieving this by reaching a certain number of sales, securing a certain market share or making a specified amount of **profit**. Ultimately, a business's survival and financial security is dependent on ensuring that more money comes into the business than it spends. If it does not achieve this, it will not survive.

For example, a cycle shop like Pompy's Cycles may set an objective such as making a certain number of sales every month. Starting up as an official local dealer of leading cycle brands will help the shop to attract customers who want to purchase a particular brand of bicycle or spare parts for the brand of bicycle that they already own. This may enable the cycle shop to attract customers who used to shop at other cycle shops in the local area but are not official dealers of particular brands. This then means that the cycle shop makes enough sales each month to meet its financial objective. This also helps the business to meet its objective to survive.

Link it up

You will learn more about business plans in Topic 1.4 *Making the business effective.*

Key terms

Profit: the amount of revenue left over once costs have been deducted.

Social objective: likely to be non-financial, such as to reduce the carbon emissions of a business or improve the quality of life for a local community.

Exam-style question

Which **one** of the following is an example of a financial objective?

(1 mark)

Select **one** answer.

- [ ] **A** To make the local community a better place
- [ ] **B** To overcome the challenge of setting up the business
- [ ] **C** To have control of the business
- [ ] **D** To increase the profit margin by 10 per cent over the next six months

Exam tip

Always read all possible answers when answering a multiple choice question. Think about financial objectives as you read each answer and justify to yourself why you think it is correct or incorrect.

Non-financial aims and objectives

Unlike financial objectives, the non-financial aims and objectives of a start-up business are more likely to vary. They will depend on the nature of the business and the sector in which the business operates. A business that sells organic or Fairtrade products may set a **social objective** as a way of measuring progress towards achieving its aim. For example, in the case study at the beginning of the topic, Toucan Wholefoods supports and encourages local artists by displaying their art for sale in its cafe. This could be one of Toucan Wholefoods' social objectives.

Entrepreneurs often set up their own businesses because they want to achieve something. This may be linked to the entrepreneurs' objectives of:

- **personal satisfaction** – they have created a thriving business that people like to use
- **challenge** – they have to make the business work
- **independence** – they have to make their own business decisions rather than working for someone else
- **control** – they get to set the business's aims and objectives and can decide the direction in which to take the business.

In particular, challenging objectives can help to keep a business and its employees focused on building on its success. These challenges should be relevant to the overall aims of the business. For example, Richard Branson is an entrepreneur who runs a group of businesses called the Virgin Group. Since its foundation, he has continuously set new challenges for the Virgin Group, which now holds more than 200 companies in over 30 countries. The group has expanded to include a railway company, a game reserve in South Africa, a mobile phone company and a space tourism enterprise.

Why businesses have different aims and objectives

Different businesses will have their own ways of operating, and this will be reflected in the aims and objectives of each business. When setting aims and objectives, the entrepreneur needs to consider the industry in which their business operates, as this will have an influence on its aims and objectives. For example, Pompy's Cycles aimed to become an official dealer of well-known brands, whereas this was not an option available to Toucan Wholefoods. If the entrepreneur knows their market well enough to know that having a dealership will attract more customers, then this is something they should consider, weighing up the cost of being a dealership against the increased sales revenue that this will bring in.

Activity ?

In pairs, choose a local business.

1 What do you think are the key financial and non-financial objectives for this business?

2 How does each objective relate to the success of the business?

3 Can you think of any other non-financial objectives that the business would benefit from adopting?

Activity ?

Think about two different businesses. You could choose local businesses or the businesses in some of the case studies you have read in this book.

Do you think that the businesses you have chosen will have the same aims and objectives? Explain your answer.

Exam tip

Always double-check that you understand what the question is asking you to do. Once you know how you will answer this question, check that your planned answer is an **explanation**, as this is what the question is asking you to do.

Exam-style question

Explain **one** reason why businesses are likely to have different aims and objectives. **(3 marks)**

Business revenues, costs and profits

Case study

Bake Me Happy

Carly Roberts started a cake-baking business called Bake Me Happy in 2014. Carly used her background in financial services to work out her set-up costs. This included considering the equipment that she would need, as well as her costs, such as electricity, water and insurance. Carly also calculated that her business would not start to make a profit until its second year and worked out how many sales she would need to make in the first and second years.

Activity

In small groups, discuss the following questions.

1 What essential equipment would Carly have needed in order to start selling cakes as soon as possible?

2 How important is it for Carly to know what her essential costs were going to be before setting up the business?

3 Discuss these costs with the rest of the small groups in your class – do you all agree on what is meant by 'essential equipment'?

It is very important that an entrepreneur can make financial calculations and know what costs will be incurred from the beginning, as this will help them to plan their business's activity in a way that will lead to success.

Theme 1: Investigating small business

Understanding and calculating business concepts

You will need to understand and know how to calculate:

- revenue
- fixed, variable and total costs
- profit and loss
- interest
- break-even level of output
- margin of safety.

Revenue

Revenue is the income that a business receives from sales. A business needs a steady revenue stream to ensure that it can survive and succeed. It is important for an entrepreneur to be able to predict their business's revenue so that they know that it can cover its costs and make a profit.

Why is it important to predict sales revenue throughout the year? What factors should be taken into consideration?

Revenue is calculated by multiplying the price of a product or service by the amount of units of that product or service that it sells:

revenue = price × quantity

Maths tip

Always double-check your answer by reversing your calculations. For example, the bread sales revenue for one day = £1.35 × 200 = £270. The reverse calculation would be £270 ÷ 200 = £1.35

Activity ?

A bakery sells 150 bread rolls and 200 loaves of bread every day. The price of the bread rolls is 25p per roll and the price of the bread is £1.35 per loaf.

1 How much revenue is made for the bread rolls per day?

2 What is the total revenue per day?

3 What is the total revenue per week if the bakery works a 6-day week?

Revenue can come from different groups of customers or customer segments, and each of these areas of revenue is known as an **income stream**. For example, a cake company like Bake Me Happy could identify the following income streams:

- customers ordering celebration cakes such as birthday and wedding cakes
- customers impulse-purchasing treats while they are out shopping
- selling cakes to a local cafe that puts in a regular weekly order of 10 different cakes.

Activity ?

Consider the three income streams listed for the cake company above.

1 Which income stream do you think is most important? Why do you think this?

2 What could the cake business do in order to create a fourth income stream?

Link it up

You learned about market segmentation in Topic 1.2 *Spotting a business opportunity*.

Key terms

Income stream: the source of regular income that a business receives. This could be through the money it receives from customers, or other areas such as investment income.

Viable: capable of working or succeeding.

Fixed, variable and total costs

Costs are what a business has to pay in order to continue operating. Costs could include the rent on a shop or office, the cost of hosting and operating an e-commerce website and the costs of the raw materials needed to manufacture products. Costs are an important factor that will determine whether a start-up business will be **viable**.

There are two different types of costs: fixed and variable costs.

- **Fixed costs** do not change, no matter how many products or services a business sells. They can be identified from the beginning and include costs such as insurance, rent, tax and salaries.
- **Variable costs** change depending on how many products or services a business sells. They include costs such as electricity bills and raw materials. For example, if a cake company like Bake Me Happy attracts more customers and sells more products, it will use more electricity and raw materials in order to produce enough products to keep up with demand. This means that the variable costs of operating will increase.

Exam-style question

Which **one** of the following is an example of a fixed cost?

(1 mark)

Select **one** answer.

- ☐ **A** Salaries
- ☐ **B** Electricity
- ☐ **C** Materials
- ☐ **D** Repairs

Exam tip

Once you have chosen your answer, look at it again and justify to yourself why you think it is the correct answer.

Theme 1: Investigating small business

A business can add together its fixed costs and its variable costs in order to calculate its **total costs**:

TC (total cost) = TFC (total fixed costs) + TVC (total variable costs)

Exam-style question

Use the information below to calculate the total costs of a business. You are advised to show your workings. **(2 marks)**

- Number of units sold: 342
- Fixed costs: £2,450
- Variable cost per unit: £1.25

Profit and loss

Profit is the amount of revenue left over once costs have been deducted. If a business has not made enough money to cover its costs, the amount left over after costs are deducted will be a negative number and the business will be said to have made a loss.

Businesses use a tool called an **income statement** to keep track of revenue and costs and to show whether they are making a profit or loss. It is good practice for all businesses to calculate an income statement every year. Key business **stakeholders** will use the information on the income statement to measure the success of the business and identify whether the business is meeting its financial targets.

Key terms

Income statement: a financial statement showing the amount of money earned and spent in a particular period and the resulting profit and loss.

Stakeholder: anyone who has an interest in the activities of a business, such as its workers, its suppliers, the local community and the government.

Losses are shown on an income statement in brackets, so if the business's income is listed as (10,000), you know that it has made a loss of £10,000.

Gross profit is the amount of profit that a business makes on a product or service before the costs of producing and selling that product or service are deducted:

gross profit = sales revenue − cost of sales

Net profit is the amount of profit that a business makes on a product or service after the costs of producing and selling that product or service are deducted:

net profit = gross profit − other operating expenses and interest

Income Statement Year 1		Income Statement Year 2	
Sales (Revenue)		**Sales (Revenue)**	
Celebration cakes	8,579.00	Celebration cakes	15,670.00
Cakes stocked in store	1,742.00	Cakes stocked in store	5,024.00
Cafe cakes	6,379.00	Cafe cakes	13,726.00
Total sales	16,700.00	Total sales	?
Expenses (Costs)		**Expenses (Costs)**	
Interest on bank loan	240.00	Interest on bank loan	240.00
Rent, business rates etc.	1,620.00	Rent, business rates etc.	1,620.00
Salaries	8,400.00	Salaries	8,400.00
Equipment & repairs	4,317.00	Equipment & repairs	138.00
Electricity, water etc.	743.00	Electricity, water etc.	1,358.00
Materials and ingredients	3817.00	Materials and ingredients	6,976.00
Total expenses	19,137.00	Total expenses	?
Net income (profit or loss)	(2,437.00)	Net income (profit or loss)	?

Table 1.3.1 Income statement comparing Years 1 and 2

Activity ?

An entrepreneur is calculating her Year 2 profit and loss sheet for her cake shop.

1 Look at the costs in Year 2 in Table 1.3.1 and then compare them with the costs in Year 1. What has changed?

2 Work out the total sales (revenue) and total expenses (costs) for Year 2, then work out the net profit or loss for Year 2.

3 Why do you think there was a loss in the first year? Use the information in the income statement as well as your knowledge about business to answer this question.

4 Do you think that the business's costs are likely to increase, decrease or remain the same in the third year? Give reasons for your answer.

Maths tip

Check your answers when working out the net income (profit or loss) on an income statement by adding the net income to the total expenses (costs). The answer should be the total sales (revenue).

Theme 1: Investigating small business

Link it up

You will also learn about interest in Topic 1.4 *Making the business effective.*

How do interest rates affect your incentive to save?

Maths tip

Go back to the formula when calculating percentages. Work through a simple sum that you know the answer to, for example, 20 per cent of £100 = £20. Be sure that you understand how you came to this correct answer and then apply these steps to the calculation you are working on.

Key term

Break-even point: the point where revenue received meets all of the costs of a business.

Interest

When businesses borrow money from a bank, they will be charged interest, which is a percentage of the amount of money borrowed that must be repaid in addition to the original amount borrowed. For most bank loans, the interest is calculated at the beginning of the loan agreement and added to the amount that is being borrowed. This total amount is then divided by the number of months over which the business has agreed to pay back the money. Interest on a loan is a fixed cost to the business.

Interest on loans is calculated using the equation:

$$\text{interest in \%} = \frac{\text{total repayment} - \text{borrowed amount}}{\text{borrowed amount}} \times 100$$

Interest can also be a form of revenue when it is paid on money that a business has saved or invested in a bank. When interest acts as revenue, it must be declared on the business's profit and loss statement and the business must pay tax on it.

Activity

Complete the following calculations.

1 What is the total amount of interest to be charged on a business loan of £2,500.00 at a rate of 7.5 per cent?

2 What would the monthly payments be if the loan was paid back over three years?

3 The bank has offered the business a reduced interest rate of 6.5 per cent if the period of the loan is reduced to 1 year. What would the interest savings be if the business chose to take up this offer?

Break-even level of output

The **break-even point** is the point at which a business's revenue exactly matches its total costs. The amount of products or services that it must sell to reach this point is known as the break-even level of output.

The break-even point can be calculated in two different ways.

- The break-even point in units tells the business how many units it needs to sell in order to meet the break-even point:

$$\text{break-even point in units} = \frac{\text{fixed costs}}{\text{(sales price} - \text{variable)}}$$

- The break-even point in currency tells the business how much money needs to be taken to meet the break-even point:

$$\text{break-even point in currency} = \text{break-even point in units} \times \text{sales price}$$

In a business's early stages, costs are likely to be greater than the revenue. This is because many items need to be paid for before the business can start selling to customers. The costs of premises, equipment and raw materials have to be made in advance of customers making orders. A business needs to work out its break-even point as this is when it will start to make a profit.

Activity ?

Ajay is starting a new business making savoury pies and needs to work out how many pies (units) he needs to sell in order to meet his break-even point. Ajay is planning to sell his pies at £1.25. The ingredients and packing for each pie costs 50p and his fixed costs are £1,524 per month.

How many units would Ajay need to sell per month to meet his break-even point?

Maths tip

Read through the question carefully and write down all the figures that you will need in order to calculate the answer. Write the figures down into the break-even point equation that you have learned.

Margin of safety

Once a business has reached its break-even point, it needs to continue to grow and increase sales in order to succeed. It is important that a trend in sales growth continues to well above the break-even point, as this will allow the business to return a healthy profit. The margin of safety is how much sales can fall before the business's break-even point is reached again:

margin of safety = actual or budgeted sales – break even sales

Activity ?

After six months, Ajay's business has grown and he is considering buying new equipment and employing additional staff. Before he does this, he needs to work out his margin of safety. The business has sold a total of 18,000 pies in its first 6 months. The business's fixed and variable costs have remained the same as in the previous activity and so Ajay has kept the selling price per pie the same.

Calculate the business's margin of safety.

Interpreting break-even diagrams

A break-even diagram is a way of showing a business's break-even point. Figure 1.3.1 is a break-even diagram. The costs and revenue are plotted against the vertical axis of the chart and the number of products or services sold against the horizontal axis.

First, the entrepreneur plots the business's fixed costs onto the diagram. As you have already learned, the fixed costs will remain the same, no matter how many products the business sells, so these can be drawn onto the diagram as a straight line.

Next, the entrepreneur needs to work out the variable cost per unit – that is, how much it will cost to make each product or service, taking into consideration all of the variables such as ingredients, electricity and so on. When a business is starting out, these costs will be estimated, as the entrepreneur does not yet know exactly how much a product will cost to make. It is only when the business has been trading for a while that a more accurate variable cost per unit can be calculated. This will allow the business to recalculate its original figures and give a more realistic picture of how well the business is doing against its break-even forecast. The variable cost per unit is then added to the fixed costs to produce the total costs. As the number of units sold goes up, so do the variable costs.

An entrepreneur planning to open a cake shop has drawn up a break-even diagram (Figure 1.3.1). She calculated that:

- her fixed costs will be £14,577
- her variable cost per unit will be £11.25
- her average price per unit will be £40.00.

She then worked out her total costs and revenue depending on the number of cakes she will sell. Her calculations are shown in Table 1.3.2, which she used to plot the diagram in Figure 1.3.1.

Units sold	Total costs	Revenue
100	£14,577 (fixed costs) + (£11.25 [variable costs] × 100 cakes sold) = £15,702 (total costs)	100 cakes sold × £40 (average price per unit) = £4,000 (gross income)
200	£14,577 + (£11.25 × 200 cakes sold) = £16,827	200 cakes sold × £40 = £8,000
400	£14,577 + (£11.25 × 400 cakes sold) = £19,077	400 cakes sold × £40 = £16,000
600	£14,577 + (£11.25 × 600 cakes sold) = £21,327	600 cakes sold × £40 = £24,000
800	£14,577 + (£11.25 × 800 cakes sold) = £23,577	800 cakes sold × £40 = £32,000

Table 1.3.2 The figures used to plot the break-even diagram for a cake shop

Activity ?

Use Figure 1.3.1 and Table 1.3.2 to answer the following questions.

1 If the cake shop sells 800 cakes in one month, calculate its profit or loss for that month.

2 What is the cake shop's break-even level of output?

3 If the cake shop sells 600 cakes, what is its margin of safety?

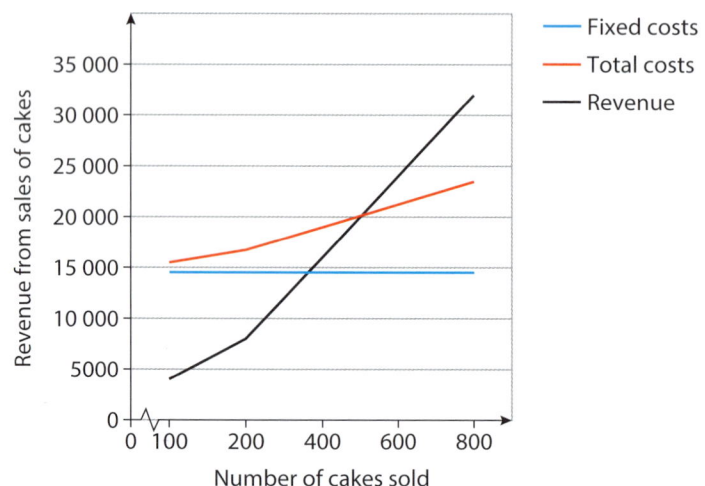

Figure 1.3.1 The break-even diagram for a cake shop

The impact of changes in revenue and costs

There are many reasons why a business's revenue and costs can change. These changes will have either a negative or positive impact on the business and its break-even point, and this would affect the margin of safety. These changes would affect the break-even calculations of fixed costs, total costs and revenue, and this would change the business's break-even diagram.

What would be the impact on revenue and cost if a similar shop opened next to your business?

When **revenue increases**, it is likely to have a positive impact on the business as long as the costs remain the same. Increased revenues can lead to an increased profit. However, if the costs rise at the same time as the revenue rises, this could reduce any profit made from increased revenues.

When **revenue decreases**, it is likely to have a negative impact on the business, unless costs also decrease at the same time. When a business can see that its revenue is decreasing, it must do everything it can to reduce its costs. For example, the business could investigate ways of making savings on costs that are within its control, such as electricity, telephone and water consumption. Even just ensuring that all lights are switched off in unused areas of the shop or office can help to reduce costs. This kind of cost-saving measure will maximise a business's profits and may even help the business to survive if its revenue is reduced.

When **costs increase**, the business has to pay them, meaning that profits will be affected negatively unless revenue can be increased. There are many reasons why costs may increase. For example, if a business rents its shop from a landlord, the cost of the rent may rise, becoming an increased cost to the business. Similarly, the cost of fuel can rise, which means that it becomes more expensive to manufacture and transport products. This cost can be paid or absorbed by the business. Alternatively, the business can pass the cost onto its customers by increasing the price of its goods.

When **costs decrease**, this can be an immediate benefit to the business as it means that it will make more money per unit sold. However, if customers are aware that costs have decreased, they may expect the business to reduce the price of its goods or services. For example, when fuel prices decrease, this is often reported in the newspapers and petrol stations pass on the reduction in costs to their customers by reducing their prices. Where price decreases are not so obvious to the customer, the business is more likely to benefit. For example, if the market price of coffee is reduced, a cafe owner is less likely to reduce their prices as customers may not be aware of the reduction in the cost, so this will increase their profits.

Exam tip

Read through the answer that you have given and imagine that the person who will read it knows nothing about this topic. Does your answer make sense? Have you explained your point well enough?

Exam-style question

Explain **one** action that a business can take when revenue decreases.

(3 marks)

Checkpoint

Now it is time to review your understanding of business revenues, costs and profits.

Strengthen

S1 What is business revenue and where does it come from?

S2 Describe the difference between fixed and variable costs.

S3 Describe the break-even point.

Challenge

C1 Write a short blog post (no more than 250 words) for a business blog to explain why it is important for a business to know when it will meet its break-even point.

C2 Using an example, explain how a business can ensure that it stays profitable.

Cash and cash flow

Case study

Skipworth Garage

Skipworth Garage specialises in the maintenance of lorries and is run by Nick Janski. Nick always pays close attention to the amount of cash in his business, because he knows that having enough cash is a very important part of business success. In the past, he sometimes struggled to get customers to pay their bills on time, which meant that he was sometimes late paying his suppliers.

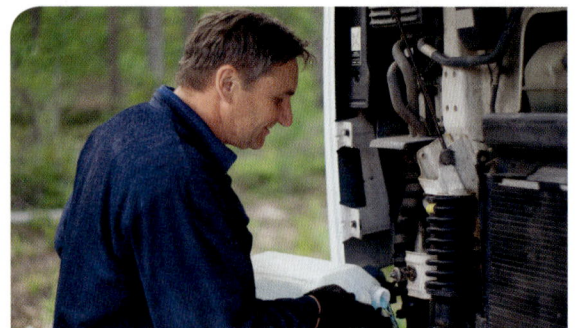

Activity ?

In small groups, discuss the following questions.

1 Think about the flow of cash into and out of Nick's business. List all of the places it comes from, and all of the places it has to go out to.

2 Why is it so important for an entrepreneur to know how much money their business is owed and how much money it owes?

3 What do you think would happen to a business that does not get its customers to pay on time?

Key terms

Credit: the amount of money that a financial institution or supplier will allow a business to use, which it must pay back in the future at an agreed time.

Overheads: fixed costs that come from running an office, shop or factory, which are not affected by the number of specific products or services that are sold.

Cash is the amount of money that a business has in its bank account. A business's cash flow is the way in which money comes into the business from customers and goes out of the business to pay suppliers. A cash flow can be either positive or negative:

- **positive cash flow** – more money coming in than going out
- **negative cash flow** – less money coming in than going out.

The importance of cash to a business

The management of a business's cash and cash flow is very important. This is because a business must have enough money in the bank to pay its regular bills and any money that it owes. A business that does not have enough cash or, a reliable cash flow, will fail, even if it is making a profit.

Managing cash flow can be difficult because not all customers pay at the point at which they receive the products or services. Instead, customers may be sent an invoice and are expected to pay when they receive the invoice, or the customer may have a **credit** arrangement allowing them to pay for the products or services within 30, 60 or even 90 days.

Paying suppliers, overheads and employees

A good relationship with suppliers is an essential part of a business's success, as a supplier is responsible for ensuring that raw materials or products arrive on time and in perfect condition to be used or sold. The supplier will only do this if the business pays them within the time limit that they have allowed. This means that a business must ensure that it has enough cash available to pay its suppliers on time. Remember that a supplier is also a business, and must also manage its own cash flow.

A business also has to be able to pay its **overheads**, such as rent and maintenance of company vehicles, as well as bills for any additional services, such as electricity and telephones. Failure to pay these costs regularly and on time could lead to the services being withdrawn. For example, failing to pay the electricity bill could lead to the supplier cutting off the business's electricity supply. Suppliers may also take the business to court in order to make it pay the money that it owes them.

Theme 1: Investigating small business

Link it up

You will learn more about taxation and the way in which this affects businesses and their employees in the section 'The economy and business' in Topic 1.5 *Understanding external influences*.

Exam tip

Read the question to ensure that you tick the correct number of boxes. This question is asking for **two** answers.

Key term

Insolvent: a business that is unable to pay its debts and/or owes more money than it is owed.

Employees also have to be paid on time every month or week. The business has to pay the additional costs of having employees, such as National Insurance contributions and tax deductions that are made on employees' wages. These are known as 'on costs' that are in addition to the wages that the employee receives from the employer.

Exam-style question

Which **two** of the following are examples of overheads? **(2 marks)**

Select **two** answers.

- ☐ **A** Raw materials
- ☐ **B** Stock
- ☐ **C** Rent
- ☐ **D** Credit arrangements
- ☐ **E** Wages

Preventing business failure

Failing to manage cash and cash flow can cause a business to fail. A business may have a lot of customers or create very innovative products or services, but can still have a negative cash flow that leads it to fail.

A business may be owed more money than it owes, so it may look like it is capable of paying its bills. However, if money owed to the business is not paid, the business cannot use it to pay its own bills and is **insolvent**.

The best way in which a business can avoid becoming insolvent is to take preventative measures.

- Arranging sensible credit agreements with suppliers and customers. A business could agree credit arrangements with its suppliers for a longer term than the term that it offers its customers. For example, if a business offers its customers 30 days in which to pay their bills, it should ask its supplier to give it 60 days to pay its bills.
- Limiting the number of customers to which it gives credit. A business should have more customers who pay for their products or services when they receive them than customers who pay later as part of a credit arrangement.

Activity

In small groups, choose a business in your local area. Thinking about this business, discuss the following questions.

1 What are the factors that need to be taken into consideration to prevent business failure?

2 What actions do you think your chosen business could take to maintain a positive cash flow and avoid failure?

The difference between cash and profit

Not all of the cash paid into a business is profit. A portion of any cash will need to be paid out to meet the business's costs. For example, when a customer pays for a product, the cash that comes in from that sale has to cover the variable costs of producing that product and a proportion of the fixed costs of the business.

Once all costs have been deducted from all revenue, the amount that is left is the profit. Although profits can be calculated for each month, businesses are likely to wait until the end of the year to calculate one set of yearly profits. However, monthly calculations will still be a good indicator to show whether the business is solvent and on target to make a profit by the end of the year.

Consider what the costs of manufacturing a pair of prescription spectacles may be compared to the profit that will be made from a sale

Link it up

Look again at the section 'Business revenues, costs and profits' in this topic to remind yourself about calculating profit and costs.

Calculation and interpretation of cash flow forecasts

A cash flow forecast is an estimate of how much cash will come into the business and how much cash will leave the business over the course of a year. Cash flow forecasts are extremely important to all businesses, but especially to small businesses. They can help a business to know how much cash it expects to take in a year and how much the business is likely to spend in costs. They also indicate when money is likely to come into and go out of the business's bank account.

This sort of information enables a business to make important decisions about the future such as:

- taking on more staff
- opening a new branch
- identifying any risk that the business could run out of cash and need to borrow money
- taking additional money out of the business to invest into a new business or to reward the owner for the success of their business.

Theme 1: Investigating small business

Creating a cash flow forecast for a new business can be challenging. The entrepreneur has no previous years' figures to help them estimate, so it involves a certain amount of guesswork. This means that they will need to watch their cash flow very carefully and compare it with the forecast to see if their estimates were realistic. An established business should also watch its cash flow and compare it with its cash flow forecast, as this will allow it to adjust its activities if the amount of cash taken does not match the forecast.

The cash flow forecast is made up of five main areas:

- cash inflows
- cash outflows
- net cash flow
- opening balance
- closing balance.

Cash inflows

The cash inflows are all of the money that comes into the business. The business is separated into different areas or categories that receive cash. The forecast cash inflow is then put against each category for each month.

In Table 1.3.3, you can see that the tool hire business has broken down its sources of income into four main areas:

- sales – used equipment
- sales – **consumables**
- hire
- repairs.

Cash outflows

The cash outflows are all of the money that will leave the business in order to pay its fixed and variable costs. A business should be cautious when estimating costs. It is best to estimate that costs will be higher than expected and have a plan in case money needs to be paid sooner than expected.

Net cash flow

The **net cash flow** is the difference between the cash inflows and the cash outflows:

net cash flow = cash inflows – cash outflows in a given period

The net cash flow will vary each month. The business can use this figure to see if there is sufficient money in the business to cover its costs. The business can also use the net cash flow figure each month to look ahead and work out if it will need to borrow money and for how long.

Opening balance

The opening balance is the amount of money in the business's bank account at the start of any period:

opening balance = closing balance of the previous period

In Table 1.3.3, the opening balance is zero because this is a new business, so there was no previous period.

Closing balance

The closing balance is the amount of money in the bank at the end of each month. To calculate the closing balance, you add the opening balance to the net cash flow:

closing balance = opening balance + net cash flow

Exam-style question ⦿

Define the term 'closing balance'. **(1 mark)**

Exam tip ⦿

'Define' means to give the meaning of something precisely and accurately. Look at your answer to the question again. Have you given a precise definition of the term 'closing balance'?

Did you know?

Every business should use a cash flow forecast. This will tell a business if it is running out of money while still turning a profit. A cash flow forecast will also tell it if the owner is taking too much money out of the business.

Table 1.3.3 is a cash flow forecast for the first 7 months of trading for a newly established tool hire business.

	Jan (£)	Feb (£)	Mar (£)	Apr (£)	May (£)	Jun (£)	Jul (£)	Total (£)
Cash inflows								
Sales – used equipment	1,500	2,000	2,000	2,500	2,500	3,000	3,000	16,500
Sales – consumables	1,000	1,000	1,200	1,500	1,500	1,700	1,700	9,600
Hire	8,000	8,000	5,000	5,000	12,000	14,000	15,000	67,000
Repairs	1,000	1,050	1,200	1,500	1,500	1,700	1,800	9,750
Total inflows	**11,500**	**12,050**	**9,400**	**10,500**	**17,500**	**20,400**	**21,500**	**102,850**
Cash outflows								
Wages	3,000	3,000	3,000	3,000	3,000	3,000	3,000	21,000
Cost of sales – used equipment	1,000	1,200	1,200	1,500	1,500	1,800	1,800	10,000
Cost of sales – consumables	600	600	700	900	900	1,080	1,200	5,980
Advertising & marketing	200	200	200	200	200	200	200	1,400
Hire equipment			1,200	800			13,500	15,500
Maintenance of hire equipment	120	120	150	165	180	210	225	1,170
Rent, rates and other fixed cost overheads	1,500	1,500	1,500	1,500	1,500	1,500	1,500	10,500
Legal and accounting	2,500	0	0	0	0	0	0	2,500
Total outflows	**8,920**	**6,620**	**7,950**	**8,065**	**7,280**	**7,790**	**21,425**	**68,050**
Net cash flow	2,580	5,430	1,450	2,435	10,220	12,610	75	34,800
Opening balance	0	2,580	8,010	9,460	11,895	22,115	34,725	
Closing balance	2,580	8,010	9,460	11,895	22,115	34,725	34,800	

Table 1.3.3 A 7-month cash flow forecast for a tool hire business

Theme 1: Investigating small business

⊞ Maths tip

Don't assume that the figures in a cash flow forecast are correct. Look at the inflows and outflows totals. If you take one away from the other, does the answer look right? You can double check using a calculator.

Activity ?

Look at the figures in Table 1.3.3 and answer the following questions

1 Which month is forecast to be the most profitable month?

2 Why is July expected to have such a low net cash flow?

3 If the business needs to buy some more equipment, which month or months would you recommend that it makes any big purchases?

Exam-style question ○

Table 1.3.4 shows the cash flow forecast for a business.

Complete the table by calculating the two missing figures (i) and (ii). You are advised to show your workings. **(2 marks)**

	March (£)	April (£)
Total money received	19,359	24,946
Fixed costs	2,468	2,468
Cost of sales	7,352	9,346
Total payments	9,820	11,814
Net cash flow	**(i)**	15,600
Opening balance	2,460	11,999
Closing balance	11,999	**(ii)**

Table 1.3.4 A cash flow forecast

Exam tip ○

Read the question and all of the information in the table carefully before you attempt to answer the question. Make sure that you understand how the figures in the table relate to each other.

Checkpoint

Now it is time to review your understanding of cash and cash flow.

Strengthen

S1 Describe why cash is important to a business.

S2 What is the difference between turnover and profit?

S3 What is cash flow?

Challenge

C1 You have been asked to give a presentation to a local group of entrepreneurs about cash flow. For this presentation, you need to explain how an accurate cash flow statement can benefit a business. Write your explanation, using examples where possible.

C2 Using an example, explain what will happen if a business's cash outflows are greater than its cash inflows?

Sources of business finance

Activity ?

Discuss the following questions with a partner or a small group.

1 What are the likely set-up costs that most businesses will need to consider?

2 Where do you think a business might be able to get funding?

3 Why might it be difficult to get funding for a new business?

How a business funds its activities is an important factor that must be considered, both when the business is starting up and also during its day-to-day operations once it is established. Equipment and stock need to be purchased and bills need to be paid on time if the business is going to be able to operate.

Short-term sources of finance

Short-term sources of finance are designed to help a business maintain a positive cash flow. They include arrangements such as **trade credit** and bank **overdrafts**. Short-term sources of finance can be particularly useful as costs are likely to be incurred in order to meet customers' needs, and this can happen before customers pay for the products or services that they are purchasing.

Some businesses will use short-term financial solutions as an emergency access to finance. Other businesses may use credit and overdrafts as part of their operating model if they know that customers will pay their invoices. This allows the business to pay off what it owes within the agreed credit limit.

Key terms

Trade credit: a credit arrangement that is offered only to businesses by suppliers.

Overdraft: a facility offered by a bank that allows an account holder to borrow money at short notice.

Exam-style question

Explain **one** reason why a business might take out a short-term loan.

(3 marks)

Exam tip

When you are asked to give a certain number of answers, ensure that you have give the correct number. This question asks for **one** reason. You should always reread your answer and check that you have given the correct number of reasons.

Overdraft

Most individuals and businesses should use overdrafts with care, or only in emergencies, as the bank will charge a high interest rate on the amount borrowed. However, they can be useful. For example, a car mechanic has to identify and buy any parts required before they can go ahead with the repair.

Once the repair is complete, the mechanic will invoice their customer. If the invoice is raised promptly, the mechanic may receive payment before their supplier has to be paid. However, if the mechanic does not receive payment before their supplier has to be paid, they may have to use their overdraft to pay the supplier, in the expectation of receiving payment from their customer.

Trade credit

A business has to apply to a supplier for a credit arrangement, and it will probably have to complete a credit application form. However, suppliers are often keen to offer credit accounts to certain businesses, as it will make the business more likely to buy from them. This is because the business does not need to have cash available in order to purchase the products or services that it needs to meet its own customers' needs.

The terms and conditions of a credit agreement are likely to include the following.

- **Credit limit** – the maximum amount of credit that a business has with a financial institution or supplier. For example, if a business has a credit limit of £1,500 with a supplier and owes £1,300, it could only purchase an extra £200 worth of supplies before it has reached its credit limit and will need to pay off the money owed to be able to order more supplies.

- **Credit period** – the maximum amount of time that a business can take to pay what is owed for a specific month. Credit periods are agreed in advance and can be 30, 60 or 90 days. The amount owed after each of these periods will be detailed on a monthly statement where all invoices that have been raised are summarised. The amount owed at the end of the agreed credit period is the amount of money that is due to be paid. For example, if the credit period has been agreed as 90 days, an invoice raised in October will be due to be paid in January.

- **Frequency of payment** – the frequency with which a business will pay a supplier. If money is owed to a supplier every month, it is usual for the business to pay the supplier on a monthly basis. However, different arrangements may be agreed, such as weekly payments.

- **Method of payment** – the way in which the business sends the money owed to the supplier. A bank transfer is most likely to be the preferred method of payment to settle credit accounts, although some businesses may want to pay by **cheque**. Cash payment is unlikely to be an appropriate method of payment as the amount owed is likely to be a large amount of money. If a credit card is accepted as a method of payment, the supplier is likely to make a small percentage charge to cover the costs of using the credit card.

- **Retrospective discount** – a discount applied when the business has purchased a certain number of goods or spent a certain amount of money with a supplier. The discount is shown on the business's credit statement as a credit or amount of money that will be deducted from the business's next order. Suppliers offer retrospective discounts as an incentive to a business to buy from them.

Key term

Cheque: a written order to a bank to pay an amount of money from an account holder's account to a specified person.

Figure 1.3.2 is an example of a typical statement received by a construction company from one of its suppliers. It details the invoices that have been raised during the period 1 October 2016 to 31 January 2017 and shows the total amount due across the credit period agreement.

Bricks and Mortar Construction Supplies Macclesfield Cheshire				STATEMENT Date 31/01/17	

For goods delivered to:
Derbyshire Construction
West Road
Buxton
Derbyshire

Invoice Date	Invoice Number	Transaction details	Total	Balance
26/10/16	133518	Invoice	128.00	128.00
14/11/16	133972	Invoice	209.16	337.16
02/12/16	134675	Invoice	1,381.25	1,718.41
16/01/17	134689	Invoice	148.52	1,866.93
23/01/17	134701	Invoice	28.02	1,894.95

Over 90 days	90 days	60 days	30 days	Current	Amount due
0	128.00	209.16	1,381.25	176.54	1894.95

Figure 1.3.2 A statement received by a business from a supplier

Activity ?

Derbyshire Construction has an agreed credit period of 90 days in which to pay its invoices from its supplier. Using the details in Figure 1.3.2, answer the following questions.

1 How much is due to be paid by the end of January 2017?
2 When will the invoices raised in December 2016 be due for payment?
3 Explain how the current balance of £176.54 has been calculated.

Long-term sources of finance

A long-term source of finance is one that is designed to be paid back over a much longer period of time than a short-term source of finance. For example, a long-term loan from a bank may be paid back over 5 or 10 years. These sources of finance are often used for large one-off costs such as purchasing expensive new equipment.

Link it up

You will learn more about rate of return and how to calculate the average rate of return in the section 'Business calculations' in Topic 2.4 *Making financial decisions*.

Key terms

Venture capital: money to invest in a business is sourced from individuals, or groups of people, who wish to invest their own money into new businesses.

Return on investment: the amount of money that an investor gets back in return for investing in a business.

Shareholders: investors who are part-owners of a company.

Share capital: money to invest in a business is raised by the business issuing shares that it then sells to those who wish to invest in the company.

Credit check: a check on the financial status of a business or individual to ensure that the business or the individual has a reliable credit history and does not have any existing outstanding debts.

Link it up

You will learn more about shares and shareholders in the section 'The options for start-up and small businesses' in Topic 1.4 *Making the business effective*, and 'Business growth' in Topic 2.1 *Growing the business*.

Long-term sources of finance include:

- personal savings
- venture capital
- share capital
- loans
- retained profit
- crowdfunding.

Personal savings

Personal savings refers to any money that the entrepreneur has saved up, either before starting the business or while they are running the business. By using personal savings rather than something like a loan, the entrepreneur avoids incurring any bank charges. However, the cost of bank charges should be weighed up against the amount of interest that they may earn if they kept their savings and took out a loan instead.

Venture capital

Money lent by a large business or successful entrepreneur to a small start-up business is known as **venture capital**. Sometimes, banks will not lend money to start-up businesses because they think the start-up business is too high-risk, whereas a venture capitalist may be prepared to take this risk if they can see that the business has potential. However, the venture capitalist will want a **return on their investment** and is also likely to want to make decisions about how the business operates.

Share capital

The amount of money invested in a business by **shareholders** is called **share capital**. Shareholders part-own the business, which means that they have certain rights, such as the right to vote on changes to the business. The entrepreneur should be aware that, if they decide to use share capital to raise funds for their business, they need to consider the opinions of the shareholders and they may lose the ability to make quick decisions.

Did you know?

Sir Charles Dunstone founded Carphone Warehouse with start-up capital of £6,000.

Loans

A loan is an amount of money lent to an individual or a business that will be paid off with interest over an agreed period of time. The interest rate on a long-term loan is likely to be fixed, meaning that the rate will not change, so the business will know exactly how much it will need to pay back each month. Interest charged on a business loan is a cost to the business, so it is included in the business's profit and loss statement.

A bank will undertake **credit checks** on an individual or business when agreeing a loan with them. This means looking at whether or not they have paid back any previous loans that they have taken out and made credit payments on time. The bank may also demand **security** from the business in the form of the business's **assets**. If the business is unable to repay the loan, the bank can then order the business to sell those assets in order to settle the loan.

If the business is new, it may not own any valuable assets. In this case, the bank may ask for a **guarantor**: a person who will guarantee to pay the monthly repayments if the business cannot pay them.

Retained profit

As a business begins to make a profit, it can leave the profit in the business or draw the profit out and use it as an extra source of income. If the profit is reinvested into the business, this is known as **retained profit** and is a cost-effective way to finance a business. If there are any shareholders in the business, some or all of the profit would need to be paid out in the form of dividends to the shareholders making it less likely that retained profit could be used as a long-term source of income.

Crowdfunding

Crowdfunding means that a business obtains funding from a large number of people who each pay a small amount of money to the business. Crowdfunding websites such as Kickstarter enable people to invest in a business by paying in just a small amount of money. If a large number of people invest small amounts into the same business, this can raise a lot of investment for a business despite the small amounts being contributed by each individual.

> ### Link it up
> You will learn more about secured loans in Topic 2.1 *Growing the business.*

> ### Key terms
> **Security:** when the lender asks the borrower to put up an asset, such as a house, or a valuable item owned by the business.
>
> **Asset:** any item of value that a business owns, such as its machinery or premises.
>
> **Guarantor:** a named person who guarantees to pay the repayments on a loan should the person who has taken out the loan not be able to make the payments.
>
> **Retained profit:** money that a business keeps, rather than paying out to its shareholders.

> ### Exam tip
> Reread your answer once you have finished to make sure that it makes sense and answers the question that you have actually been asked.

> ### Exam-style question
> Explain **one** reason why a business may set up a credit agreement with a supplier. **(3 marks)**

Checkpoint

Now it is time to review your understanding of sources of business finance.

Strengthen

S1 Give two examples of long-term funding options for a business.

S2 Give two examples of short-term funding options for a business.

S3 Describe what a credit arrangement is and how it works.

Challenge

C1 Using an example, describe one reason why a business might prefer to take a short-term funding solution rather than a long-term solution.

C2 An entrepreneur is considering using their savings to fund their business when bank interest rates are low. What would you advise the entrepreneur to do, and why?

1.3 Putting a business idea into practice

1   Which **one** of the following is a short-term source for a business loan?   *(1 mark)*
    Select **one** answer.

    ☐   A   *Bank loan over 10 years*

    ☐   B   *Personal savings*

    ☐   C   *Crowd funding*

    ☐   D   *Trade credit*

2   Define the term 'margin of safety'.   *(1 mark)*

Student answer

A margin of safety is the amount of sales that a business needs to generate above the break-even point.

Verdict

A good answer. The student has given a correct definition and has avoided giving a more detailed explanation, which would not have earned them any more marks.

3   Explain **one** reason why having a positive cash flow is important.   *(3 marks)*

Student answer

A positive cash flow means that the business has available cash in the bank. It means that more money is coming into the business than is leaving it. It is important that a business has a positive cash flow so that it can pay all of the bills, such as rent, insurances and everyday expenses.

Verdict

The answer given is correct. However, the first two sentences describe what positive cash flow is, rather than answering the question, which asked the student to explain the importance of positive cash flow. The student only answers the question in their final sentence.

Read the following extract carefully, then answer Questions 4, 5 and 6.

Alexei and Anna Vygotsky have put their business idea into reality by opening up a gym in their local town. The gym has been open for 6 months and has attracted more customers than expected.

Customers have suggested that they would like a cross trainer in the gym. As the business is doing well, Anna thinks that they should take out a business loan to pay for the cross trainer. They complete a cash flow forecast that includes the cost of the cross trainer, and the result shows their inflows are greater than their outflows.

Alexei investigates the cost of a bank loan for the cross trainer. They would need to borrow £1,200 to cover the cost of the cross trainer. This would be repaid over 2 years and they would pay back a total of £1,414.56.

4   Explain **one** way in which having greater financial inflows than outflows will impact on the business's cash flow.   (3 marks)

Student answer

It will mean that there is more money coming into the business than is leaving it.

Verdict

The answer does not actually answer the question that has been asked. The student has defined what it means to have greater inflows than outflows but has not explained the impact of this on the business. Try underlining the words in the question that will help you to answer the question properly. In this example, the student could have underlined 'explain' and 'impact'.

5   Calculate the monthly payments that Alexei and Anna would pay on their loan. You are advised to show your workings.   (2 marks)

Student answer

£1,200 + £1,414.56 = 2,614.56/£108.94

Verdict

This answer is incorrect. The student has added the loan amount including interest to the loan amount. The student should have taken the loan amount including interest (£1,414.56) and divided it by 24. This would give them the amount of money to be paid every month over 2 years.

Alexei and Anna decide that they do not want to pay the interest on a loan so are considering two other options.

Option 1: They could take the money from their personal savings.

Option 2: They could wait until they have enough profit in the business to purchase the cross trainer.

6   Justify which **one** of these two options Alexei and Anna should choose.   (9 marks)

Student answer

I would advise Alexei and Anna to take the money from their personal savings. They have already had feedback from their customers that they would like a cross trainer in the gym and so they should purchase it as soon as possible. If they do not do this, it could lead to customer complaints and, even worse, customers would choose to go to a different gym as the facilities are not meeting their expectations and their comments are not being listened to. By keeping the customers happy with the additional piece of equipment, it will lead to more business with an increase in the amount of cash that is coming into the gym and contribute to a positive cash flow. As the business is doing well, they could then take money out of the business in the future to replace their savings.

Verdict

This is a correct answer. The student gives a full and detailed justification. The answer is balanced and the student looks at a number of different benefits of the option that they have chosen to justify.

Topic 1.4 Making the business effective

Topic overview

This topic considers the range of factors that will influence whether a small business is successful or not. This will include looking at the ownership of the business, the choice of location, the marketing mix and how the elements of the marketing mix must work together. It also looks at the role and importance of a business plan.

Case study

York Cocoa House

Sophie Jewett had a love of chocolate from a very young age. She started baking when she was just four years old and had developed her own chocolate fudge recipe by the age of eight. Now the proud owner of York Cocoa House, Sophie is able to combine her passion with running a successful business.

Sophie moved to York to study at York University. The city is popular with tourists and has a strong chocolate heritage. Sophie enjoyed learning more about both the city and how chocolate is made, and was fascinated by their impact on the world. This, combined with her desire to open her own business, led her to spot an opportunity. She started making chocolates in her own kitchen and teaching chocolate making at weekends. She soon became so busy it was time to scale up the operation.

In November 2011, Sophie's dream came true. She created a home for chocolate lovers, the York Cocoa House Chocolate Emporium. The emporium is a chocolate shop, a chocolate cafe and a chocolate school. All of the products are also available in the online shop, www.yorkcocoahouse.co.uk.

Activity

In 2013, Sophie won a national competition where her prize included a year's mentoring from Deborah Meaden, the well-known star of the BBC's *Dragons' Den*. The business continues to grow, offering a wide range of special events and even a 5-day chocolate apprenticeship where customers can learn the art of chocolate making.

1 Why is York a good location for the Cocoa House?
2 What are the advantages to Sophie of offering a range of both goods and services?
3 What planning would Sophie have needed to do before opening York Cocoa House?

Theme 1: Investigating small business

Your learning

In this topic you will learn about:

- the options for start-up and small businesses – the concept of limited liability, the types of business ownership for start-ups and the option of starting up and running a franchise operation
- business location – factors influencing business location
- the marketing mix – what the marketing mix is, the importance of each element of the marketing mix and how the elements of the marketing mix work together
- business plans – the role and importance of a business plan and the purpose of planning business activity.

The options for start-up and small businesses

Case study

Mo Bro's

Mo Bro's is a beard grooming company selling high-quality handmade goods for men with beards and moustaches. These include products such as soaps, oils, brushes and other related accessories. The business was launched in 2014 by three brothers in Leicester. While growing beards to support the charity, Movember, they realised they needed special attention to keep their beards looking good and came up with ideas to solve the problem. These specialist products are now sold all over the world from their website www.mobros.co.uk.

Activity

In groups, discuss the following.

1 Why might the brothers behind Mo Bro's want to set up in business together rather than individually?
2 Would you prefer to set up a business by yourself or with family or friends?
3 Do you think this business has the potential to grow in the future?

The concept of limited liability

Setting up and running a business involves risk. An entrepreneur and other investors will have risked their own money to help establish the business. One of the first decisions to be made will be the type of business ownership, as this will determine the amount of liability (risk).

Limited liability exists when an entrepreneur's risk is limited to the amount they have actually invested or promised to invest. This means that their personal **assets** cannot be used to pay the business's debts. Businesses that have limited liability are known as **incorporated**. These are seen as less risky to the investor.

Unlimited liability exists when an entrepreneur's risk includes their own personal assets, such as their house and car. This means that if the debts of a business cannot be covered by the business's assets, the entrepreneur will have to use their own assets to pay the debts. Businesses that have unlimited liability are known as **unincorporated**.

Partners in a limited liability partnership are not personally liable for debts that the business cannot pay

The main implication of limited and unlimited liability for a business owner is the risk to their own assets.

Exam-style question

Explain **one** disadvantage to an entrepreneur of unlimited liability.

(3 marks)

The types of business ownership for start-ups

When setting up a business the entrepreneur has to decide on the type of business ownership. This is known as the legal structure of the business.

Sole trader

A **sole trader** is when one person sets up a business on their own. They are the sole owner. A sole trader is an unincorporated business and therefore has unlimited liability. Although the entrepreneur is the only owner this does not mean that they cannot employ the help of others. It is normal for a sole trader to use the help of specialists, for example a web designer

Key terms

Limited liability: the level of risk is limited to the amount of money that has been invested in the business or promised as an investment.

Assets: property, such as a house or car.

Incorporated: a business that is registered as a company, so the business and the owners are separate in the eyes of the law.

Unlimited liability: the level of risk goes beyond the amount invested, so the personal assets of the business owner can be used to pay off the business's debts.

Unincorporated: a business that is not registered as a company, so the owners and the business are the same body in the eyes of the law.

Sole trader: a type of unincorporated business that is owned by just one person.

Exam tip

State a disadvantage and explain why it is a disadvantage to an entrepreneur.

Link it up

In Topic 1.1 *Enterprise and entrepreneurship*, you learned about the risks and rewards of business activity, including the financial risks. The potential for financial loss is directly linked to the concept of liability.

Theme 1: Investigating small business

Key terms

Partnership: a business that is owned by a group of two or more people who share the financial risk, the decision-making and the profits.

Deed of partnership: a legal document that defines the terms of a partnership.

Private limited company: an incorporated business that is owned by shareholders.

Shareholders: investors who are part-owners of a company. They invest in the business in return for a share of the profits and voting rights at the AGM

Link it up

In Topic 2.1 *Growing the business*, you will learn about types of business ownership for growing businesses. This includes public limited companies (PLCs), which can sell their shares to the public via a stock market.

Exam tip

Read through all of the answers carefully before selecting an answer. As you read each answer, justify why you think it is correct or incorrect in order to help you eliminate answers.

or accountant. They may also need to employ staff, even if on a part-time basis, to help with the day-to-day running of the business. Sole traders are often seen as the easiest way of setting up a business as there are no legal requirements – an entrepreneur can just start trading. For this reason, they are a popular type of business for small businesses such as florists, mechanics and market traders. The business's financial information is not published, but the sole trader must declare their earnings to Her Majesty's Revenue and Customs (HMRC) as they have to pay income tax on the profits of the business.

Partnership

A **partnership** is when two or more people join together to set up and run a business. They share the financial risk by investing their own money in the business, but they also share the decision-making and the rewards. Partnerships are often set up by doctors, lawyers or accountants. Traditionally, partnerships have had unlimited liability, but it is now possible to set up a limited liability partnership. A partnership is set up using a **deed of partnership**. This legal document outlines who the partners are, the amount invested by each partner, how profits will be shared, the voting rights of each partner and also the actions to be taken if a partner wishes to leave or they want to bring in a new partner.

Private limited company

A **private limited company** is an incorporated business that is owned by **shareholders**. The shareholders must be known to the entrepreneur, so they would usually be family, friends or business contacts. The shareholders have limited liability. A private limited company must have 'Ltd' after its name. To set up a private limited company it must be registered at Companies House, which is part of the UK government. This involves submitting both a Memorandum of Association and Articles of Association. The Memorandum of Association gives details such as the name of the company, its trading activities, its registered office and the amount to be invested in shares. The Articles of Association give details about the voting rights of the shareholders, how profits will be distributed and the running of the annual general meeting (AGM). At the AGM, all shareholders are invited to vote on important decisions. The number of votes held by each shareholder is determined by the number of shares that they hold.

Exam-style question

Which **one** of the following is a characteristic of a private limited company? **(1 mark)**

Select **one** answer:

- [ ] **A** Can sell shares to anyone
- [ ] **B** Shareholders work for the business
- [ ] **C** Has limited liability
- [ ] **D** Is unincorporated

The advantages and disadvantages of each type of ownership

Type of ownership	Advantages	Disadvantages
Sole trader	• The sole trader makes all of the decisions by themselves, which is quick and does not lead to disagreements. • Quick and easy to set up. • The sole trader keeps all of the profits. • Financial information is kept private.	• The sole trader has unlimited liability. • It may be difficult to raise enough money to establish or grow the business. • Puts a lot of pressure on just one person. • Can be difficult to run if the owner is ill or takes time off.
Partnership	• The business owners may have wider expertise and can share ideas and decision-making. • The risk is shared. • Can be easier to raise finance to establish or grow the business. • The business's financial information is kept private.	• Decisions made by one partner can affect all partners. • If a partner leaves, the business no longer exists. • The profits are shared. • There may be disagreements between partners.
Private limited company	• The owners have limited liability. • The term 'Ltd' after the business's name may make it appear to be a bigger or more long-established business. • Can be easier to raise finance to establish or grow the business. • The business continues to trade even if shareholders change.	• More complex to set up than a sole trader or partnership. • There may be disagreements between shareholders. • The business's financial information is published. • More requirements to report information to organisations such as HMRC and Companies House.

Table 1.4.1 The advantages and disadvantages of different types of ownership

Activity ?

In teams of two to four people, produce a deed of partnership. Remember that, in a partnership, all partners are bound by the decisions and actions made by any one partner.

The option of starting up and running a franchise operation

When setting up a business, an entrepreneur may decide to set up as a **franchise** rather than an independent business. A franchise is when one business, the **franchisor**, gives permission to an entrepreneur, the **franchisee**, to set up a business using its brand name and selling its products. In return, the franchisee pays the franchisor an initial fee and an ongoing share of the profits. As the franchisor's business is already established and successful, starting up a franchise is seen as a less risky option than setting up independently.

Key terms

Franchise: when one business gives another business permission to trade using its name and products in return for a fee and share of its profits.

Franchisor: an established business that gives permission to an entrepreneur to trade using its name and products.

Franchisee: an entrepreneur who pays a fee to trade using the name and products of an established business.

The franchisor provides help and support to the franchisee while they are setting up and also on an ongoing basis. This usually includes training for both the entrepreneur and their employees. The franchisor also makes key decisions, such as choosing suppliers, setting prices, deciding what goods or services are offered, setting wages and determining uniforms. Brand recognition is often a key part of a franchise, so the franchisor usually wants to ensure that each franchise uses its branding correctly.

The franchisee benefits from the fact that the franchise is already successful, so they will be more confident in the success of their individual start-up. However, initial fees can be expensive and the franchisee has to share their profits with the franchisor.

Each franchise will have different terms and conditions that will be set out in its franchise agreement

Link it up

You will study marketing decisions in more detail in Topic 2.2 *Making marketing decisions*. In particular, you will look at promotional strategies, including branding in the section Promotion.

Activity ?

A McDonald's franchise has to make annual payments for various services provided by the franchisor, including:

- monthly rent: 10–18 per cent of sales (based on sales and profitability)
- fees to use McDonald's systems: 5 per cent of sales
- contribution towards marketing costs: 4.5 per cent of sales.

If a new McDonald's franchisee made sales of £250,000, what would be its:

a annual fee to use the McDonald's system?

b annual contribution towards marketing costs?

⊞ Maths tip

Remember to check your calculations and always express them in the correct format. Here, your answer should be expressed in pounds.

Advantages of franchising	Disadvantages of franchising
• Lower risk than setting up independently, as the business model is already successful. • Support and training are provided by the franchisor. • Franchisees benefit from national marketing campaigns.	• Franchisees have to pay an initial fee as well as ongoing fees and/or a share of their profits. • Franchisees cannot make independent decisions. • Brand reputation can be damaged by other franchisees if they do not maintain standards.

Table 1.4.2 The advantages and disadvantages of operating a franchise

Activity ?

Design an advert to recruit new franchisees for a national franchise chain. Your advert should be for a specific franchise of your choice and in a chosen format, such as at a bus stop, in a newspaper, on the franchisor's webpage or social media.

Exam-style question

Read the following extract carefully, then answer the question.

Eva is thinking of opening a small coffee shop in Manchester. She has looked at premises near the train station but the rents are very expensive. There is also a lot of competition in the town centre from big coffee shop chains such as Costa Coffee and Starbucks. She is therefore thinking of starting up a franchise operation.

With a minimum investment of £5,000, she could start a Coffee-Bike franchise. This is a mobile coffee franchise where coffee is freshly made and sold from an adapted bicycle. The franchisor would provide Eva with her own bike, equipment and all the necessary training.

Analyse the benefits to Eva of operating as a franchise to set up a mobile coffee shop. **(6 marks)**

Exam tip

Clearly state two benefits and explain why these are benefits.

Checkpoint

Now it is time to review your understanding of the options for start-up and small businesses.

Strengthen

S1 What is the difference between limited and unlimited liability?
S2 Draw a mind map to show three types of business ownership for start-ups. For each type, include:
   a) definition   b) characteristics   c) advantages   d) disadvantages.

Challenge

C1 If you were setting up a fast-food business, would you prefer to be an independent business or a franchise? Make a decision, then write a paragraph of at least four sentences to justify your decision. Start your paragraph with the words, 'I believe that setting up a franchise/independent (delete as appropriate) business is the best decision because…'
C2 Summarise in 125 words the implications of limited and unlimited liability for a business owner.

Theme 1: Investigating small business

Business location

Factors influencing business location

Choosing the correct location is an important decision for any business. A poor choice of location could result in the failure of a business, especially when the business is newly established. If customers struggle to get to the business or potential customers do not know about it because it is not in a convenient or visible location, the business will not do well. The choice of location will also have a major impact on the business's costs. For example, premises on a busy street in a city centre will be a lot more expensive than premises on the outskirts of a town or city.

Link it up

In the 'Business revenue, costs and profits' section of Topic 1.3 *Putting a business idea into practice*, you learned that one of the major costs of a start-up business is the cost of its premises. This is a fixed cost and has an impact on a business's ability to break even and achieve a profit.

Proximity to key factors

'Proximity' means nearness to something. A business may want to be close to or far away from the following key factors: market, **labour**, materials and competitors. These choices will depend on the business's activities, so the decisions may vary widely for different kinds of businesses.

Proximity to market

This means how close a business is to its customers. The importance of proximity to market will depend on how important convenience is to the customer. For example, a customer is unlikely to travel a long way to buy fish and chips or a daily newspaper. Businesses selling these products need to be close to their market. However, a customer is more likely to travel further for more specialist products such as wedding dresses or custom-built cars. Before choosing to set up in a particular location, a business may look at the **footfall** of the location or research the **demographics** of the area to see if it matches their customers.

Key terms

Labour: workers or the workforce.

Footfall: the number of people passing a particular location within a given time period.

Demographics: the characteristics of the population, such as gender, age, religion and wealth.

Proximity to labour

A business may want to locate itself in an area where there is plenty of labour (a lot of potential workers). 'Labour' can include the number of workers in an area and the availability of workers with the right skills in that area. Certain parts of the UK are associated with highly skilled workers in certain fields or industries. For example, a technology company may choose to locate close to the M25 around London, where there are plenty of workers with technology skills. The availability of workers in a certain area may also affect the wages that a business will need to pay. For example, if a business needs to recruit a large number of unskilled workers, they may choose to locate in an area with high unemployment, as this area should contain a large number of workers willing to work for the **National Living Wage**. This would help to keep costs down.

> **Key term**
>
> **National Living Wage:** the minimum amount that a business is legally allowed to pay its employees.

> ## Activity   ?
>
> In pairs, research the National Living Wage.
>
> 1 How much is it for employees aged:
>
>   **a** over 25
>
>   **b** 21–24
>
>   **c** 18–20
>
>   **d** under 18?
>
> 2 How much is the National Living Wage for an apprentice?
>
> 3 Hold a class debate on the topic: 'Is the National Living Wage a fair wage or should employers pay more?' Try to think of it both from the point of view of the business and of the employees.

Proximity to materials

A business may locate itself as close as possible to the raw materials that it uses to produce its finished products. For example, there are lots of commercial orchards that grow apples and similar fruits in the south-west areas of the UK, where the climate is suitable for this kind of crop. Apple juice and cider producers also choose to locate in these areas in order to be close to these orchards, which are the source of their raw materials.

Often, businesses need to choose between locating close to their raw materials and locating close to their market. Their decision depends on whether the business's products are bulk-gaining or bulk-reducing.

A **bulk-gaining product** is one where the end product is bigger (and more difficult or expensive to transport) than the raw materials. This means that it is sensible for the business to locate close to the market in order to reduce transportation costs. For example, a manufacturer of soft drinks may have bottling plants across the UK, as it is cheaper to transport the flavoured syrups and then add water at a location much closer to the market than it would be to distribute the finished bottles of drinks.

> **Key term**
>
> **Bulk-gaining product:** an end product that is bigger than the raw materials used to make it, such as a bicycle.

Theme 1: Investigating small business

Are soft drinks a bulk-gaining or bulk-reducing good?

A **bulk-reducing product** is one where the end product is smaller than the raw materials. For example, a wholesale fish distributor would not transport whole fish to a factory that manufactures fish fingers, as much of the raw material, such as skin and bones, would be disposed of as soon as it reached the factory. Instead, it is more efficient to dispose of the waste as close as possible to the source of the raw material. This will avoid wasting money by unnecessarily transporting it.

Proximity to competitors

Some businesses choose to locate themselves away from their competitors. A business selling a **convenience good**, such as a newsagent's, is unlikely to locate close to its competitors as this would probably just split the local customers between the two businesses, reducing the number of their potential customers.

However, if the business sells what is known as a **shopping good**, they might want to be close to competitors. For example, if a customer wants to buy a new car and knows that one part of town contains one car dealership but another area contains five car dealerships, they are likely to go to the area with more dealerships. This area offers them a wider choice and the ability to shop around for the best deal with ease, as the dealerships are all in one place. In this case, the dealership located away from its competitors has lost out before the customer has even arrived in the area.

This is true for a range of businesses. For example, in many cities it is easy to see particular types of businesses grouping together, such as in an area with lots of restaurants or clothes shops.

Nature of the business activity

The location chosen by a business may be partly determined by what the business does on a day-to-day basis – that is, its activities. There are many instances in which business activity could have an impact on choice of location, including:

- businesses that import or export goods that locate close to a seaport or airport
- businesses that distribute goods around the UK that locate in the centre of the UK with easy access to major roads and motorways
- agricultural businesses that need a certain type of **topography**, climate or soil in order to grow particular crops or rear particular animals
- tourist-related businesses such as bed and breakfasts, souvenir shops or attractions that locate in areas that attract large numbers of tourists, such as famous cities or seaside towns

- specialist support services or providers of raw materials that locate in an area containing businesses that will buy their products, such as a producer of car headlights locating in an area containing car factories
- businesses in industries traditionally associated with certain areas that choose to locate in these areas, such as cotton mills in Lancashire or boot and shoe manufacturers in Northampton, where luxury shoemakers Crockett & Jones still manufacture their products.

However, some business location decisions are based on personal preference or **inertia**. Inertia is when a business is located in a certain area because that is where it was first set up, possibly the entrepreneur's home town. The business stays in that location not because of any particular reason or benefit but just because it is easier.

> ### Key terms
>
> **Inertia:** a tendency to keep things as they are rather than change.
>
> **E-commerce:** using the internet to carry out business transactions.
>
> **M-commerce:** using mobile technologies such as smartphones and tablets to carry out business transactions.

> ### Activity ?
>
> Certain areas of the UK are well known for specific industries. In pairs look at each of the areas listed below. Can you identify the industry that is historically located in each area? You might need to carry out some research.
>
> **a** Sheffield
>
> **b** Savile Row, London
>
> **c** the North East (Newcastle or Sunderland)
>
> **d** Stoke-on-Trent
>
> **e** Dover
>
> **f** the Lake District
>
> In each case, try to explain a possible reason for the industry's location based on the business activity.

> ### Link it up
>
> In the section 'Business and globalisation' in Topic 2.1 *Growing the business*, you will learn why some businesses choose to locate abroad or choose their location due to operating in international markets.

> ### Exam-style question
>
> Explain **one** advantage to a business of locating in an area of high unemployment. **(3 marks)**

> ### Exam tip
>
> Identify an advantage, then explain why it is an advantage to a business.

The impact of the internet on location decisions

The internet has led to buyers and sellers being able to trade online. This means that there is no need for fixed premises. This can benefit start-up businesses in particular, as it provides a lower cost option than having to buy or rent, insure and furnish premises. It is not even necessary for the business to have its own website. Some businesses start trading using the platforms provided by other businesses, such as eBay or notonthehighstreet.com.

When buyers and sellers trade in a virtual location, this is called **e-commerce**. Increasingly, businesses are using e-commerce and **m-commerce** as a cost-effective way of attracting customers.

Key term

Multi-channel: using a number of methods to reach the customer, including physical stores and e-commerce.

Link it up

You will consider the impact of e-commerce in more detail in the section 'The marketing mix' later in this Topic. This will be revisited in the section 'Business and globalisation' in Topic 2.1 *Growing the business*, when you will look at the use of technology by businesses that trade internationally.

Did you know?

It is estimated that by 2020 online spending in the UK will reach £62.7 billion.

It is estimated that by 2020 17.1 per cent of all sales in the retail sector will be made online.

Benefits of e-commerce include:

• lower operating costs, such as not needing retail premises or staff
• ability to reach a wider audience
• ability to trade 24 hours a day, 7 days a week
• ability to respond to changing consumer buying habits, such as by making a website mobile-friendly to allow purchases from mobile devices.

Many businesses use a **multi-channel** approach to reach their customers. This means that they still operate traditional stores as well as operating an e-commerce site. This allows the businesses to maximise the number of customers that they can reach.

Activity

In pairs select an industry, such as fashion. Produce a table to show examples of businesses within this industry that operate:

• physical stores only
• e-commerce only
• physical stores and e-commerce.

Checkpoint

Now it is time to review your understanding of the factors influencing business location.

Strengthen

S1 Describe why some businesses may choose to locate close to their competitors whereas others may choose to locate away from competitors.

S2 List three reasons why the nature of a business's activity affects location decisions.

S3 Using an example, describe the difference between bulk-gaining and bulk-reducing goods. How does this difference affect location decisions?

Challenge

C1 Produce a revision card to summarise the factors influencing business location. Describe each factor stated in just one sentence.

C2 Choose a business in your local area. Identify four factors that may have influenced its location decision. Prioritise these factors, with one being the most important and four being the least important.

The marketing mix

The marketing mix and the importance of each element

The marketing mix is the combination of the four 'P's of marketing: price, product, promotion and place. A business uses the marketing mix to attract its customers. In order to be effective, the marketing mix should be informed by market research to ensure that the business understands the needs and expectations of existing customers and potential new customers. It is important that the four elements of the marketing mix complement each other and work together, rather than contradicting each other. For example, a product that is of relatively low quality is unlikely to succeed if it has a high retail price.

Price

Price is the amount of money that a customer will need to pay to receive the product. Prices can be set high if customers are willing and able to pay that high price. Factors influencing price will include:

- the amount of competition from other businesses
- customers' opinions about the product's value.

Product

Product is the actual good or service that the business is offering for sale. A good is a product that can be touched, such as a smartphone or a scooter. A service is a product that cannot be touched, such as a taxi ride or buying car insurance.

Promotion

Promotion is the range of activities undertaken by a business to make customers aware of its products and to encourage customers to buy them. This can include a variety of activities, such as:

- offering discounts
- television or billboard advertising
- using social media such as Facebook and Twitter
- sponsoring people or organisations, such as sports teams or individual athletes.

Theme 1: Investigating small business

In Topic 2.2 *Making marketing decisions*, you will look at each of the four 'P's of marketing in more detail.

Link it up

In Topic 2.2 *Making marketing decisions*, you will look at each of the four 'P's of marketing in more detail.

Exam tip

Read through all of the answers carefully before selecting the answers you think are correct. As you read each answer, justify why you think it is correct or incorrect in order to help you eliminate answers.

Read the instructions carefully so that you select the correct number of answers.

Key terms

Undercut: sell the same product for a lower price than competitors.

Price war: when competing businesses try to undercut each other by lowering prices. This leads to an ongoing battle where only the customer benefits, not the businesses.

Product differentiation: designing a product with some unique features that distinguish it from similar products sold by competitors.

Brand loyalty: a customer's willingness to buy a product from a particular business rather than from its competitors.

Market share: the percentage of the total sales of a product in a market that is taken by one business in that market.

Place

Place is where the customer can purchase the product, such as:
- online
- through a retailer
- direct from the manufacturer.

Place can also be used to refer to the route that a product takes to get from the manufacturer to the end customer.

Exam-style question

Which **two** of the following are part of the marketing mix for a mobile phone? **(2 marks)**

Select **two** answers:

- [ ] **A** monthly tariff of £30
- [ ] **B** the competitor is Samsung
- [ ] **C** raw material costs are £50 per phone
- [ ] **D** an advert on a major supermarket's website
- [ ] **E** manufactured in China

Activity ?

Choose a product and draw a diagram to show the marketing mix for that product.

How the elements of the marketing mix work together

The way in which the four elements of the marketing mix work together will be influenced by a variety of factors. These factors may include the competitive environment, changes in consumer needs or trends and changes in technology.

Balancing the marketing mix based on the competitive environment

The 'competitive environment' refers to the number and relative power of businesses competing in one market. A business will balance the aspects of its marketing mix based on the competitive environment – that is, in response to the actions of its competitors. Examples of how a business may respond to its competitors include:

- changing a product's price to match or **undercut** its competitors, though businesses have to be careful that this strategy does not result in a **price war**
- altering aspects of an existing product or bringing out a new product with a unique feature to achieve **product differentiation**
- undertaking promotional activities to boost brand awareness in order to encourage more **brand loyalty**
- changing the place or increasing the number of places where products are available to the customer in order to maintain or increase **market share**, such as introducing an e-commerce site.

Activity ?

Look again at the marketing mix diagram you drew earlier (page 102).

1 Draw lines linking each component of the marketing mix to the others. Along these lines, write an explanation of how the connected components work together.

2 For your chosen product, rank the four components of the marketing mix in order of importance, with one being the most important and four being the least important. Justify your ranking.

Link it up

In Topic 2.2 *Making marketing decisions,* you will look at the importance to a business of differentiating a product in more detail.

The impact of changing consumer needs on the marketing mix

Businesses respond to changing consumer needs by adapting aspects of their marketing mix. For example, many businesses introduced e-commerce to meet consumers' need for the increased convenience of internet shopping. Other examples could include:

- launching new products to respond to consumer trends, such as veganism or wholefood diets

- changing prices in response to economic conditions, such as customers reducing the amount that they spend during a **recession**

- opening more small local stores to make products more easily accessible to consumers who do not own cars.

Key term

Recession: a period of economic decline characterised by the fact that the economy has failed to grow for 6 consecutive months.

How has the growth of the internet affected the availability of information to consumers?

The impact of technology on the marketing mix

Constant changes in technology create both opportunities and threats for businesses. Businesses need to respond to these changes in order to remain competitive. This will have an impact on the marketing mix.

For example, a business may change its **promotional mix** to use increasingly popular uses of technology. Examples of this include:

- introducing e-commerce or m-commerce to meet customer needs
- using more digital communication such as blogging and social media activity to promote products and keep customers interested in the brand
- changing aspects of product design by incorporating new technologies into the product
- lowering prices due to savings made by using efficient technologies in the production process
- changing prices as a result of greater availability of information to customers, such as through price comparison websites.

Exam-style question

Read the following extract carefully, then answer the question.

Tyres on the Drive is a mobile tyre-fitting business. It offers customers the convenience of having tyres fitted either at home or at their place of work. They can be booked any day of the week and are on average 40 per cent cheaper than competitors working from garages and workshops. They invite customers to review their services using an online review package called Trustpilot. Its service has a 5 star rating, classifying it as excellent.

Analyse the impact on Tyres on the Drive, concentrating on just one element of the marketing mix. **(6 marks)**

Exam tip

Analyse how two or more elements of Tyres on the Drive's marketing mix complement each other and explain why.

You do not need to explain all four 'P's in the context of Tyres on the Drive: focus on the interrelationship between them.

Checkpoint

Now it is time to review your understanding of the marketing mix.

Strengthen

S1 Describe what is meant by the term 'marketing mix'.
S2 Using your local cinema or leisure facility as an example, describe the four elements of the marketing mix.

Challenge

C1 Considering the four elements of the marketing mix, write a promotional tweet for #cadburycremeegg with a maximum of 140 characters.
C2 In 125 words or fewer, describe why the elements of the marketing mix must work together.

Business plans

Chez Liz Resto Bar

Chez Liz Resto Bar opened in Cornwall, Canada, in 2016. It is owned by husband and wife team Lizanne and Gilles, and the running of the business is supported by their two sons Derik and Janik. The restaurant seats 97 people, with seating both inside and on the patio. It took several weeks to renovate the premises before opening the doors.

Activity

Why would it be necessary for Lizanne and Gilles to plan the opening of their restaurant?

The role and importance of a business plan

Setting up a business is complex. It involves carrying out a range of activities and coordinating a number of resources. For this reason, it is important that entrepreneurs plan these activities before they start to set up a new business.

A **business plan** is a document that outlines the details of an entrepreneur's idea, the financial forecasts for the new business and how the entrepreneur will set up the business. The process of writing a business plan encourages the entrepreneur to collect all of the relevant information together in a logical manner and to think through each step that they need to take before they can start to trade. Once the business is up and running, the entrepreneur can then continue to use the business plan as a guide and to check their progress against their original targets. The business plan is also likely to be shared with external parties, such as banks or potential investors.

Key term

Business plan: a document that outlines how an entrepreneur is going to set up a new business.

Activity

Reread the case study about Chez Liz Resto Bar.

1 Draw a spider diagram showing all of the activities that Lizanne and Gilles would have completed before they could open their restaurant.

2 Now compare your list with the items listed in Table 1.4.3 on page 106. If you missed out any activities, add them to your list.

Why would a bank manager want to see a business plan before offering a loan?

Theme 1: Investigating small business

Factor	Details about the identified factor
Business idea	A brief description of the goods and/or services that the business will provide on a day-to-day basis.
Business aims and objectives	An outline of what the business wants to achieve. These aims and objectives should be **SMART** (Specific, Measurable, Achievable, Realistic and Time-bound), as this will allow the entrepreneur to measure their later performance easily against their original objectives.
Target market	A summary of the **market research** findings and details about the business's target market. This will include potential size of the market and any identifiable trends in that market.
Forecast **revenue**, cost and profit	These forecasts are based on market research. They also include the estimated costs of setting up the business and running it on a day-to-day basis, as well as the business's predicted **profit**.
Cash flow forecast	A forecast of the amount of money that will come into and go out of the business, and the times at which money will come and go. This is very important, as even a profitable business can fail due to cash flow problems.
Sources of finance	The total amount of money that is needed in order to start up and run the business, and where this money will come from.
Location	An outline of where the business will operate from. This could include a retail outlet, a factory, offices or even the entrepreneur's home address if they are going to run the business from home.
Marketing mix	A short description of each of the business's four 'P's. This will include: • what products the business will sell • what price it will charge for each product • where the products will be made available to customers • how the business will promote itself. Each of these decisions should be backed by market research findings and reflected in the forecast revenues and costs.

Table 1.4.3 The factors that should be identified in a business plan

Key terms

SMART objectives: objectives that are Specific, Measurable, Achievable, Realistic and Time-bound.

Market research: the process of gathering information about the market and customers' needs and wants in order to help inform business decisions, including product design and marketing.

Target market: the group of people that a business has identified as potential customers.

Revenue: the money that will come into a business from sales.

Profit: the amount of revenue left over once costs have been deducted.

Cash flow: the amount of money coming in and going out of the business and the timing of its movement.

Activity ?

Write a SMART objective for each of the following businesses.

a A market trader selling fruit and vegetables at the weekend.

b A children's nursery offering pre-school care in your local area.

c A chain of three fish and chip shops in Cumbria.

d A manufacturer of ladies' clothes selling to a high-street fashion chain.

Link it up

You have already looked at some of the items included in a business plan, such as the section 'Market research' in Topic 1.2 *Spotting a business opportunity* and other set-up activities like setting aims and objectives and financial forecasting (Topic 1.3 *Putting a business idea into practice*).

The purpose of planning business activity

Minimising risk

Setting up a business involves risk, such as the potential loss of invested money and time. A business plan can help to minimise risk, but it will not eliminate risk.

Risk can be reduced by:
- very detailed planning that makes the entrepreneur think through the issues that may arise
- setting clear objectives and aims to help provide direction when making business decisions
- conducting market research to help inform decision-making
- making financial forecasts so that the entrepreneur can set **budgets** and monitor spending
- using a cash flow forecast to identify any times when there may be a **negative cash balance** and to plan for this in advance (for example, by arranging an **overdraft**).

Obtaining finance

A business plan is also important when obtaining finance. If an entrepreneur is trying to raise finance from a bank, such as a **bank loan**, the bank manager would review their business plan before granting the loan in order to see how the entrepreneur intends to repay the money. Similarly, if an entrepreneur approached an investor for finance, the investor would want to see a thorough and realistic business plan, as this would show them that the business is well-researched and has the potential to succeed.

Exam-style question ○

Explain **one** difficulty that a new entrepreneur may experience when writing a business plan.   **(3 marks)**

Checkpoint

Now it is time to review your understanding of business plans.

Strengthen

S1 Write a list of the components of a business plan.

S2 Describe two advantages to an entrepreneur of a producing a business plan.

Challenge

C1 Design a leaflet or webpage for a high street bank that explains the following to new entrepreneurs:
- the contents of a business plan
- the purpose of a business plan
- top tips for writing a business plan.

Key terms

Budgets: pre-set financial targets for a business to achieve, like a sales budget, or abide by, such as an expenditure budget, in a given period of time.

Negative cash balance: occurs if the business's opening balance results in a negative amount at the end of the period, leading to a cash shortage.

Overdraft: a facility provided by a bank allowing a current account holder to withdraw more money than there is in the account.

Bank loan: a fixed sum of money lent by a bank to an individual or a business for a specific purpose, which must be repaid with interest in set payments over an agreed period of time.

Exam tip ○

State one difficulty and then explain why a new entrepreneur may experience this difficulty.

An important clue in this question is that the entrepreneur is a 'new' entrepreneur.

Maths tip

Remember that the interest charged on a bank loan is a cost to the business and will therefore impact on profits. Interest rates are shown as a percentage (%).

1.4 Making the business effective

1. Which **one** of the following definitions of 'the marketing mix' is correct? *(1 mark)*

   Select **one** answer:

   ☐ A Product, price, profit, promotion

   ☐ B Promotion, profit, people, place

   ☐ C Place, product, price, proximity

   ☐ D Price, place, product, promotion

2. Explain **one** factor that will influence the location decision of a retail business. *(3 marks)*

   ## Student answer

   One factor is the proximity to the market. This means they will want to be close to customers. This will increase the number of customers visiting the shop and therefore increase sales.

   ## Verdict

   The student clearly identifies a factor that is relevant to location, showing good knowledge. The factor selected is also relevant to a retail business. This is followed by an explanation of why this factor influences the choice of location.

3. Explain **one** benefit to a new business of setting up as a private limited company. *(3 marks)*

   ## Student answer

   The business and the owner are seen as separate in the eyes of the law. Customers may see the business as more successful because it is a Ltd.

   ## Verdict

   This student has good knowledge but fails to answer the question successfully. They then give more information about limited companies rather than explaining why having limited liability is an advantage.

Read the following extract carefully, then answer Questions 4, 5 and 6.

Joe runs an Italian delicatessen in Bath. He enjoys being his own boss and making all of his own decisions. In his business plan, he set a target to achieve 10 per cent growth on sales each year and maintain a positive cash balance. This year, Joe noticed a fall in repeat customers and became concerned that he might not achieve his target. He thought that his customers might be put off by a lack of variety in his products.

Saskia is one of Joe's friends and is a successful businessperson. She worries that, by operating as a sole trader, Joe is putting too much pressure on himself. Saskia has ideas to help expand his business and she offers to invest £120,000 in Joe's business in return for a 50 per cent share of the business. Her marketing skills could help to develop the profile of the business and allow it to expand, and in the long term she thinks that the business should operate as a franchisor.

4. Explain **one** advantage to a business of extending its product range. (3 marks)

Student answer

One advantage would be this offers customers a wider choice. This will encourage customers to keep going back as they will not get bored. This will help a business achieve an increase in sales.

Verdict

The student gives a very strong answer focused on the business in the extract. There are a number of steps in their argument that are linked together to form a complete answer.

5. Outline **one** advantage to Joe of having a business plan. (3 marks)

Student answer

One advantage is that it will allow Joe to see how he is performing against the plan. This will help him know if he will meet his targets.

Verdict

There is some explanation of an advantage, but the student fails to link this effectively to the extract. For example, they could have mentioned Joe's sales target or cash flow target, which are explicitly mentioned in the extract.

Joe is considering two options: continue to operate as a sole trader or accept Saskia's proposal and change to being a private limited company

6. Justify which **one** of these two options Joe should choose. (9 marks)

Student answer

Joe has set a target of growth in his business plan. This means he will need to continue to attract new customers while maintaining repeat customers in order for sales to increase. This can be achieved by effective marketing. This will require a budget and expertise but as a sole trader Joe is already under a lot of pressure. Yet if he were to use the expertise of Saskia by accepting her proposal he would lose the ability to make all of the decisions himself.

Option 2 is the best option for Joe as he would benefit from Saskia's knowledge of marketing and her previous success as a businessperson. As a Ltd company, Joe and Saskia would share the decision-making and enjoy limited liability, which is important as the business grows. It is unlikely that Joe would be able to grow the business as well by himself.

Although Joe would lose some of his independence, this should not be a major problem as he and Saskia are friends so should be able to work well together.

Verdict

This student has given a well-balanced argument that makes good use of the case material. The response clearly answers the question by stating which option is best and justifying why it is the best option. It is particularly good that the student recognises there is a negative to this decision but that it is not a big enough concern to sway the decision in the opposite direction.

Topic 1.5 Understanding external influences

Topic overview

This topic will help you to understand external influences on a business and the ways in which businesses respond to these influences. External influences are factors outside a business's control. They include stakeholders, technology, legislation (law) and the economy.

Case study

Funky Pigeon

Funky Pigeon is one of the top online card retailers operating in the UK. Funky Pigeon produces personalised greeting cards and other gifts using digital technology: customers upload their images to the website to have them added to greetings cards and other products, which are then sent directly to customers.

The website was established in 2007 by an entrepreneur called Richard Pepper, as part of a limited company called Spilt Ink. Pepper made good use of new technology when he established Funky Pigeon, as advances in technology enabled him to provide personalised goods in a way that had not previously been possible. Customers reacted well to this service, and soon other websites were also established to cater for this demand.

Before online card retailing, it was possible for customers to go into a shop and order a greetings card with a photograph on it. However, the customer would have to wait days or weeks for the card to be produced. The technology used by Funky Pigeon transformed customers' expectations about the length of time that they were prepared to wait for a personalised greetings card.

Funky Pigeon was so successful that, in May 2010, it was bought by high-street retailer WHSmith. After the sale, Richard Pepper continued to work at the company, making use of new advances in technology to expand the business even further. For example, Funky Pigeon's cards and other gifts can now be produced using smartphones, and the number of possible gift options has now increased to include items such as personalised foods and clothing.

Activity ?

1 Describe the influence that technology has had on Spilt Ink using information from the case study.
2 How have customers, as stakeholders, helped to influence the success of the business?
3 Funky Pigeon is an online business. How far do you think the law will have an impact on the way that this website operates?

Your learning

In this topic you will learn about:

- business stakeholders – who business stakeholders are and their different objectives, and the relationship between stakeholders and businesses
- technology and businesses – different types of technology used by business and how technology influences business activity
- legislation and business – the purpose of legislation and the impact of legislation on businesses
- the economy and business – the impact of the economic climate on businesses
- external influences – the importance of external influences on business.

Theme 1: Investigating small business

Business stakeholders

Activity ?

Give three benefits to Wiggle of receiving awards from **stakeholders** like BikeBiz. You may want to look up Wiggle and BikeBiz online to help you complete this activity.

Stakeholders and their objectives

All businesses have stakeholders that influence the way in which the business operates. Each stakeholder or group of stakeholders also has their own set of objectives. The number of stakeholders and the influence that each stakeholder has over the business depends on the type of business and the way in which it operates. There are eight main types of stakeholder.

Key terms

Stakeholder: anyone who has an interest in the activities of a business, such as its workers, its suppliers, the local community and the government.

Shareholders: investors who are part-owners of a company.

Private limited company: an incorporated business that is owned by shareholders who invest in the business in return for a share of the profits and voting rights at the annual general meeting (AGM).

Public limited company: an incorporated business that can sell shares to the public (also known as a PLC).

Stock exchange: a place where shares in PLCs can be bought and sold.

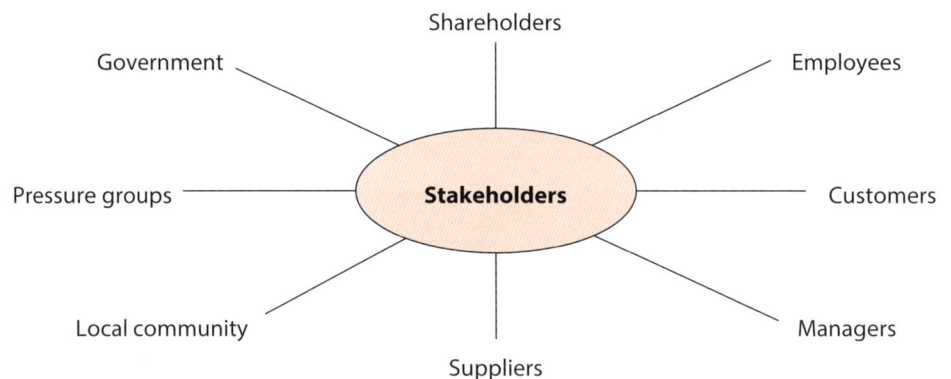

Figure 1.5.1 The eight different types of stakeholder that may influence businesses

Shareholders (owners)

Shareholders influence the way in which a business is run because they own a part of the business by holding a share or a number of shares in it. People can hold shares in two different types of business:

- **private limited companies** – shares in these businesses can only be bought privately, that is by people who know the entrepreneur setting up and running the private limited company
- **public limited companies** (PLCs) – shares in these businesses can be bought through a **stock exchange** by members of the public who are not known to the original entrepreneur.

112

Shareholders have a big influence on a business because they have invested their money in the business, and expect to receive something in return. This means that their objectives are:

- to make money by being given a share of the **profits** of the business in return for their investments
- to make money if they sell their shares – if the business grows and its value goes up, the value of each individual share increases and the shareholder will make a profit when they sell their shares.

Shareholders may be able to vote on matters such as the appointment of new chief executives who will run the business on a day-to-day basis. Shareholders can also have a big influence on the business if they decide to buy enough shares that they own a significant percentage of the business. A shareholder who owns 10 per cent of the business's shares owns 10 per cent of the business, and they can influence the way in which it is run.

Employees

Employees are key stakeholders in a business because they actually do the business's work. If they do their jobs as well as possible, the business should do well as a result. However, if they do not do their jobs well, this could lead to bad customer service and a decrease in sales. Employees are also influenced by the performance of the business: if the business does well, their jobs are more secure and they are more likely to receive pay rises or bonuses. The way in which a business treats its employees can have a big impact on the reputation and overall performance of a business, so managing employees well is vital.

The main objectives of employees are:

- to get the best possible pay and rewards for doing their jobs
- to keep their jobs and to ensure that their job is secure.

> ### Exam-style question
>
> Explain **one** advantage to a business of having satisfied employees as stakeholders. **(3 marks)**

Customers

Customers are stakeholders with an influence over businesses because they buy a business's products and services. If they buy a lot from that business, its sales will increase and the business will do well. If customers stop buying the business's products, the business's sales will decrease and, over time, this will lower that business's profits. Customers also influence the quality and delivery of a business's product or service. The way that a customer is treated has a huge impact on the way that customers feel about a business and therefore whether or not they recommend the business to other people.

> ### Key term
>
> **Profit:** the amount of revenue left over once costs have been deducted.

> ### Link it up
>
> You have already learned about shareholders of private limited companies in the section 'The options for start-up and small businesses' in Topic 1.4 *Making the business effective*. You will explore the role of shareholders in more detail when you learn about public limited companies (PLCs) in Topic 2.1 *Growing the business*.

> ### Exam tip
>
> Remember to give only **one** advantage, not more, and include two additional points about why this is an advantage.

> ### Did you know?
>
> Many customers make judgements about how and where to buy products based on reviews. Customer service is often a key part of reviews, so ensuring that employees are trained and motivated to give excellent customer service is extremely important.

Customers' objectives are:

- to get the best possible quality service or product (this may include excellent delivery or problems being resolved quickly)
- to get the best value for money for that product or service.

Activity ?

Think about the cafeteria in your school or college. Think about how much influence you have over the quality, choice and price of the food that it sells to you. In small groups, discuss how much influence you, as stakeholders, have over this service. Then make a judgement about how you could influence the service even more in the future.

Managers

Managers are senior employees within a business. They can influence a business because they ensure that the business's employees work well, either in teams or individually. This then has an influence on the way in which employees provide customers with the products or services they want. Like other employees, managers are also influenced by the business because it pays their wages.

The objectives of managers are:

- to make sure that the business succeeds so that they get paid
- to ensure that their jobs are secure.

Suppliers

Suppliers can have a big influence on businesses because they provide the goods or services that the business needs in order to keep on operating. Suppliers need to trade with businesses to increase their sales and are dependent on the success of the businesses that buy from them. For example, if customers buy more from a business that they supply, the supplier is also likely to make more money.

It can be very important for a business to have a good relationship with its suppliers. This makes it more likely that the business will be able to negotiate better **payment terms** or savings that they can pass on to their customers. This should help to increase the business's sales and profits, meaning that they will probably buy more from their suppliers, leading to a positive outcome for the suppliers and the business.

Like any other business, a supplier will have very clear objectives, including:

- to increase sales and profits
- to encourage businesses to buy from them again in the future
- to grow their business.

Local community

The local community is made of the people who live and work in the area around a business. The local community is a business stakeholder because the work of the business has an influence on them. The local community can

---

Key term

Payment terms: the period of time that a business has to pay its suppliers.

Activity ?

Businesses often ask their suppliers for offers and special arrangements, such as requesting that a supplier holds stock in a warehouse for them until they need it. In pairs, research other ways in which a supplier can influence a business to buy from them.

also influence the business because they can support or object to the way in which it operates.

If a business affects the local community by causing parking problems or noise from late-night deliveries, people can complain to their local council. If a business wants to expand, it may also have to seek permission from the local council and the local community. On the other hand, businesses can affect the local community in positive ways. They may sponsor local activities or invest in local infrastructure such as roads, schools and leisure facilities.

The local community has one major objective: to look after the local area and the people within it.

Pressure groups

A pressure group is a group of people who join together to try to influence businesses or the government for a particular cause. There are lots of different pressure groups in the UK, and each one focuses on a particular issue or concern. Many pressure groups focus on **ethical** issues, such as the environment or animal testing. Other pressure groups look after groups of people, usually based on the type of work that they do. These groups include trades unions, such as the National Union of Teachers (NUT), and professional associations, such as the Association of Accounting Technicians (AAT). Depending on the pressure group, its members may pay a membership fee.

The size and influence of a pressure group will often depend on the topic that it is concerned about. However, each group has an influence on the way in which businesses operate. This influence can take many different forms, such as:

- encouraging consumers to increase the amount of a product or service that is used – for example, customers increasing their use of low energy light bulbs
- persuading customers to boycott or stop buying from a business – for example, buying free range eggs rather than eggs from caged hens
- encouraging businesses to behave in more ethical ways that help other stakeholders – for example, pressuring a coffee shop chain to stock Fairtrade coffee.

Pressure groups have all sorts of objectives, depending on their purpose. However, all pressure groups try to change something, whether it is the environmental impact of a chocolate manufacturer or working conditions for doctors.

Link it up

You will learn more about business ethics and pressure groups in the section 'Ethics, the environment and business' in Topic 2.1 *Growing the business*

Did you know?

Stansted Airport is a very busy airport close to London. Like many businesses and organisations, Stansted has a corporate social responsibility (CSR) policy. This policy sets out the ways in which it tries to support the local community, such as investing in local schools, reducing its impact on the local environment and reducing the impact of aircraft noise on local residents.

Key term

Ethics: moral principles or standards that guide the behaviour of a person or business.

Pressure groups influence businesses by trying to get them to change the way that they operate

Activity ?

Working in pairs, choose one of the following categories: environment, working conditions, health or animal welfare. Create a mind map showing all of the different pressure groups that you can think of in your chosen category. How do the pressure groups that you have included influence businesses?

Link it up

In the section 'The economy and business' later in Topic 1.5, you will learn more about how the economy influences businesses and the link between government actions and business success.

Exam tip

Read the question carefully to ensure that you choose the correct number of answers.

Government

Governments have a very large influence over businesses because they are responsible for running the country. Governments influence all aspects of how a business operates. This includes the amount of tax that it pays, the way it treats its employees and its impact on the environment. They do this through the laws or legislation that they pass. The way in which the government manages the national economy can also influence businesses.

Exam-style question

Which **two** of the following are not stakeholders of a business? **(2 marks)**

Select **two** answers.

- ☐ **A** Shareholders
- ☐ **B** Profits
- ☐ **C** Government
- ☐ **D** Productivity levels
- ☐ **E** Suppliers

Stakeholders and businesses

The relationship between stakeholders and a business is defined by the way in which:

- the business affects stakeholders

- stakeholders have an impact on a business

- a business must try to satisfy all of its different stakeholders and manage any **conflict** between them.

Business activity affecting stakeholders

Everyday business activity affects different stakeholders in different ways. Whether the activity's effect on stakeholders is positive or negative depends on the point of view of each stakeholder.

Case study

Richardson's Boating Holidays

Richardson's Boating Holidays is a business offering boating holidays in Norfolk. It has lots of different stakeholders.

- Richardson's has an impact on its customers by offering different types of boat for hire, maintaining the boats and giving special offers and deals.

- Richardson's has an impact on its employees by paying their wages and offering good working conditions.

- Richardson's has an impact on its owners by maintaining or increasing sales, keeping costs low and improving the business's profits.

- Richardson's has an impact on its local community by ensuring that its customers respect the local wildlife and obey the speed restrictions on the Norfolk Broads.

- Richardson's has an impact on the government by paying taxes.

Activity ?

1 How do you think Richardson's might affect its suppliers?

2 Find out whether any pressure groups operate close to the Norfolk Broads. Do you think that they are a stakeholder? How might they be affected by Richardson's?

Stakeholders impacting on business activity

As you have already seen in this topic, businesses can have a big impact on stakeholders. However, stakeholders can also have an impact on a business's activities. Some of these are shown in Table 1.5.1 on page 118.

Theme 1: Investigating small business

Stakeholder	Impacts on business activity
Shareholders (owners)	• Set the aims and strategy for the business, including how it behaves. • Provide funding and investment to start up and expand a business.
Employees	• Provide good service, which usually results in higher sales and profits (or have a negative impact on a business's profits and reputation if they do not do their jobs well).
Customers	• Buy products and services. • Make recommendations for how to improve products and services. • Recommend the business to friends and on social media.
Managers	• Manage employees who do the day-to-day work of the business. • Communicate employees' needs to senior management. • Communicate the business's needs to employees.
Suppliers	• Provide the business with the materials it needs for its products or services. • Affect the amount of products or services that can be produced and sold (for example, if a supplier cannot provide raw materials on time, production may be stopped), which can have an impact on the business's sales and reputation.
Local community	• Support their local business by buying its products or services. • Object to the business if it has a negative impact on the local community or local environment.
Pressure groups	• Change the business's practices, such as its delivery times or the packaging it uses. • Improve employees' conditions, such as health and safety in the workplace or fair wages. • Influence customers' opinions of the business and their buying habits.
Government	• Changes the amount of tax that the business has to pay. • Passes new laws relating to the business and its industry. • Promotes different types of business activity by providing special funding for particular activities. For example, the availability of grants for wind farms has increased the number of businesses installing and operating wind farms.

Table 1.5.1 Examples of stakeholders' impact on business activity

Businesses have to try to make sure that all stakeholder groups are satisfied, or as satisfied as they can be, because this will encourage them to work with the business rather than against it. This means that businesses will change the way in which they operate due to the influence of these stakeholder groups.

Case study

FareShare

FareShare is a charity that aims to influence the way in which supermarkets, food manufacturers, processors, distributors, packers and wholesalers deal with surplus food. It is important to FareShare that food is redistributed so that it does not become food waste. FareShare encourages businesses to reduce their food waste by redistributing good, unsold food to charities and organisations such as homeless shelters, children's breakfast clubs, older people's lunch clubs, domestic violence refuges or community cafes.

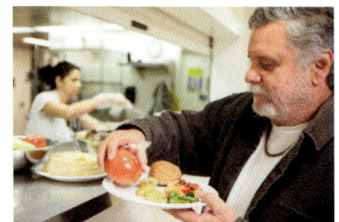

Activity ?

In pairs or small groups, research FareShare and the businesses it works with, then discuss the following questions.

1 What are the benefits to businesses of working with FareShare?

2 How have businesses been influenced by FareShare?

The pressure group Which? had an impact on the way in which some takeaway restaurants operated when it influenced the government to set up the National Food Crime Unit. This saw the establishment of a confidential helpline, which can be used to report crimes in the production and supply of food and drink. The unit also carries out random testing of takeaway meals.

Possible conflicts between stakeholder groups

Each stakeholder group has its own objectives. These objectives may not always agree, which means that stakeholder groups may be in conflict with one another. For example, the shareholders or owners of a business may want the business to make the biggest possible profit, while employees and pressure groups may want the business to pay better wages. While it is very important that a business tries to satisfy all its different stakeholders, sometimes this may not be possible because of the conflict between stakeholders' objectives.

One major reason why a business wants to avoid stakeholder conflict is because it can have a direct impact on the service provided to customers. For example, if employees who are members of a trades union go on strike as part of a campaign for better working conditions, this may affect the level of service offered to customers. In turn, this can have a negative effect on sales and on the business's profits.

Ensuring that the needs and objectives of different stakeholder groups are met can be difficult. If one group is in direct conflict with another, a business may have to choose which group it feels has the most influence over it and its decisions. For example, a pressure group may try to influence an oil company to stop operating in a particular location because of environmental concerns, whereas the oil company's shareholders may want it to expand its operations in this location. Unless the pressure group can influence customers to stop buying oil from that business, it is likely that the business will listen to its shareholders rather than the pressure group.

Did you know?

The pressure group Which? had an impact on the way in which some takeaway restaurants operated. Which? influenced the government to set up the National Food Crime unit. This included a confidential helpline, which can be used to report crimes in the production and supply of food and drink, as well as random testing of takeaway meals.

Exam-style question ⚪

Discuss the disadvantages to a business when two of its stakeholders are in conflict with each other. **(6 marks)**

Exam tip ⚪

Include at least two disadvantages of stakeholder conflict and give details for each disadvantage. Try to include business terminology in your answer and link the different points of your argument together.

Theme 1: Investigating small business

Technology and business

Case study

Hannah Banana Bakery

Hannah Banana Bakery is a small business that was founded by Hannah in Southampton in 2011. The business produces vegan cakes. Hannah Banana Bakery uses technology to promote itself, for ordering and updating customers on new recipes and products on offer. Hannah also uses Instagram to promote her ranges and also uses the latest packaging that has been made using technology to ensure that she can send her products all over the UK.

Activity ?

Using information from the case study and your own ideas, describe three ways in which technology has influenced, and continues to influence, the way in which Amazon operates.

Link it up

In the section 'The dynamic nature of business' in Topic 1.1 *Enterprise and entrepreneurship*, you learned about the way in which changes in technology can affect businesses.

Technology changes rapidly. Changes in technology can produce new ways of working, as well as new products and services, and this can have a huge impact on businesses and the way in which they operate. The fact that technology advances very quickly also means that something that was popular or innovative 10 years ago may now seem old-fashioned and out of date, and this can affect businesses as well.

Different types of technology used by business

The influence of technology on most businesses is very strong. This is particularly true of businesses that are able to operate worldwide thanks to the internet. There are many different technologies that businesses can use, but the most significant are:

- e-commerce
- social media
- digital communication
- payment systems.

E-commerce

E-commerce is the process of using the internet to carry out business transactions. This covers the use of desktop computers and laptops, as well as the use of mobile devices such as smartphones, which is known as m-commerce.

E-commerce has a significant impact on businesses. This impact can be positive, such as allowing businesses to trade with customers around the world, and negative, requiring businesses to keep up to date with the latest technological developments such as the use of smartphones.

One major challenge for businesses that trade online is ensuring that potential customers can find the business among the hundreds or thousands of other businesses on the internet. They must also ensure that their business ideas are not easily copied by their competitors. Some of the advantages and disadvantages of e-commerce are shown in Table 1.5.2.

Advantages of using e-commerce	Disadvantages of using e-commerce
• Can trade around the world, at any time of day or night. • Can process order immediately. • Can give **real-time** order updates to customers. • May be able to avoid running a retail shop or other outlet and so reduce costs. • Easier ordering process for customers.	• Can be expensive to keep up with technology. • Customers may have security concerns over fraud and the security of their account details. • Can make it harder to build relationships with customers, leading them to make purchase decisions because of price rather than brand loyalty.

Table 1.5.2 The advantages and disadvantages of using e-commerce

Social media

Social media is a term that covers a number of online channels that influence businesses, including Facebook, Twitter, YouTube, Instagram and Flickr. It is very important for a business to keep up with social media and respond to it, as it allows the business to talk to customers, read customer comments about its products and services, and respond to customers about any positive or negative reviews. This means that it is an effective way for customers and other stakeholders, such as pressure groups, to influence a business. Social media platforms also allow businesses to communicate with each other.

Did you know?

Many businesses look at the social media profiles of people who apply for jobs with them. This helps give them a sense of the sort of person the job candidate is and gives an insight into how they might behave.

Link it up

You looked at e-commerce in Topic 1.1 *Enterprise and entrepreneurship*, and Topic 1.4 *Making the business effective*. It will come up again in Topic 2.1 *Growing the business* and Topic 2.2 *Making marketing decisions*.

Key term

Real-time: live or as it happens.

Link it up

You will learn more about the use of social media for promotion in the section 'Promotion' in Topic 2.2 *Making marketing decisions*.

Theme 1: Investigating small business

Exam tip

Read all of the possible answers and decide which ones you think are incorrect, justifying your reasons to yourself. This will help you to narrow down the correct answers.

Exam-style question

Which **two** of the following are advantages of using e-commerce for a business? **(2 marks)**

Select **two** answers.

- ☐ **A** Increasing bank charges
- ☐ **B** 24/7 ordering
- ☐ **C** Customers being local
- ☐ **D** High levels of emails
- ☐ **E** Easy ordering for customers

Digital communication

Digital communication includes email or SMS (text message) and communication through websites or social media platforms. This ability to communicate digitally with customers and other stakeholders has a huge influence on the way in which businesses operate. For example, businesses and customers can communicate with each other any time of the day or night, and many businesses provide real-time updates on the delivery status of customers' orders.

Being able to communicate using technology has also changed the way that people work, as they can meet and work together virtually using communication and file-sharing services such as Skype, Google Hangout and Dropbox, rather than having to be in the same office or even in the same country. This is much quicker and cheaper than travelling long distances in order to meet in person, so it should mean that businesses' costs are lower, that decisions can be made faster and that employees' time is used as efficiently as possible.

Advances in technology mean that organisations do not necessarily need to have an office that employees travel to every day. Many businesses now have staff who use technology in order to work from home. This means that the costs of having many employees in one place – rent, heating and lighting – can be reduced, allowing that money to be used elsewhere.

Activity ?

Do some research into VoIP (voice over internet protocol) applications such as Skype and Google Hangout. List the possible ways in which businesses can communicate with stakeholders using VoIP software and the benefits to the business of each use.

VoIP software allows virtual meetings to take place, saving travel time and costs

Technology can also help businesses to operate in other countries. It allows quick, cheap communication between countries that are very far apart. It can even help people to understand one another, with online translation services to help businesses communicate with overseas customers and suppliers.

Payment systems

Advances in technology have made it very easy to pay for products and services. Payments can be made in many different ways, including through websites (e-commerce) and using mobile technology (m-commerce). Digital payment systems are extremely efficient, meaning that payments happen quicker, and they also cut down on the costs of payment processing and paperwork for businesses. They even allow a large organisation to use bank accounts in different parts of the world so that its customers can buy its products in their local currency.

Even small businesses can benefit from using digital payment systems to take debit and credit card payments, such as Sage Pay and PayPal, which are convenient for customers and ensure that payments are processed quickly. Other payment systems include Barclays Pingit and Apple Pay, which allow customers to make payments using their smartphones.

Benefits of payment systems	Drawbacks of payment systems
• Easy. • Fast. • Open 24 hours a day, 7 days a week. • Allow people to order immediately, which is good for customer service. • Trends in sales (such as increases or decreases) can be identified quickly. • Can work in many different currencies. • Customers have come to expect it and may choose not to shop with a business if digital payment is not available.	• May be vulnerable to fraud. • May be additional fees to be paid by the business.

Table 1.5.3 The benefits and drawbacks of digital payment systems

Case study

PayPal

In 2015, PayPal had 173 million users. PayPal offers businesses the ability to trade in 203 countries in 26 different currencies, 24 hours a day and 7 days a week. This means that orders can be made and payments taken all day, every day.

Businesses are constantly changing the way in which they take orders and process payments

How technology influences business activity

As you have seen, technology has a huge impact on the way in which businesses trade with each other and with customers. There are three main influences that technology has on the activities of a businesses:

- influence on sales
- influence on costs
- influence on the marketing mix.

Influence on sales

Sales refers to the number of products or services that a business sells. Technology ensures that sales can be made at any time, from any location in the world as long as it has an internet connection. Sales can even be made on days when physical shops are closed, such as bank holidays or religious festivals such as Christmas. This means that technology can help a business to increase its sales.

Having high sales is an important factor in a business's growth and survival. Any opportunities to increase sales, especially at times when people would not otherwise be able to make purchases, are very important. It is also very important that, if sales of physical products are high, the demand can be met. It is common now for businesses to use technology in their warehouses to track the amount of stock available. Many businesses also show customers on their websites how many of a product or service is available before customers make a purchase decision. This use of technology helps to increase customer satisfaction: either they get the product they want because enough of it has been kept in stock, or they are not disappointed when they are informed after purchase that the item is no longer available.

Activity ?

In recent years, online sales on Christmas Day have increased. Find out which other days in the year have very high online sales and why this happens.

Influence on costs

Technology has also had a huge influence on the costs of running a business. Communicating through the internet often means that costs are kept low, meaning that an entrepreneur can start up a business with a very small investment. Other ways in which technology can help to reduce costs include:

- avoiding paperwork by using online record keeping
- enabling real-time purchasing through online transactions
- enabling real-time monitoring of business performance
- reducing travel costs by hosting online meetings
- not needing an office or a high-street shop because staff can work from home and sales can be made through an e-commerce site
- sharing and reading documents online, rather than printing them out
- using email to communicate with customers rather than sending letters and newsletters by post.

As technology has developed, its costs have reduced and it has become more accessible to everyone. Now, even online services that used to be expensive and difficult to use without a lot of technical knowledge can be used by small start-up businesses. For example, a start-up business can create its own website using pre-made templates without needing any technical knowledge or a lot of funding.

Activity ?

Most companies use emails to communicate with their customers rather than using postal mail. What are the benefits to a business of using email and other technology to communicate? Are there any disadvantages?

Influence on the marketing mix

Technology also influences the marketing of a business and its products and services. The marketing mix is the combination of things that a business uses to attract customers: price, product, place and promotion. Technology has a big impact on all four elements, as shown in Table 1.5.4 on page 126.

Link it up

You have already learned about the marketing mix and its elements in the section 'The marketing mix' in Topic 1.4 *Making the business effective*. You will examine the marketing mix in more detail in Topic 2.2 *Making marketing decisions*.

Element of the marketing mix	The impact of technology
Price	• Customers shopping online will have a lot of businesses to choose from, so technology helps businesses to lower their prices in order to compete. • Customers can use online price comparison websites to compare deals, which also encourages businesses to lower their prices. • Businesses can operate more efficiently and reduce costs, allowing them to lower their prices and attract more customers while still making a profit.
Product	• Businesses can use technology to take advantage of the latest methods to produce goods and services, such as using robots to manufacture products so that products can be produced 24 hours a day, 7 days a week. • Businesses can use technology to offer new ways to access products or services, such as offering downloadable books and e-readers instead of, or as well as, selling printed books. • Customers can also customise their product choices, which can be produced quickly using robotics or manufacturing technology, such as custom trainers or personalised mugs.
Place	• Businesses can use social media platforms to make customers aware of their brands, products and services, and to make them feel positive about their brands. • Businesses can create reliable, easy-to-use e-commerce websites that make purchasing easy for customers. • Customers can be impressed by a good e-commerce website or put off by a bad e-commerce website.
Promotion	• Businesses can use cheap digital promotional materials, such as email newsletters, promotional codes and online advertising, which cost less than physical promotional materials such as billboards and adverts in magazines. • Businesses can target their advertising at customers by using **cookies** to track what a particular customer has been looking at online.

Table 1.5.4 The impact of technology on the marketing mix

Key term

Cookies: small files stored on a customer's computer when the customer visits a website, which record details about that visit and can be accessed by the website when the customer visits it again.

Exam tip

Give your **one** advantage and then include two additional points about why this is an advantage.

Activity

In pairs, write a list of all the offers that you have been sent through email, text message and social media, then discuss the following questions.

1 What are the advantages of receiving offers in this way?
2 Which ones did you think were the best and why?
3 Are there any disadvantages of promoting goods and services to customers in this way?

Exam-style question

Explain **one** advantage to a business of using an online payment system.

(3 marks)

Legislation and business

Case study

GAME

GAME sells games and other electronic equipment online and on the high street. GAME sells new and pre-owned games, offering a 12-month warranty on pre-owned games. This means that, if the game goes wrong, GAME has an opportunity to repair the game for the customer. It also protects the customer's rights under the Consumer Rights Act 2015.

Legislation means the laws of a country, and this can have a big impact on a business. Whether a business trades online or offline, it still has to follow the laws of the country and these can affect the way that it trades.

The purpose of legislation

There are lots of reasons why legislation exists in the UK. However, when thinking about businesses, there are two key purposes of legislation:

- protecting the rights of consumers through consumer law
- protecting the rights of employees and employers through employment law.

Principles of consumer law

Consumer law relates to the quality of products or services offered by businesses and the rights of consumers relating to those products or services. This means that a business has to provide a product or service that is of a reasonable quality and that is fit for its intended purpose – for example, selling a bicycle helmet that can and will protect a cyclist's head if they fall off their bicycle. This also means that a business has to respect its customers' rights – for example, repairing or replacing a faulty toaster.

Activity ?

In small groups, look up your rights as a customer under the Consumer Rights Act 2015. What does this piece of legislation mean for you as a customer and for businesses like GAME when it trades online and on the high street?

Key term

Legislation: the laws that a country must comply with.

127

In 2015, the government introduced the Consumer Rights Act 2015, which brought together a number of other laws into one consumer law that ensures that consumers are protected when they buy goods or services from businesses. Businesses are also protected by the Consumer Rights Act when they are buying from each other – for example, when a business purchases goods from a supplier. The Consumer Rights Act requires that:

- products must be of satisfactory quality, be fit for the purpose for which they are supposed to be used and are as they were described to the customer (for example, new or second hand)
- customers have the legal right to reject goods within 30 days if there is something wrong with them (with some exceptions, such as food)
- after 30 days, customers have the right to a repair, replacement or refund for a faulty product
- digital content, such as films streamed online or games played online, should also be of a suitable quality
- the retailer is responsible for the safe delivery of the goods
- a business providing a service must provide the service with **reasonable care** and, if they do not, the service should be redone or corrected
- businesses are not allowed to enforce unfair terms when selling goods or services, and this may even lead to a court cancelling a contract that is judged unfair.

Activity ?

Which? is a well-known consumer organisation that seeks to influence the way that consumer law is implemented and updated. Find out more about Which?, including its latest reports and its campaigns for consumers.

The Consumer Rights Act ensures that customers receive goods and services of the right quality and gives them legal protection if standards are not met

Having clear consumer law that sets out the rights of consumers helps businesses as well as customers, as it helps them to understand what must be provided and the consequences of not doing the right thing.

Exam-style question

Define the term 'consumer law'. **(1 mark)**

Exam tip

A good answer to this question will give one sentence that explains the term.

Principles of employment law

Employment law relates to the way in which employees are hired and treated by businesses and sets out the responsibilities that businesses have towards their staff. Like consumer law, it also has a significant impact on businesses. Employment law not only ensures that employees' rights are protected, but it also helps businesses to make sure that they are behaving in a legal way and will not be sued. The key areas of employment law relate to:

- recruitment
- pay
- discrimination
- health and safety.

Recruitment

Employment law covers the way that businesses recruit staff, including the way in which they advertise vacancies and interview candidates. Employment law ensures that employers do the following things in a fair way:

- advertising vacancies
- selecting candidates
- interviewing candidates
- offering a candidate the job
- preparing the employee to start their job
- producing the employee's contract of employment
- conducting the employee's **induction** programme once they start their job.

The law relating to recruitment is very complicated and there are lots of different pieces of legislation that cover all the elements that a business has to **comply** with. These elements include the rights of a person to work for a particular employer or arrangements for sick leave, including time off and sick pay. It also includes any checks that must be made before someone can do a particular job. For example, someone applying to be a teacher must have a Disclosure and Barring Service (DBS) check conducted before they can start work, which looks at whether they have a criminal record.

Link it up

You will explore employment law in more detail in Topic 2.5 *Making human resource decisions*.

Key terms

Induction: the period of time after an employee starts a job when they must be shown how to work safely and within the employer's expectations.
Comply: obey a command or meet a set of standards.

Activity

In pairs, look at the bullet list above showing the different stages of the recruitment process and choose one of them. Try to find out as much as possible about how employment law influences that stage of the recruitment process.

Theme 1: Investigating small business

Exam tip

Always read the question carefully. This question asks you to give **two** answers.

Key terms

Minimum wage: the lowest legal rate of pay for employees, depending on their age and their type of employment.

Discrimination: when someone is treated differently to someone else because of a particular characteristic, such as a disability, their ethnicity or their sex.

Activity

Find out about the current rates for apprentices, employees under the age of 25 and employees aged 25 and over, then discuss the following questions in pairs or small groups.

1 What do you notice about the minimum rates?

2 What are the advantages and disadvantages to a business of having set rates of pay for different groups of workers?

Exam-style question

Which **two** of the following do not comply with the principles of employment law? **(2 marks)**

Select **two** answers.

- ☐ **A** Fair advertising
- ☐ **B** Giving a job to your friend
- ☐ **C** Ensuring that there is equal treatment of candidates
- ☐ **D** Selecting the most attractive person for a job
- ☐ **E** Ensuring a potential employee is given a contract of employment

Pay

Employment law relating to pay is very complex and different laws regulate how much a person must be paid, depending on their age. In the UK, there are **minimum wage** requirements, as shown in Table 1.5.5.

Minimum wage requirement	Implication for a business
Apprenticeship	Businesses must pay a specified minimum rate to any apprentice employed by them in their first year. This rate is set by the government and changes each October. After their first year, the apprenticeship rate goes up to the National Minimum Wage or National Living Wage, depending on the apprentice's age.
National Minimum Wage	Businesses must pay a specified minimum wage rate to any employee under the age of 25. These rates are set by the government and there are different levels of minimum wage depending on the employee's age: • under 18 • 18–20 • 21–24.
National Living Wage	Businesses must pay a specified minimum wage to any employee over the age of 25. When the National Living Wage was introduced in 2016, it was set at £7.20 per hour.

Table 1.5.5 Different minimum wage requirements and their implications for a business

Discrimination

Employment law also requires that employees are treated fairly and equally at work. This means that businesses cannot **discriminate** against certain groups of people. For example, businesses have to make adjustments for some employees, such as a wheelchair user, to ensure that they have equal access to employment. It also means that businesses cannot refuse to give a job to a candidate because of their race, sexual orientation or any other **protected characteristic**. Law that prevents discrimination comes from the Equality Act 2010.

The law requires that all employees are treated fairly and have equal opportunities

Health and safety

Health and safety is another very important aspect of employment law. It ensures that everyone in the workplace is responsible for looking after each other's health and safety, and that it is the responsibility of both employers and employees to make sure that the workplace is safe.

Most health and safety law is set out in the Health and Safety at Work Act 1974 (HASAWA). This Act states that employees and employers have to look after each other. There are also lots of health and safety regulations that businesses must follow in order to avoid breaking the law.

HASAWA requires that:

- businesses provide safe places to work
- businesses maintain and provide suitable equipment for employees to use
- businesses provide training for employees in how to use suitable equipment and how to keep themselves safe
- employees report any accidents or near misses that they have at work
- employees report to their employer anything that they think might hurt them or someone else in the workplace
- businesses report very serious accidents in the workplace to the Health and Safety Executive (HSE) and allow the HSE to investigate what happened if necessary
- businesses ensure the safety of anyone who comes into their premises
- businesses have public liability insurance, which covers them in case a member of the public has an accident on their premises.

Key term

Protected characteristic: characteristics that cannot be used in the recruitment process to reject a candidate, such as age, disability, sex or gender, marriage status, pregnancy, race, religion or belief, or sexual orientation.

Activity **?**

In small groups, look up three different protected characteristics and find out more about what they mean, then answer the following questions.

1 How does employment law protect people who have these characteristics?

2 Can you find any examples where an employer has been taken to court for discriminating against someone with one of your chosen characteristics?

Activity ?

1 The HSE is a government agency responsible for promoting and monitoring health and safety in the workplace. Find out more about its work and the latest health and safety news.

2 Choose one area of health and safety from the list on the previous page and research it. Try to find a real-life example of an employer or employee who has not complied with that health and safety law or regulation. Tell your partner about your example.

Exam-style question

Explain **one** principle of consumer law that a business has to follow and how it affects the way in which that business trades. **(3 marks)**

The impact of legislation on businesses

Each year, lots of new legislation is approved and businesses need to make sure that they follow it. Businesses need to keep up to date with changes in legislation and ensure that the way in which they operate complies with the law. This has two main implications: the cost of adapting the business to comply with the law and the consequences of meeting or not meeting the business's legal obligations.

Cost

Each time the law changes or is updated, there are potential cost implications for businesses. Some of these cost implications are as follows.

- **Training** – this may need to be retaken and updated to comply when the law has changed so that staff know what they need to do differently. Training costs include the costs of staff being on a training course and not doing their jobs, the cost of travelling to the training and any accommodation, such as hotel rooms or a conference room, or the cost of getting the trainer to come to the business.
- **Equipment** – this may need to be changed or updated, especially if the business has to alter the way in which work is carried out.
- **Pay** – this may need to be increased in line with rises in the apprenticeship wage, National Minimum Wage and National Living Wage, so any changes must be budgeted for.
- **Administration** – administration costs may increase if a business has to update its websites, paperwork, guides and manuals to reflect what the law says. This may involve paying physical costs for paper and printing, as well as time costs if an employee has to update information on the website.
- **Licences or professional services** – these costs include payments to specialists like solicitors and accountants, who may have to advise a business on any changes in employment and consumer law.

A business has to keep up to date with changes to the law and this often involves retraining its staff

Consequences of meeting and not meeting legal obligations

Legislation changes frequently, so businesses may need to meet new legal obligations every few years. Many changes to legislation are put into place to make sure that businesses operate as safely and fairly as possible. This can lead to positive consequences if a business meets its legal obligations, as well as negative consequences if the business does not meet those legal obligations.

Positive consequences	Negative consequences
• The business has a positive reputation. • Customers and other stakeholders, such as employees, feel that they are being treated fairly by the business. • Higher sales due to customers being attracted to buy from the business because of its good reputation. • Better candidates for jobs with the business, because people are attracted to work for the business.	• The business may be taken to court, resulting in fines or even prison sentences for members of staff, including the owners. • Negative media stories about the business, leading to a bad reputation. • A customer or employee is injured, suffers ill-health or is even killed as a result of the business's failure to meet legal obligations. • The business is closed down temporarily or permanently.

Table 1.5.6 The positive and negative consequences of meeting or not meeting legal obligations

Activity ?

In small groups, choose an aspect of consumer or employment law. Find out what sort of fines and other penalties have been paid by businesses that have not followed this aspect of the law.

Did you know?

Businesses can face fines that run into millions of pounds. In 2016, Tata UK was fined £1.98 million by the HSE for failing to protect two employees who were injured when operating machinery in the workplace.

Checkpoint

Now it is time to review your understanding of legislation and business.

Strengthen

S1 Describe two principles of consumer law that influence businesses.

S2 Name the four key areas of employment law.

S3 Describe how legislation can lead to increases in costs for business. Use examples to explain your answer.

Challenge

C1 Choose a business – for example, a high street clothes retailer. Write a case study examining the impact on your chosen business of failing to follow consumer law.

C2 Discuss the statement: 'good employment law is the only way to ensure that businesses look after their employees'. Do you agree or disagree? Justify your decision.

The economy and business

Key term

Levy: a tax on a particular product or service.

Activity   **?**

In pairs, research and answer the following questions.

1 How has the money raised from the carrier bag levy been used for good causes in your area?

2 What are the benefits to businesses of introducing this levy and are there any disadvantages?

Did you know?

As a result of the introduction of the carrier bag levy, some retailers found that the number of plastic bags used by their customers decreased by up to 80 per cent.

Businesses are affected by what is happening in the economy. The performance of a national economy affects lots of different factors, including the number of people that are available for work and how much money consumers and businesses have available to spend on purchases and investments.

Exam tip

It may help you to think about an example of the term that you are defining. In this case, you could think about what makes up the UK economy.

Exam-style question

Define the term 'the economy'.   **(1 mark)**

The impact of the economic climate on businesses

The economic climate refers to the performance of the economy. When the economy is growing, the economic climate is positive. If the economy goes into recession or shrinks, the economic climate is negative.

The state of the economic climate can impact on businesses in six key ways, as shown in Figure 1.5.2. Businesses respond to these different impacts in different ways.

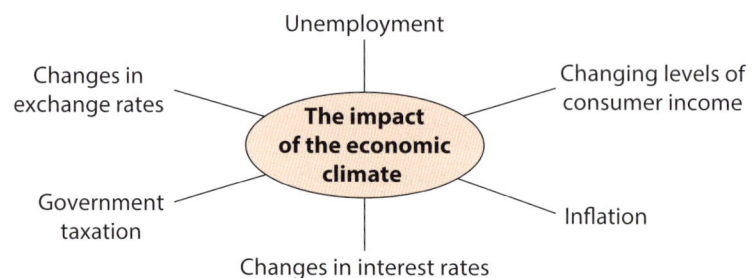

Figure 1.5.2 Aspects of the economic climate that have an impact on businesses

Unemployment

Figures measuring unemployment take into account the number of people of working age who are able to work but are not currently in work. This number is usually measured by the government by counting the number of people claiming the unemployment benefit, Jobseeker's Allowance. This is not necessarily the total number of people who are not working, but it is the measure used by the government to see if the number of people who are unemployed is going up or down.

According to the Office for National Statistics (ONS), the unemployment rate in June 2015 was 5.6 per cent. By May 2016, it had gone down to 4.9 per cent. This means that the number of people counted as unemployed had gone down, meaning that fewer people were available for work in May 2016. The highest levels of unemployment in the UK were in 1984, when unemployment was around 12 per cent. The lowest unemployment rate in the UK was counted in 1973, when it was only 3.4 per cent.

When unemployment is low and falling, this affects businesses because:

- there are fewer potential employees that they can hire

- they may need to put up their wages in order to attract potential employees to work for the business

- people's income is higher, so they have more money to spend on products and services because they are in work and receiving wages

- employees are happier because their jobs feel secure as the economy is doing well.

However, having low levels of unemployment does not always mean that a business will struggle to attract the right number of staff. Similarly, sometimes even when unemployment is high, a business may struggle to find candidates who are qualified or who have the skills to do the job. Due to **globalisation**, businesses may not be affected at all by the level of unemployment in the UK if their business uses staff overseas. This may also be true if they rely on technology such as robotics to do a lot of their manufacturing processes.

> ### Key term
>
> **Globalisation:** when businesses operate on an international scale and gain international influence or power.

Link it up

You will learn more about globalisation and its impact on business in the section 'Business and globalisation' in Topic 2.1 *Growing the business*.

Activity ?

Working in pairs, go to the website of the Office for National Statistics (www.ons.gov.uk). Look up the latest unemployment statistics. Is unemployment rising or falling? What impact could this have on businesses?

Theme 1: Investigating small business

Exam tip

Always read through all the answers carefully before choosing the ones that you think are correct, even if the answers look obvious at first glance.

Exam-style question

Which **two** of the following are advantages of low unemployment for a business? **(2 marks)**

Select **two** answers.

- ☐ **A** People having more money to spend
- ☐ **B** More skilled people being available
- ☐ **C** Fewer potential employees being available
- ☐ **D** Employees asking for higher wages
- ☐ **E** Employees feeling happier in their jobs

Changing levels of consumer income

Consumer income is the amount of money that people are paid. Consumer income is affected by the number of people who are in work, and the level of consumer income that is available for consumers to spend on products and services. Table 1.5.7 lists the effects of consumer income on the businesses that produce and sell these products and services.

Low levels of consumer income	High levels of consumer income
• Consumers are more restricted so they are more likely to buy lower-priced products or go to budget shops and supermarkets.	• Consumers have more money to spend and so they are more likely to buy higher-priced goods or luxuries.
• The number of products and services that are bought is also likely to go down, as people make do with the things that they already have.	• The number of products and services that are bought is likely to rise, as people are happier to replace existing possessions such as cars or computers.
• Consumer confidence is likely to be low, meaning that they are less likely to make a big purchase, such as a car, and will put it off until their income is higher.	• Consumer confidence is likely to be high, meaning that people are happy to make a big purchase immediately because they are not worried about their income and the security of their job.

Table 1.5.7 The effects of consumer income on businesses

Activity

Working in pairs, discuss the effect that you think falling levels of consumer income might have on the following businesses:

a a holiday park

b a corner shop

c a car showroom

d a chemist.

Inflation

Inflation is the increase of prices over time. Inflation can have a huge impact on the performance of businesses. For example, if inflation is high or going up, the cost of everyday items goes up. If wages do not rise at the same rate, the amount of money that people have left over to spend on products and services goes down. The rate of inflation changes every month and this is monitored by the **Bank of England**.

Most of the time, inflation is positive, meaning that the cost of living is going up. However, in 2015, inflation became negative, meaning that the cost of products and services went down. A decrease in the cost of everyday items is not necessarily good for businesses. Sometimes it can encourage consumers not to buy a product or service immediately but wait for the price go down again in the future. Prices going down also may mean that businesses do not feel as confident about the state of the economy and whether they will survive. This may lead them to reduce the amount that they invest in business activities or cut their costs, which can make prices go down again.

Low inflation can benefit a business because it means that the amount that it pays its suppliers should remain low. Low inflation also means that employees are less likely to ask for pay increases and that employers can give very small pay increases, as the cost of living is not increasing very much.

Table 1.5.8 shows the rates of inflation in the UK during 2015 and the first half of 2016.

2016	Jan	Feb	Mar	Apr	May	June						
Rate	0.2%	0.3%	0.5%	0.3%	0.3%	0.4%						
2015	Jan	Feb	Mar	Apr	May	June	Jul	Aug	Sep	Oct	Nov	Dec
Rate	0.3%	0%	0%	-0.2%	0.1%	0%	0.1%	0.1%	-0.1%	-0.1%	0.2%	0.2%

Table 1.5.8 UK inflation rates during 2015/16

Looking at Table 1.5.8, you can see that, in 2015, there was negative inflation in April, September and October, because the rate is preceded by a minus sign. However, in the first 6 months of 2016, inflation was low but remained positive.

Activity

When inflation is 0 per cent, a television costs £200. If inflation increases to 0.1 per cent, what will the price of the television be?

Key term

Bank of England: the central bank of the United Kingdom. It manages the country's debts, sets interest rates and influences the exchange rate between the pound and other currencies.

Did you know?

In the UK, the rate of inflation is worked out using the consumer price index (CPI) or retail price index (RPI). Do some research to find out how these measures work.

Maths tip

Inflation is worked out as a percentage (that is, out of 100). If the cost of an item goes up from £1.00 to £1.05, you would calculate the increase in inflation using the equation: $\frac{£0.05}{£1.00} = 5\%$.

Theme 1: Investigating small business

Exam tip

Explain just one advantage and link together the different parts of your explanation to ensure that you focus on just one advantage.

Exam-style question

Explain **one** advantage to a business of having low inflation. **(3 marks)**

Changes in interest rates

Interest is the amount of money that a bank charges for borrowing money. A bank will also pay interest to someone who keeps their money in that bank. The interest rate is the percentage rate used to work out the amount of interest that must be paid.

The Bank of England not only monitors inflation, but it also sets interest rates. The rate set by the Bank of England is known as the 'base rate'. This rate of interest is then used by all other banks operating in the UK, although each bank will add an additional percentage to that figure in order to produce the final interest rate that it charges or offers businesses and customers.

The impact of interest rates on businesses and individuals depends on whether they have savings or whether they are borrowing money.

Interest rate	Impact on savers	Impact on borrowers
High	Savers are paid more money for keeping their money in the bank, meaning that they have more to spend.	Borrowers have to pay more money to borrow from a bank, meaning that they have less to spend.
Low	Savers are paid small amounts of money for keeping their money in the bank, meaning that they have less to spend.	Borrowers have to pay a smaller amount of money to borrow from a bank, meaning that they have more left over to spend.

Table 1.5.9 The impact of high and low interest rates on savers and borrowers

Interest rates influence businesses in two ways.

- **They influence the way in which consumers behave.** Low interest rates generally mean that consumer income levels are higher because the amount of money that it costs to borrow money is lower. However, this is only useful if the business sells to customers who buy a lot more products or services when their income levels are higher. If a business sells to groups of consumers that rely on their savings to pay for goods and services, such as pensioners, low interest rates may not be so good for them.

- **They affect the way in which businesses spend their money or borrow.** When interest rates are low, businesses are more likely to be able to borrow money to expand or invest in their business at a cheaper rate. However, if sales are also low, the business may not be confident enough to do this. Low interest rates may mean other costs, such as wages or supplier costs, are also low. However, if interest rates are high, this means that costs are likely to go up and staff will start to ask for higher wages.

Activity ?

Working individually, find out the latest base interest rate set by the Bank of England. Find out what the rate was 6 months ago. Has the base rate gone up or down? How do you think this might affect businesses in your local area?

Now, in small groups, discuss and compare your findings.

Link it up

You will learn more about the effect of the economy on the way in which businesses trade overseas in Topic 2.1 *Growing the business.*

Checkpoint

Now it is time to review your understanding of the economy and business so far.

Strengthen

S1 Describe one way in which businesses are affected when unemployment levels are low.

S2 What are the benefits to a business selling luxury cars of having high levels of consumer income? Explain why this is the case.

S3 Describe how an increase in inflation can have an impact on businesses.

Challenge

C1 Research the impact on a business of negative inflation.

C2 Discuss the statement: 'low interest rates are always good for businesses'. Do you agree or disagree? Justify your opinion.

Government taxation

Taxation is the collection or payment of **taxes**. Individuals and businesses pay taxes to the government to fund public services such as hospitals, schools and colleges, and the police. There are different types of tax in the UK, as shown in Table 1.5.10.

Key term

Tax: a proportion of an individual's income or a business's profits that must be paid to the government.

Government tax	Description
Income tax	Individuals pay income tax from their wages. The percentage of their wages that they pay as tax depends on how much they earn.
National Insurance	Individuals pay this insurance to cover their state pensions and other benefits. Employers also pay a National Insurance contribution on behalf of their employees. As with income tax, the amount depends on how much the employee earns.
Value added tax (VAT)	Individuals pay VAT when they buy goods and services, as VAT is added on to the price of those products and services. VAT is also paid by businesses when they buy from their suppliers.
Corporation tax	Businesses pay corporation tax on any profits that they make.
Council tax	Individuals pay council tax to pay for services that are provided in their local community.
Business rates	Businesses pay business rates to pay for services that are provided for them locally.
Excise duties	Individuals pay these extra taxes when they buy certain products, such as cigarettes or alcohol, because excise duties are added to the price of these products.
Other taxes	Several other taxes are paid by individuals and businesses, such as the carrier bag levy.

Table 1.5.10 The different types of tax collected by the UK government

The amount of tax that needs to be collected in order to pay for public services affects the level of taxation charged on individuals' wages, businesses' profits and the cost of products and services. It also affects the amount of money that consumers have left over to spend. If taxation is high, meaning that people and businesses have to pay a lot of tax, consumers will not have much money left over and they will have less to spend. If taxation is low, meaning that people and businesses pay less tax, consumers will have more money and might be more likely to spend it on products and services.

Activity ?

1 Find out the amount that businesses must pay for their business rates in your area. You could do this through online research or by talking to local businesses. Was the amount higher or lower than you thought it would be? What services are provided for businesses in your area?

2 The standard rate of VAT on goods and services is 20 per cent. If a product costs £250 before VAT is added, how much will the customer pay once VAT is added?

3 Using the internet, look up the other two rates of VAT that customers could pay on different types of goods or services. How would these rates affect the selling price of the product in question 2?

Maths tip

VAT is worked out as a percentage of the selling price. If the rate of VAT is 20 per cent, this means that 20 per cent of the product's price has to be added to the price. If a product is priced at £100 + VAT, the customer will pay £100 + VAT= £120. You work out the VAT by multiplying the selling price before VAT by the rate of VAT: in this case 20 per cent or 0.2.

For example: £350 × 0.2 = 70. This means that the price including VAT will be £350 + £70 = £420.

Exam tip

Give one clear sentence explaining that the term means.

Exam-style question

Define the term 'government taxation'. **(1 mark)**

Key terms

Imports: the flow of goods and services into a country from another country.

Exports: the flow of goods and services out of a country to another country.

Changes in exchange rates

An exchange rate is the measure of the value of one currency in another currency. For example, the exchange rate between the pound (£) and the US dollar ($) might be £1 to US $1.30. This means that £1 in the UK is equivalent to US $1.30 in the USA. The value of the pound against other currencies has a big impact on many businesses, especially those that buy their supplies from overseas that **import** goods or services and **export** goods or services.

Due to globalisation and advances in technology, most businesses trade in more than one country. Because different countries use different currencies, businesses need to exchange their currency into another. Think back to the case study about PayPal on page 123. PayPal operates in more than 200 countries, meaning that it has to deal with a large number of different currencies.

Large businesses will have bank accounts in many of the countries in which they operate, meaning that local customers can buy in their own currency. However, many small and medium-sized businesses do not have enough business in other countries to make this possible. This means that, in order to trade overseas, they need to go to a bank to change money using the exchange rate on that day. This means that changes in the exchange rates can have a big impact on a business's sales and profits.

Imagine that you run a business importing T-shirts from the USA. The standard cost of the T-shirt that you purchase in the USA is US $5, and you sell each T-shirt in the UK for £10. Any changes in the exchange rate will have an impact on the profits of your business, as shown in Table 1.5.11.

Exchange rate	Cost of importing	Gross profit per T-shirt
£1 is worth US $1.30 Weak £ – the value of the pound is low in comparison with the dollar.	Each T-shirt costs £3.85 to buy in the USA.	£10.00 – £3.85 = £6.15 **gross profit**.
£1 is worth US $2.50 Strong £ – the value of the pound is high in comparison with the dollar.	Each T-shirt costs £2.00 to buy in the USA.	£10.00 – £2.00 = £8.00 gross profit.

Table 1.5.11 The impact of changes in the exchange rate on a business that imports

Key term

Gross profit: the amount of profit that a business makes before the business's costs are deducted.

Link it up

You learned about profits in the section 'Business revenues, costs and profits' in Topic 1.3 *Putting a business idea into practice*.

Table 1.5.11 shows that your business's profits are reduced just because the value of the pound is low in comparison with the dollar, which is not something that the business can control.

The impact of the change in currency works in reverse if your business is exporting T-shirts to the USA, as shown in Table 1.5.12. Your T-shirts cost £5 to manufacture in the UK, and you sell each T-shirt in the USA for US $15.

Theme 1: Investigating small business

Exchange rate	Cost of exporting	Gross profit per T-shirt
£1 is worth US $1.30 Weak £ – the value of the pound is low in comparison with the dollar.	Each T-shirt costs US $6.50 to manufacture in the UK.	US $15.00 – US $6.50 = US $8.50. US $8.50 = £6.50 gross profit.
£1 is worth US $2.50 Strong £ – the value of the pound is high in comparison with the dollar.	Each T-shirt costs US $12.50 to manufacture in the UK.	US $15.00 – US $12.50 = US $2.50. US $2.50 = £1 gross profit.

Table 1.5.12 The impact of changes in the exchange rate on a business that exports

These examples show you that:
- when the value of the pound is low/weak – imports are more expensive
- when the value of the pound is high/strong – imports are cheaper
- when the value of the pound is low/weak – exports are cheaper
- when the value of the pound is high/strong – exports are more expensive.

Activity ?

A business exports computer games to Europe. Each game costs £3.00 to produce. Working in pairs, discuss what would happen if the value of the euro changed from £1.00 = 1.50 euros to £1.00 = 1.25 euros. What would be the impact on the business?

Maths tip

Working out the currencies means dividing or multiplying one by the other. If you have £5.00 and you want to work out how much it is worth in dollars when the rate is £1.00 = US $1.50, multiply £5.00 by US $1.50 to get the amount in dollars (in this case US $7.50). To convert dollars to pounds, you do this in reverse.

The value of one currency against another has a huge impact on a business when it trades overseas

As you have seen, if a business trades overseas, then a change in exchange rate can be an advantage or disadvantage depending on whether the business is exporting or importing. If changes in exchange rates benefit a business, it is likely to make more money and therefore more profit. It may even be able to reduce its prices in order to attract more customers while still making plenty of profit. However, if changes in exchange rates have a negative effect on a business, it is likely to have to put up its prices or cut its costs. Higher prices may mean that fewer customers buy the business's products and services, and so the business may see its sales fall.

Activity ?

Find out the latest exchange rate information for the following currencies against the pound:

a the US dollar ($)

b the euro (€)

c the Swiss franc (Fr)

d the Chinese yuan (¥).

Look at the trends of those currencies. Is the pound getting stronger or weaker against them? What does this mean for businesses exporting from the UK to countries that use those currencies?

A country's rate of interest can also have an impact on exchange rates. If the rate of interest in the UK is high, investors from overseas may wish to put their money into the UK to get paid that high rate of interest on their money. If the demand to put money into the UK goes up, the value of the pound will also go up. The same is true if the UK becomes less attractive for investors from overseas. If fewer people want to put their money into the UK, the value of the pound is likely to go down.

Checkpoint

Now it is time to review your understanding of taxation and exchange rates.

Strengthen

S1 Describe one way in which the UK government taxes businesses.

S2 What are the disadvantages to a business exporting goods overseas of having a strong pound?

S3 Describe how the value of the pound becoming lower or weaker may benefit a business.

Challenge

C1 Consider the impact of government taxation on consumer income. What are the potential consequences of raising or lowering taxes?

C2 Consider the statement: 'a strong pound is best for business'. Do you agree or disagree? Justify your opinion.

External influences

Case study

E.E. Green & Son

E.E. Green & Son is a family business serving the construction industry. The business used to have a strong focus on its skip hire services. However, in response to changes in legislation relating to recycling and reusing materials, E.E. Green & Son diversified its business by offering more recycling services. As a result, the business now recycles all sorts of different materials.

Activity

Choose a business in your local area. List the ways in which you think that business might have been affected by technology, legislation or the economic climate. Compare your answers with a partner.

External influences on businesses can have a huge impact on business operations. Different businesses respond to the external influences of technology, legislation and the economic climate in different ways. The way in which businesses respond to external influences can lead to their survival, growth, decline or failure.

Responding to changes in technology

If a business does not adapt to changes in technology, it may lose its reputation. In turn, this could lead to lower sales and a continuing decline in reputation. There is also the risk that its competitors will adapt to the changes and either become more efficient or attract the business's customers. If the change in technology means that the technology used or sold by the business becomes **obsolete**, then it may lead to the business failing completely. For example, Blockbuster was a business that rented out films on video tapes and DVDs. However, due to the rise of internet-based subscription services such as Netflix, Blockbuster closed down in 2013.

Key term

Obsolete: out of date or not used anymore.

Can you think of other examples of businesses that have been affected by rapidly changing technology?

Link it up

You learned about Blockbuster and the impact of technology becoming obsolete in the section 'The dynamic nature of business' in Topic 1.1 *Enterprise and entrepreneurship*.

Responding to changes in legislation

If a business ignores changes in legislation, there is a risk that it will be penalised through being fined, having its staff members or owners imprisoned or even being closed down. While complying with new legislation may cost a business money, choosing to ignore the change in legislation could damage people, equipment, the environment or the reputation of the business.

Responding to changes in the economic climate

If a business does not embrace changes in the economic climate, there is a risk that it will experience negative consequences. These include the following examples.

- If consumer incomes go down, a business may lower its prices to ensure that sales remain high or it may look for customers in other places, such as in overseas markets. If it does not do this, it may fail to make enough sales, experience a cash flow problem and collapse.

- If interest rates go up, a business may have to decide to slow down any plans to expand its activities in order to avoid borrowing money. If it goes ahead with its plans by borrowing money, the cost of borrowing will be greater than expected and this may have a negative consequence on the business's finances.

- If taxation falls, a business may respond by hiring more people as it can afford to pay more staff. This may make the business more effective, increase its sales and put it ahead of any competitors who have not responded to the change in the economic climate.

Checkpoint

Now it is time to review your understanding of how businesses respond to external influences.

Strengthen

S1 Describe one way in which an export business could respond to the pound getting weaker.

S2 How might a construction business respond to changing health and safety legislation? What additional costs do you think it might incur?

S3 List the potential consequences to a business of failing to keep up with changes in employment law.

Challenge

C1 Discuss the following statement: 'it is always best for a business to use the latest technology'. Do you agree or disagree? Justify your opinion.

C2 Choose a business in your local area. Analyse the impact of increased interest rates on your chosen business and propose two possible ways in which the business could respond to the change.

1.5 Understanding external influences

1 Which **two** of the following are most likely to be the objectives of employees? (2 marks)

Select **two** answers.

- ☐ A Secure jobs
- ☐ B Increasing pay and conditions
- ☐ C Lower prices
- ☐ D Higher levels of taxation
- ☐ E Longer working hours

2 (a) Explain **one** benefit to a business of using social media to communicate with customers. (3 marks)

Student answer

The benefit to the business of using social media is that it is very fast and cheap and young people are using it. Social media is very fast to communicate so it means that customers get the latest information about the business.

Verdict

This answer gives three benefits, two of which are unnecessary. It then goes on to explain that the benefit of using social media is the speed of communication. However, the student could have provided more detail about this benefit in order to improve their answer.

(b) Explain **one** disadvantage to a business of not keeping up to date with health and safety legislation.

(3 marks)

Student answer

Health and safety legislation means the law at work relating to health and safety. If a business does not keep up to date one disadvantage could be that they break the law. If a business breaks the law by not operating safely, this could lead to someone being hurt and then the business getting a fine or even the owners or managers going to prison. The publicity from someone getting hurt could lead to a bad reputation for the business and sales going down.

Verdict

This is a very good answer. It identifies that not keeping up to date could lead to the business not operating safely, and then goes on to describe the potential consequences of this, including damage to the reputation and sales of the business.

Read the following extract carefully, then answer Questions 4, 5 and 6.

Seajacks is a company that maintains structures in the sea such as wind turbines, and oil and gas platforms. Seajacks operates five 'jack-up' vessels that it uses to maintain and construct offshore structures for its clients. Seajacks operates in the Netherlands and Denmark as well as the UK, but it has its head office in Great Yarmouth, Norfolk. The business has expanded significantly since 2006. Seajacks is a key employer in Great Yarmouth and has a policy of recruiting as many of its staff from the local area as possible. Seajacks also invests a lot of money in the local community, sponsoring local events and investing in community facilities. Health and safety is very important to Seajacks – its vessels comply with strict legislation and guidelines.

4   Define the term 'stakeholder'.   (1 mark)

Student answer

Stakeholders are anyone that is affected by a business.

Verdict

This is a good answer as it gives a clear, well-worded definition.

5   Outline **one** advantage for Seajacks of investing in its local community.   (2 marks)

Student answer

By investing in the local community, Seajacks are working with one of their local stakeholders to make sure that their needs are met. Investing in the local community means that their reputation is likely to be good as local people are happy and if they need to expand further that there are likely to be less objections.

Verdict

This is a very good answer. It gives a clearly stated advantage (good reputation) and then builds on the information given in the case study about the business's expansion to explain how it may help the business to expand more easily in the future.

Seajacks is considering two options to grow the business at a time when the pound is weak and interest rates are low.

Option 1: Investing in a new vessel by borrowing money from the bank and offering more services to its existing clients

Option 2: Offering its services further afield to countries such as China

6   Justify which one of these two options Seajacks should choose.   (9 marks)

Student answer

Seajacks should choose to invest in a new vessel by borrowing money from the bank. This is because interest rates are low which means the amount that Seajacks would have to pay to borrow the money would be low. By increasing the business they have with existing clients or countries, the risk is low. The pound is also weak which means it would be better to increase the business offered in the UK and export overseas as exports are cheaper when the pound is weaker. Seajacks do not have experience of working with China so this is higher risk and the law in China will be different than European law which Seajacks know well.

Verdict

This answer is okay but could be improved. The student has shown that they understand the impact of low interest rates and a weak pound on the way in which Seajacks operates. They have given a judgement about which option they would choose and have highlighted and explained the risks of both options. The student could have improved this answer by increasing the level of detail and expanding their justification to give a more in-depth conclusion.

Topic 2.1 Growing the business

Topic overview

This topic considers a range of factors that a business needs to look at when it is growing. This includes methods of achieving growth, as well as how and why a business changes its aims and objectives as it grows. It also explores the impact of globalisation, and the ethical and environmental factors that a business must consider.

Case study

Co-op

The Co-op is a large retail business with food stores across the UK. The Co-op food website www.co-operativefood.co.uk states: "Local convenience, great value food and ethical trading are what Co-op Food is all about."

In 2016, the Co-op opened approximately 100 new stores. In 2017, it will open another 100 stores, costing £70m. It will focus on opening new stores in London and the south east of England. The business has ambitious plans to continue to grow.

The Co-op is owned by members. The members include customers and employees who own the business.

Activity ?

1 What are the likely advantages to the Co-op of growing as a business?
2 How might the Co-op fund its ambitious expansion plans?
3 To what extent do you think the Co-op behaves in a way that benefits stakeholders such as its workers, local communities and customers?

Your learning

In this topic you will learn about:
- business growth – methods of business growth and their impact, the types of business ownership for growing businesses and sources of finance for growing and established businesses
- changes in business aims and objectives – why and how business aims and objectives change as businesses evolve
- business and globalisation – the impact of globalisation on businesses, barriers to international trade and how businesses compete internationally
- ethics, the environment and business – the impact of ethical and environmental considerations on businesses.

Theme 2: Building the business

Business growth

Case study

Merging firms

Two firms of chartered accountants in York joined forces by merging. Both businesses were keen to grow and saw the merger as an opportunity to build on their existing customer bases. Working together allows the two firms to offer a wider range of products, while continuing to serve small and medium-sized businesses in the area.

Activity ?

In groups, discuss why joining together two businesses might be a good way of achieving a growth objective.

Methods of business growth and their impact

Business growth is when a business increases the scale of its operations. This can be achieved through internal growth or external growth.

Internal growth

Internal growth occurs when a business expands by itself, by bringing out new products or by entering new markets. It is also known as organic growth. Two common methods of internal growth are:

- introducing new products
- entering new markets.

A business can expand by bringing out new products. **Research and development** is the process by which a business researches new products and starts to produce them. Such **innovation** can be relatively high risk as research and development takes time, can be expensive and does not always succeed. Innovation should also be informed by market research, to ensure that customers want a particular product before researching and developing it, and to make sure that the finished product will meet their needs.

Alternatively, a business can expand by entering new markets, which means selling existing products to a new group of people. This could be achieved by changing elements of the product's marketing mix, such as an extension strategy on an existing product (for example, bringing out a new variety of an existing chocolate bar) or changing the promotion strategy in order to attract new customers.

Businesses can also reach new markets by taking advantage of technological developments. For example, increased use of the internet has led to businesses using **e-commerce** platforms. This makes it easier for businesses to reach new markets, not only in their own country but abroad. A business could expand into a new overseas market by setting up high street stores in that country, which could be complex and expensive, but e-commerce may be an easier alternative. Like new products, new markets are usually seen as high risk: the business may not understand the wants and needs of its new customers, and so it may not succeed in that market.

Internal growth can be achieved by regularly bringing out new products. Can you think of examples of businesses that demonstrate this?

External growth

External growth occurs when a business expands by joining with another business. It is also known as inorganic growth. Two common methods of external growth are:

- **mergers**
- **takeovers**.

A merger is when two or more businesses agree to join together and operate as a combined business. In this instance, a new business is normally formed to represent the merged businesses. Well-known examples include the international accountancy firm PricewaterhouseCoopers and the food manufacturer Tate & Lyle. PricewaterhouseCoopers was originally two separate companies, Price Waterhouse and Coopers & Lybrand, while Tate & Lyle dates back to a 1921 merger between sugar refineries Henry Tate & Sons and Abram Lyle & Sons.

In comparison, a takeover occurs when one business takes complete control of another business. Following a takeover, one of the businesses will no longer exist. This happened, for example, when the supermarket chain Morrisons bought Safeway in 2004, rebranding most stores as Morrisons and selling the rest off, so that the Safeway name disappeared from UK high streets. US telecoms company AT&T is currently in the late stages of a multi-billion dollar takeover of the entertainment company Time Warner, which owns *Game of Thrones* and the news channel CNN.

> **Key terms**
>
> **Merger:** when two or more businesses join together to operate as one business.
>
> **Takeover:** when one business buys another business and incorporates it into their own business.

Theme 2: Building the business

Exam-style question

Which **two** of the following are examples of organic growth? **(2 marks)**
Select **two** answers:

☐ **A** A merger   ☐ **B** Developing new products

☐ **C** Entering new markets   ☐ **D** A takeover

☐ **E** External growth

The types of business ownership for growing businesses

A business's ownership type can have an impact on its ability to raise finance in order to fund its growth. As you have seen, one example of this is the fact that only **public limited companies (PLCs)** can raise share capital. This is an advantage, but it does mean that their shareholders become part-owners of the business. The shareholders have a voting right which is proportional to the number of shares they own. This means that PLCs are at risk of hostile takeovers: if anyone gains control of 51 per cent of the shares in the business, they effectively have control of the business.

Advantages of being a PLC	Disadvantages of being a PLC
Ability to raise additional finance.	More complex accounting and reporting procedures.
Limited liability.	Risk of hostile takeovers.
Seen as more prestigious and potentially more reliable.	Increased media attention.
May be able to negotiate better prices with suppliers.	Less privacy in relation to financial performance.

Table 2.1.1 The advantages and disadvantages of being a PLC

As a business grows, it may also start to expand into new countries, by either selling or producing its products or the raw materials for its products abroad. This would make it a **multinational** business. Examples of multinationals include a retailer having sales outlets in several countries, like The Body Shop and Zara, or a manufacturer having production plants in different countries, such as Toyota and Coca-Cola, or a combination of both of these.

Advantages of being a multinational	Disadvantages of being a multinational
Wider target market.	Loss of focus on key markets.
Ability to take advantage of cheaper labour and utilities abroad.	Cultural and language differences between different countries.
Can spread risk between operations in different countries.	Uncertainty regarding profits based on exchange rates that change on a regular basis.
Reputation as a market leader.	Potential damage to reputation if found to be operating unethically.

Table 2.1.2 The advantages and disadvantages of being a multinational

Key terms

Public limited company: an incorporated business that can sell shares to the public (also known as a PLC).

Multinational: a business with operations in more than one country (also known as a multinational corporation or MNC).

1 In pairs, draw a spider diagram containing at least 10 big businesses.
2 Research each of the businesses that you have named to find out whether it is:
   a a PLC
   b a multinational.
3 Can you think of a big business that is neither a PLC nor a multinational?

Link it up

You will learn more about ethics in business in the section 'Ethics, the environment and business' later in this topic. You will also look at the impact of operating globally in the section 'Business and globalisation'.

Exam-style question

Explain **one** advantage to a business of being a public limited company.
(3 marks)

Exam tip

State one advantage and explain why it is an advantage, remembering to show that you understand why it can boost a business's performance.

Sources of finance for growing and established businesses

As a business grows, it needs to invest money in its activities, such as developing new products or buying other businesses. There are two main sources of finance: internal sources and external sources.

Case study

Time Out

Time Out is a website and magazine brand that lists places to go and things to do in major cities around the world. There are 30 different editions of its magazines, including *Time Out London* and *Time Out Beijing*.

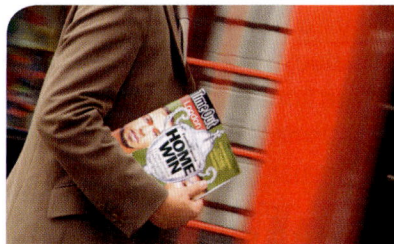

In 2016, Time Out Group raised £90 million for marketing and web development by selling shares to external investors. Time Out's founder, Tony Elliott, still owns 10 per cent of the business.

Activity ?

In pairs, discuss the potential disadvantages of raising finance from external investors.

Internal sources of finance

Internal sources of finance are found within the business and can include:
• retained profit
• selling **assets**.

Profit is the amount of revenue left after costs have been deducted. This can be used to either pay dividends to shareholders or kept in the business to fund future business activities. The advantage of this is that there is no need to repay the finance and there are no **interest** charges. However, the amount available may be limited and investors, for example shareholders, may be frustrated by the lack of dividends.

Selling assets is the process by which a business sells items that it owns in order to raise finance.

Key terms

Assets: items owned by a business, such as premises, equipment or stock.

Interest: the cost of borrowing, or a percentage of the amount of money borrowed that must be repaid in addition to the original amount borrowed.

Theme 2: Building the business

This provides the business with an immediate lump sum of money, but the business loses the use of the asset itself. This may not be a disadvantage if the assets are no longer needed, but selling assets can be expensive if the business later needs to lease or buy back the assets.

External sources of finance

External sources of finance are found outside the business, such as:

- loan capital
- share capital.

Loan capital is finance borrowed from a financial institution such as a bank. The money has to be repaid over a specified period of time and with interest. Loan capital is often acquired for a specific purpose, such as in order to buy an asset, in which case it can be **secured** against that asset. This reduces the risk being taken by the lender, which makes it more likely to lend the business money. For example, if a printing firm wanted to buy a new four-colour printing press, it could secure the printing press against the loan. If the printing firm then stopped repaying the loan, the lender can take possession of the press and sell it to regain its losses.

Share capital is finance raised by selling a percentage of the business to external investors. Investors buy part of the business as shares in return for a share of the business's profits, in the form of **dividends** and increases in the value of their shares. Only limited companies can raise share capital. A private limited company can only sell shares to family and friends. However, as a business grows, it may undertake a **stock market flotation**. This means that the business's form of ownership changes from a private limited company to a public limited company, and this allows it to sell shares to the public through a **stock exchange**.

Link it up

In Topic 1.4 *Making the business effective*, you looked at types of legal structure including private limited companies.

Exam tip

Show that you understand the key term in the question by defining what is meant by 'bank loans'.

Exam-style question

Explain **one** disadvantage to a business of using bank loans as a source of finance. **(3 marks)**

Maths tip

- In the UK, share prices are given in pence, so a share price of 780 means that each share is worth £7.80. Divide the share price by 100 to get its price in pence.
- Remember to check your calculations.

Checkpoint

Now it is time to review your understanding of business growth.

Strengthen

S1 Using examples, describe the difference between internal and external methods of growth.

S2 Using examples, describe the difference between internal and external sources of finance.

S3 Describe why the type of business ownership used may change as a business grows.

Challenge

C1 Choose a large business. Do some research into the business's history and draw a timeline to show how it has grown. Annotate key moments in its growth using business terminology.

C2 Choose two businesses on the Financial Times Stock Exchange (FTSE) 100 and look at their current share prices. Calculate how many shares you would own if you invested £1,000 in each business today. After a week, check the share price again. Has the value of your 'investment' gone up or down?

Changes in business aims and objectives

Case study

Bill's

Bill's is a national chain of restaurants. Bill Collison started with a small greengrocer's shop in Lewes, East Sussex. After the shop was flooded in 2000, he reopened it and included a cafe, which proved to be very popular. By 2016, there were 74 Bill's restaurants in the UK, including 20 in London. The basic values of Bill's restaurants are the same as the values of his original cafe: to provide good food and good service to every customer.

Activity ?

In groups, discuss how you think the business aims and objectives of Bill's might have changed as the business evolved.

Businesses change as they grow and become established. It may be that their original aims and objectives are no longer appropriate, either because the company is much larger than it was or because the external environment in which it operates has changed.

Why business aims and objectives change as businesses evolve

As businesses evolve, their aims and objectives will change in response to:

- market conditions
- technology
- performance
- legislation
- internal reasons.

Link it up

In the section 'Business aims and objectives' in Topic 1.3, *Putting a business idea into practice*, you studied the types of objectives that businesses would set when starting up, including both financial and non-financial objectives.

Theme 2: Building the business

Market conditions

Market conditions include the size of the market and the **degree of competition**. In particular, the environment will change as other businesses enter and leave the market, and this may affect a business's objectives. For example, a business may have an objective of growth, but if new competitors enter the market it may need to change this objective in order to focus on survival instead. Alternatively, if a business has an objective of increasing its **market share**, the arrival of new competitors may mean that it needs to review this objective.

Technology

Technology is constantly changing, which means that it offers opportunities and poses threats to a business. For example, if a business spots an opportunity to use new technology to introduce an innovative product into the market, it would probably change its objectives to focus on product development. Alternatively, a business may set an objective to enter new markets using e-commerce, or an objective to minimise its costs by using new technologies in its production process.

Performance

A business may review and amend its aims and objectives in light of its performance. This could be financial performance, using benchmarks such as profits and cash flow, or non-financial performance, using benchmarks such as market share or the productivity of its workforce. For example, if the business is performing poorly, such as receiving poor ratings on review websites like TripAdvisor or Trustpilot, it might set a short-term aim to fix this problem.

Legislation

A business's aims and objectives are also influenced by legislation – the laws that determine how a business operates. Specific laws influence a range of business activities, such as how businesses promote their products or treat their employees. Existing legislation that affects businesses includes the Health and Safety at Work Act (1974) and the Equality Act (2010). The government can also introduce new laws that affect business behaviours, and a business will have to abide by these laws. These may also affect other objectives. For example, the introduction of the National Living Wage may affect an objective of profit maximisation or growth.

Activity ?

Working in pairs, select one large organisation, such as Kellogg's or Marks & Spencer. Research how they are affected by two different pieces of legislation in the UK.

Internal reasons

Changes within a business can also affect its aims and objectives. For example, a new chief executive may have different priorities for the business's profit or environment, or they may set more ambitious objectives. Other internal reasons could include the **culture** of the organisation and the attitudes of workers.

156

Exam-style question

Discuss the factors that influence why a business changes its aims and objectives as it evolves. **(6 marks)**

Exam tip

Choose two influencing factors to discuss – there is no need to cover every factor.

How business aims and objectives change as businesses evolve

The market conditions and the performance of a business affect whether a business focuses on survival or growth as it evolves. During times of increased competition or poor economic conditions, a business may focus on survival. It may do this through initiatives to cut costs, such as looking for cheaper suppliers or reducing the size of the workforce. This is a short-term objective, ensuring that the business continues to trade. When a business is performing well, it is likely to focus on growth, such as by opening new stores or bringing out new products. At first, a new business is likely to focus on short-term survival, but over time it will change this to focus on profit and then on growth.

As a business evolves, it will enter new markets in order to grow, and it will exit existing markets (also known as **retrenchment**). A business will set an objective to enter new markets if it wants to grow. It can do this by targeting new markets within the country where it operates, such as a women's clothing retailer bringing out a range of men's clothes. It can also do this by entering new markets abroad. These strategies may be high-risk due to the potential for failure, but they may be necessary if the business wants to achieve objectives such as growth, establishing itself as the market leader or maximising its profits. Alternatively, a business may reduce the size of its operations. This may involve closing down less profitable stores or withdrawing from a market in order to focus investment elsewhere. These actions could be taken to achieve an objective of cost minimisation. They may even be necessary for survival during poor economic conditions.

Key term

Retrenchment: when a business downsizes the scale of its operations by reducing the number of employees or closing less profitable branches.

Case study

Tyrrells English crisps

In 2002, farmer William Chase decided that it would be easier to make a profit by manufacturing crisps than by selling potatoes to supermarkets. He established Tyrrells Potato Crisps Ltd, which makes high-quality crisps and savoury snacks on a farm in Herefordshire. Tyrrells now sells in more than 30 countries, with reported sales in excess of £80 million in 2015. In 2016, the business was bought by American firm Amplify. Now listed on the US stock market, Tyrrells aims to become a global brand.

Activity

In pairs, discuss how Tyrrells' objectives are likely to have changed between 2002 and 2016.

Theme 2: Building the business

A change in the size of a business's operations is also likely to affect the size of its workforce. As it grows, it will recruit new employees and may change its **organisational structure**. This may affect objectives such as human resources targets, which would change from focusing on recruitment to focusing on retaining employees. Alternatively, a business may want to reduce the size of its workforce for a number of reasons, such as introducing new technologies or withdrawing from a market.

A business will also change aspects of its marketing mix as it grows, often by increasing or decreasing its product range. A business may therefore change its objective to becoming a market leader through increasing consumers' awareness of the brand and innovation. As a business grows, it is likely to introduce new and innovative products to its range. Having a broader **product portfolio** helps a business to spread the risk of loss of revenue. It also builds brand loyalty by encouraging customers to come back again for new or varied products. Increasing the range of products allows a business to use its promotional budgets more effectively as it can advertise its brand or product range rather than an individual product. A business may also remove products from its range if a product is no longer in demand, usually due to being replaced by a new product, changes in technology or consumer preferences. A business does not want to hold stock of products that are out of date and cannot be sold.

Business and globalisation

The impact of globalisation on businesses

In the modern world, many businesses operate across a number of countries. **Globalisation** is the process by which more and more businesses operate on an international scale: selling to, buying from and operating in multiple countries. This has led to the growth of multinationals, which often have a great deal of international influence.

Globalisation affects businesses in three key ways:
- **imports**
- **exports**
- business locations.

Imports

Imports are goods brought into a country from abroad, meaning that money moves out of the country. For example, if the UK imports cheese from France, money flows from the UK to France.

The arrival of imports in a country creates competition for **domestically** produced goods. This will have a negative impact on demand for domestically produced goods and therefore on the profits of domestic businesses. However, a business may import goods from abroad, either to sell on to domestic customers or to make its own products. This can allow the business to stock a wider range of products or buy the raw materials for its own products more cheaply than if it purchased them domestically. Both of these outcomes have a positive impact on the business and should lead to higher profits.

Exports

Exports are goods produced in a country that are then sold abroad, meaning that money flows into the country. For example, if the UK exports lamb to France, money flows from France to the UK. Being able to export goods abroad provides domestic businesses with a wider target market, as it gives them the opportunity to sell their goods and services around the world.

Did you know?

The BBC exports many of its television programmes around the world. *Top Gear* and *Doctor Who* are two of its most popular exports. The 50th anniversary special of *Doctor Who* was aired simultaneously in 94 countries, gaining it a Guinness World Record for the largest ever simultaneous broadcast of a television drama.

Link it up

In the 'Business location' section of Topic 1.4 *Making the business effective*, you looked at factors influencing location decisions, including proximity to markets and labour. These influences are also relevant to international location decisions.

Activity ?

In June 2016, the total value of imports to the UK was £40.2 billion, an increase of £4.1 billion on May 2016. The total value of exports from the UK was £24.9 billion, an increase of £1.7 billion on May 2016. This meant that the value of net imports (imports minus exports) in June 2016 was £15.3 billion.

What was the value of net imports in May 2016?

Maths tip

- Work through the problem logically: first, calculate the value of imports in May 2016, then the value of exports, then the value of net imports.
- Remember to check your calculations.
- Always express your answers in the correct format. Your answer to this question should be expressed in £ billions.

Business locations

Globalisation also affects where businesses choose to locate their offices or premises. The fact that international trade, communication and travel is so easy in the modern world allows businesses to locate abroad. This can include opening outlets abroad in order to enter new markets. For example, as countries such as China and Russia become increasingly wealthy, retailers may want to locate in these countries in order to enter the market and increase their sales. Businesses may also locate their manufacturing facilities abroad, usually to take advantage of cheaper labour and utility costs.

Exam tip

Identify and define the key term in the question: in this case, 'importing'.

Exam-style question

Discuss the likely benefits to a business of importing goods from abroad.

(6 marks)

Barriers to international trade

> ### Case study
>
> **Taxing imported goods**
> Politicians can have a huge impact on businesses. In 2016, there was a presidential election campaign in the United States of America. Donald Trump, who was elected President of the United States, stated that, if he was elected president, he would impose a 45 per cent tax on all goods imported from China.

International trade is the buying and selling of goods and services between countries. However, barriers can prevent businesses from engaging in international trade.

One barrier is a **tariff**, which is a tax imposed by a country on imported goods and services. A tariff makes a particular product or service more expensive, with the aim of reducing the demand for imported goods and switching demand to domestically produced goods. Tariffs are a **protectionist measure** put in place to protect a country's businesses and employment by reducing competition from abroad.

Tariffs can be imposed on imports from specific countries or on particular types of product

> ### Activity ?
>
> A car is manufactured in country A and is intended to sell in country B for US $25,000. However, when the car is exported to country B, a 20 per cent tariff is imposed on its price.
> What is the price of the car in country B?

Another barrier to international trade is a **trading bloc**. A trading bloc is created when the governments of different countries agree to act together to promote trade among themselves. These agreements give member nations of the trading bloc preferential treatment in other countries within the trading bloc, to encourage trade between the countries.

> ### Activity ?
>
> In pairs, discuss the reasons why a politician might choose to make imports more expensive.

> ### Key terms
>
> **Tariff:** a tax imposed on imports or exports.
> **Protectionist measure:** an action taken by a government to reduce the flow of imports into the country.
> **Trading bloc:** a group of countries that agree to act together to promote trade between themselves.

> ### Link it up
>
> In the section 'The economy and business' in Topic 1.5 *Understanding external influences on businesses*, you looked at the impact of the economic climate on businesses, including unemployment and consumer incomes. Barriers to international trade will affect the level of unemployment in a country.

> ### Maths tip
>
> - Remember to show your workings.
> - Always express your answers in the correct format. Your answer to this question should be expressed in dollars (US $).

For example, members of the European Union (EU) can trade freely with each other without additional taxes being charged on goods that are imported and exported between the member countries.

Examples of trading blocs include:

- the EU
- the Association of Southeast Asian Nations (ASEAN)
- the North American Free Trade Agreement (NAFTA).

Please note that the United Kingdom voted to leave the EU in 2016.

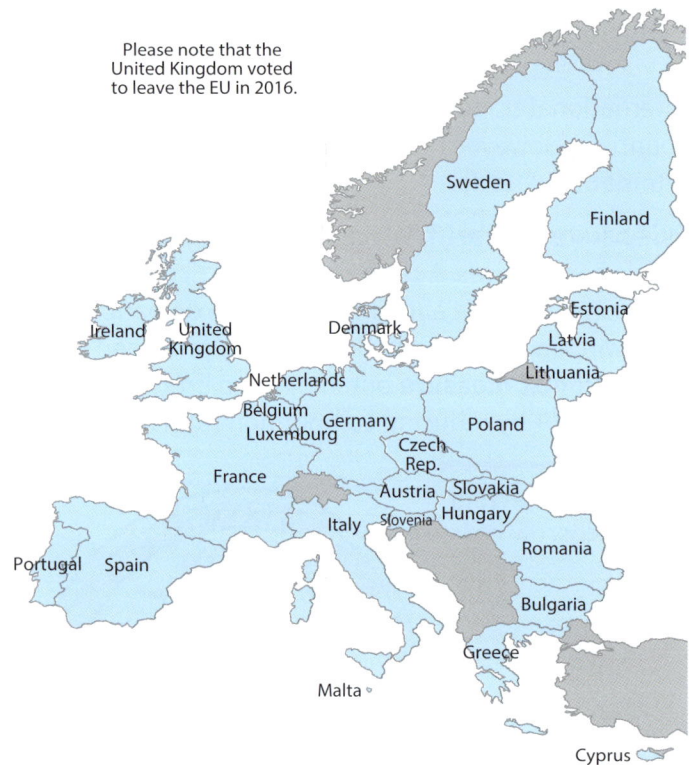

Figure 2.1.1 Why do you think these trading blocs are between countries that are geographically close to each other?

The countries within a trading bloc are normally located relatively close together, such as the nations of the EU. Countries within a trading bloc can benefit from sharing workers, knowledge and expertise. Different countries may specialise in producing particular goods or services, meaning that their production may be more efficient, which could lower the cost of these products in all member nations. Businesses may also be able to change location within the trading bloc to benefit from economic variations between member countries, such as lower tax rates or lower wages.

However, the creation of a trading bloc provides trade barriers for countries outside the trading bloc. These countries may increase their own barriers, reducing the ability of member countries to trade outside of the bloc. While trading blocs normally operate without the use of protectionist measures, they can use tariffs or other protectionist measures. For example, in 2016 the EU imposed tariffs on steel produced in China in order to protect steel-producing businesses within its member nations.

Exam style questions

Which **one** of the following is an example of a barrier to international trade? **(1 mark)**

Select **one** answer:

- ☐ **A** Import
- ☐ **B** Export
- ☐ **C** Tariff
- ☐ **D** Globalisation

Exam tip

Read through all of the answers and try to justify why you think each one is correct or incorrect. This will help you to eliminate answers.

How businesses compete internationally

Case study

Foodpanda

Foodpanda is an online service that allows customers to order their favourite takeaway food and have it delivered to their door. It operates in more than 500 cities across five continents. Foodpanda's success is partly due to the fact it **localises** its model to meet the needs of different countries. For example:

- in Moscow it delivers to customers using the underground rail system
- in Hong Kong it delivers by bicycle
- in other countries it delivers by moped or motorbike.

Activity

In groups, do some research to identify the steps that Foodpanda has taken to compete internationally.

Key term

Localise: adapt to suit the local area and its needs, particularly in terms of culture, language or geographical location.

International markets are very competitive. Increased globalisation has increased the ease with which businesses can enter new markets, which increases the level of competition.

Using the internet and e-commerce

Businesses compete internationally using the internet and e-commerce. The internet allows businesses to communicate with existing and potential customers around the world through social media and review websites. This form of promotion can give a business a competitive advantage by allowing them to build brand loyalty.

E-commerce is one key use of the internet that helps businesses to compete internationally. It allows business to trade 24 hours a day and 7 days a week across the world. Through the internet, businesses have access to a global marketplace in which they can buy and sell goods and services.

Theme 2: Building the business

Businesses can compete internationally by launching their own websites

Activity ?

In pairs, revisit the section 'Technology and business' in Topic 1.5 and the technologies that businesses use. Write two sentences about each use of technology, explaining how it could be used to help a business compete internationally.

Changing the marketing mix

Businesses may need to change elements of their marketing mix in order to compete internationally. The amount by which they need to change their marketing mix may vary, as it depends on the level of difference between the culture of the business's home country and the culture of the new market. For example, a business from the UK trading in Italy may have to make fewer changes to its marketing mix than a business from the UK trading in China.

There are many examples of how and why a business may change elements of the marketing mix. Some of these examples are shown in the table below.

Changes to the marketing mix	Reasons for changes to the marketing mix
Changes to price	• Different currencies. • Potential fluctuations in exchange rates. • Tariffs. • Different tax laws. • Different standards of living and average incomes of potential customers.
Changes to place	• Availability of technology, such as e-commerce, that can be used to reach global markets. • Cultural differences, such as whether people shop at market stalls, independent stores or supermarkets.
Changes to promotion	• Language differences, such as avoiding unintended meanings in translation. • Cultural differences, such as the connotations of particular animals, colours or gestures.
Changes to product	• Cultural or physical differences, such as average family size or average height and weight. • Technological differences, such as socket type or wattage. • Tastes and cultural preferences, such as religious dietary requirements or the level of sweetness or spiciness preferred in foods.

Table 2.1.3 Ways in which the marketing mix may be changed in order to compete internationally

Exam-style question

To coincide with the 2016 Olympic Games in Brazil, Starbucks launched a new range of summer beverages inspired by nations around the world. In Brazil, they sold a 'Brigadeiro Frappuccino' based on the country's favourite chocolate truffle; in Asia, shops sold a 'Fruit Jelly Yogurt Frappuccino'; in the USA and Canada, customers could buy a 'Vanilla Sweet Cream Cold Brew'.

Analyse the impact on Starbucks of opening new restaurants in foreign countries. **(6 marks)**

Exam tip

Identify how Starbucks has changed its marketing mix and explain how this will affect the performance of the business.

Checkpoint

Now it is time to review your understanding of business and globalisation.

Strengthen

S1 Write down a definition of each of the following words:
- import
- export
- globalisation
- tariff
- trading bloc.

S2 Draw a table that shows three advantages and three disadvantages of globalisation to UK firms.

Challenge

C1 Chose one business that you are familiar with that operates in the UK, such as a supermarket or a fast-food restaurant. How would you change its marketing mix in order to help it trade in another country, such as the USA or India?

C2 Produce an advert, in any format of your choice, promoting the UK as a location for foreign businesses. What factors would influence a business to locate in a different country?

Similar to Starbucks, McDonald's changed its marketing mix and launched a new product for Japan. The McFry Potato Chocolate Sauce. Can you think of other examples of products that have been designed specifically for a foreign market?

Ethics, the environment and business

Activity ?

In pairs, identify the advantages to Primark of inspecting all of the factories that it uses. Are there any disadvantages?

The impact of ethical and environmental considerations on businesses

How ethical considerations influence business activity

Ethics are the moral standards that guide people's actions. A business that behaves ethically will act in a way that is seen to be morally correct (doing the 'right thing'), including the way in which the business deals with its **stakeholders**.

Ethical behaviour includes:

- treating workers fairly – not discriminating against people, paying fair wages, providing safe working conditions and taking action against workplace bullying
- treating suppliers fairly – making payments on time and paying a fair price
- ethical sourcing of materials – not tested on animals, not produced by child labour, not damaging the environment
- caring for the community – not permitting antisocial behaviour and supporting local causes
- treating consumers fairly – giving clear and accurate information about products and services, and charging fair prices
- meeting government requirements – paying all required taxes and abiding by legislation.

Key terms

Ethics: moral principles or standards that guide the behaviour of a person or business.

Stakeholder: anyone who has an interest in the activities of a business, such as its workers, its suppliers and the government.

Link it up

In the section 'Legislation and business' in Topic 1.5 *Understanding external influences on business* you looked at how a truly ethical business will abide by the law, but it will also voluntarily choose to do what it considers to be 'right'.

Trade-offs between ethics and profit

Behaving ethically has advantages for a business. Consumers are sometimes willing to pay a higher price for a product that they know has been ethically sourced. For example, a business can charge higher prices for goods such as free-range eggs or cosmetics that have not been tested on animals.

A business that does not behave ethically is likely to attract negative media attention, which can damage its reputation and brand value. By behaving ethically, it can avoid such negative attention and can even attract positive media attention. Employees are also more likely to be happy if they work for an ethical business, which makes it easier to recruit and retain talented staff.

However, there can be a **trade-off** between ethics and profit. Sometimes, the actions taken to behave ethically can have a negative effect on the business's profit. If behaving ethically increases costs, this will reduce a product's **profit margin** if the product's price is kept the same. Increased costs could occur as a result of paying a fair rate to suppliers or improving working conditions for employees.

Key terms

Trade-off: a balance between two different or opposing objectives, such as making a profit and spending money on ethical activities that will enhance the business's reputation.

Profit margin: the proportion of revenue left over after costs have been deducted.

Activity ?

In a leading supermarket in the UK, a box of six barn eggs is £0.70. These eggs are laid by chickens that can wander freely around inside a barn. In the same supermarket, a box of six free-range eggs costs £1.00.

In a competing low-cost supermarket, a customer can buy a box of 15 eggs for £1.25. These eggs are laid by chickens that are battery farmed, which means that they are kept indoors in cages.

1 Calculate the unit cost of one egg for each of the three options: barn eggs, free-range eggs and battery-farmed eggs.

2 As a class, discuss the following questions.

   a What is the trade-off between competing on price and selling goods that are ethical?

   b Should supermarkets be free to choose what types of eggs they stock?

   c Which would you buy?

Maths tip

- Always express your answer in the correct format. Your answer to this question should be expressed in pence per egg.

- Always compare like-with-like for a fair comparison. This is why you calculate the cost per egg rather than comparing the cost per box, as the boxes are different sizes.

How environmental considerations influence business activity

Businesses can have a negative impact on the environment, and they must take this into account when making decisions. Environmental considerations to take into account when making business decisions can include:

- pollution to air and water, noise pollution and light pollution
- the use of non-renewable resources such as oil and coal
- long-term damage to the environment, such as global warming or damage to the ozone layer
- waste disposal, such as the safe disposal of toxic or dangerous waste
- reducing the use of unnecessary and excessive packaging
- carbon footprint, such as the carbon dioxide emissions caused by manufacturing or transporting goods.

Did you know?

In 2010, an oil rig operated by BP called Deepwater Horizon caused a huge oil spill in the Gulf of Mexico. In 2016, BP estimated that this environmental disaster cost the business US $61.6 billion.

Key term

Green audit: a detailed review of a business's impact on the environment, either conducted by the business itself or by an independent organisation.

Activity ?

1 In pairs, select one business with which you are familiar, such as your favourite retailer or a factory near your school. Draw a spider diagram to list the ways in which it has a negative impact on the environment.

2 For each negative impact listed on your spider diagram, identify steps that the business could take to reduce these impacts.

Behaving in an environmentally friendly way can give a business a competitive advantage and help build brand loyalty among customers. It will improve the business's reputation among key stakeholders, such as customers, suppliers and employees. It can also help a business to avoid negative media attention and expensive clean-up operations following environmental disasters.

Large businesses normally carry out a **green audit** to assess their impact on the environment. This allows them to set environmental targets and to measure their performance against these targets.

Case study

easyJet

The low-cost airline, easyJet, aims to reduce its negative impact on the environment. One of its SMART objectives is 'to reduce carbon emissions per passenger kilometre by 8 per cent by 2020', compared with carbon emissions data from 2013. It also aims to minimise environmental inconveniences, such as noise pollution, to reduce the impact on people living close to airports.

Trade-offs between the environment, sustainability and profit

There can be trade-offs between the environment, **sustainability** and profit. Businesses may need to increase costs in order to reduce their impact on the environment. For example, a business may place filters on factory chimneys and cooling towers in order to reduce pollution. This will reduce its negative impact on the environment, but will cost the business money and thereby reduce its profits.

Some businesses that use wood in their manufacturing processes have a policy of planting a tree for every tree that they cut down and use. Trees are a **finite resource**, so replacing them like this improves the business's sustainability. However, there is a long delay between planting a new tree and the new tree growing to full size in order to replace a tree that has already been cut down. The process is positive from an environmental point of view, but it could negatively affect a business's profits.

> ## Activity ?
> Discuss the advantages to easyJet of acting in an environmentally responsible way.

> ## Key terms
> **Sustainability:** acting to ensure that natural resources are used responsibly, to protect the environment for future generations.
>
> **Finite resource:** (also known as a non-renewable resource) a resource that does not renew itself quickly enough to meet society's consumption of that resource, such as oil and natural gas.

> ## Exam-style question
> Which **two** of the following are environmental considerations? **(2 marks)**
>
> Select **two** answers:
>
> ☐ **A** Pollution
> ☐ **B** Workforce
> ☐ **C** Fair payment to suppliers
> ☐ **D** Sustainability
> ☐ **E** Paying taxes

> ## Exam tip
> Read the instructions carefully so that you select the correct number of answers.

Potential impact of pressure group activity on the marketing mix

> ## Case study
> **#antibiotics**
> Fast-food chains such as McDonald's and KFC are being put under pressure to stop using meat from animals treated with antibiotics to improve their growth. There are concerns that this practice may be helping to make bacteria resistant to antibiotics. One group, ShareAction, encourages people to email the CEO of McDonald's to express their concerns. Protestors also use social media sites to raise the campaign's profile, using hashtags such as #antibiotics and #takeaction.

> ## Activity ?
> In pairs or small groups, discuss how far you think the public can influence decisions made by large businesses such as McDonald's and KFC.

Key terms

Pressure group: a group of people who join together to try to influence government policy or business policy for a particular cause.

Boycott: refusing to buy from or interact with a particular business or organisation.

Viral marketing: using online channels, such as video-sharing or social media sites, to spread a campaign message by encouraging people to share it with their friends.

Lobbying: trying to influence the government or other organisations.

A **pressure group** is a group of people who join together with the aim of influencing public opinion or the policies of governments or businesses for a particular cause. Pressure groups use strength of numbers to raise awareness of a campaign in order to force people, businesses or governments to take action. Examples of pressure groups include Greenpeace, the Fairtrade Foundation, World Wide Fund for Nature (WWF) and the Confederation of British Industry (CBI).

A pressure group may use a wide range of activities to attract media attention and put pressure on their target. These include:

- a **boycott** of a specific business, product or country
- social media campaigns
- **viral marketing**
- public protests
- online petitions
- media campaigns, such as speaking to television and radio news and newspapers
- **lobbying**.

Exam-style question

Explain **one** reason why a business may respond to a pressure group.

(3 marks)

Exam tip

Explain briefly your chosen reason why a business would respond to a pressure group.

Many of these actions are often high profile, attracting a lot of media attention, and this can help pressure groups to achieve their aim.

A pressure group may campaign for a business to change the way it operates, which means that pressure groups can affect the business's marketing mix. Examples of the impact of pressure groups on the marketing mix are shown in Table 2.1.4.

Link it up

In the section 'The marketing mix' in Topic 1.4 *Making the business effective*, you looked at the marketing mix in relation to a small business. You will look at the marketing mix in relation to bigger businesses in Topic 2.2 *Making marketing decisions*.

Element of the marketing mix	Impact of pressure groups on an element of the marketing mix
Product	• Change key ingredients to use ethically sourced raw materials. • Remove a product from the range because it is considered socially unacceptable.
Price	• Increase price as a result of paying a fair price to suppliers or improving conditions in which farm animals are kept. • Applying a government-imposed minimum price on goods that are deemed harmful to society.
Place	• Not opening stores in certain locations due to local campaigns to support small local businesses. • Sourcing local products or raw materials to reduce carbon footprint.
Promotion	• Including complete and honest information on packaging. • Obeying legislation banning the promotion of certain products, such as cigarettes. • Reviewing product placement in stores, such as supermarkets removing confectionery from child-height displays at checkouts.

Table 2.1.4 Ways in which pressure groups can influence a business's marketing mix

Checkpoint

Now it is time to review your understanding of ethics, the environment and business.

Strengthen

S1 Write a tweet for the campaign against fast-food restaurants' use of chickens treated with antibiotics.

S2 Describe how both ethical and environmental considerations can lead to trade-offs.

S3 Using an example, describe how pressure from a campaign group may influence a business's marketing mix.

Challenge

C1 Write down three reasons why a business should behave ethically and then prioritise them in terms of their importance.

C2 Write a letter to your local newspaper complaining about the negative impact of one local business on the environment. The business could be any size, from a newsagent's near your school generating litter to a big business causing road congestion from delivery lorries. What effect do you think this sort of complaint might have on the business?

2.1 Growing the business

1. Which **one** of the following is an advantage of being a public limited company? **(1 mark)**

   Select **one** answer:

   ☐ A Owned by the government
   ☐ B Able to raise additional capital
   ☐ C Is a multinational
   ☐ D Has unlimited liability

2. Explain **one** advantage to a business of using share capital to fund growth. **(3 marks)**

   ### Student answer

   One advantage is that it does not have to be paid back with interest. However, the shareholders do have a voting right in the business and will expect a share of the profits.

   ### Verdict

   The student identifies an advantage, but instead of explaining why this is an advantage they go on to give a disadvantage.

3. Explain **one** advantage to a business of behaving in an environmentally friendly way. **(3 marks)**

   ### Student answer

   One advantage is that it avoids bad publicity, giving the business a good reputation. This means that people will be more willing to use the business on a regular basis leading to a rise in brand loyalty.

   ### Verdict

   The student states one possible advantage and explains it with a short logical argument.

Read the following extract carefully, then answer Questions 4, 5 and 6.

Nestlé is a multinational corporation, selling products in more than 189 countries and operating factories in 85. It sells a wide range of products in various food and drink sectors, such as KitKat chocolate bars, Felix cat food and Nesquik drinks. The wide range of products is the result of internal and external growth. For example, in 2015, Nestlé took over an American pet food business, Merrick Pet Care, and sold off Davigel frozen foods.

Nestlé buys the cocoa for its confectionery from African farmers. The Nestlé Cocoa Plan is designed to help these farmers and their communities, including by building or renovating local schools.

Palm oil is used in many consumer products, such as chocolate bars, but some palm oil producers are damaging the Indonesian rainforest, which is home to critically endangered orang-utans. In 2010, the environmental pressure group Greenpeace successfully campaigned against the use of irresponsibly farmed palm oil in Nestlé products.

4. Outline **one** method of external growth that might be appropriate for Nestlé. (2 marks)

Student answer

External growth can be achieved through takeovers or mergers. Nestlé is a big business that could take over competitors such as when they brought Merrick Pet Care which was a competitor to their Felix brand.

Verdict

The student shows a good understanding of external growth and makes good use of information provided in the extract to support their answer.

5. Explain **one** impact on a business of globalisation. (3 marks)

Student answer

One impact is the ability to sell in other countries. This gives the business access to a much bigger potential market. Which allows the business to grow.

Verdict

The student has correctly identified one impact and then developed that impact.

6. Evaluate whether Nestlé behaves in an ethical way. You should use the information provided as well as your knowledge of business. (12 marks)

Student answer

Ethical businesses do the morally 'right thing'. Nestlé is an ethical business as it is aiming to support its farmers in Africa. It is doing this by having a plan in place to help the farmers and their community. The building of schools is a good thing to do as it will help educate the children so they can have a better future. This shows they are looking after suppliers which is ethically correct. However, this is likely to have a trade-off as it will cost money to build and run the school.

However, Nestlé used to use a raw material that had a negative impact on the rainforest. They had to be forced to change this by the pressure group Greenpeace. This shows that they were not ethical because they did not want to change even though what they were doing was damaging the environment. However, they did change so they are not doing this now so they are ethical again.

Overall, I think Nestlé are ethical because they are voluntarily supporting their suppliers and no longer destroy the homes of orang-utans.

Verdict

The student shows a good understanding of ethics and uses business terminology well in their answer, such as 'trade-offs' and 'suppliers'. They also apply their understanding to Nestlé and use information from the extract. There is some analysis, although this could be developed a little further. Judgements within each main paragraph are good, but the conclusion could be better justified.

ENGLISH STRAWBERRY
2 FOR £1.50

Topic 2.2 Making marketing decisions

Topic overview

This topic considers the use of the marketing mix in business. It examines how each element of the marketing mix is managed and how businesses use the marketing mix to inform the decisions that they make about their products and services. It also considers the importance of developing an integrated marketing mix that can give a business a competitive advantage in its market.

Case study

The Snowdonia Cheese Company®

The Snowdonia Cheese Company was founded in 2001. The business's aim was to create a new variety of premium cheeses using local Welsh ingredients. The Snowdonia Cheese Company offers a range of different types and flavours of cheese, including an extra mature Cheddar ('Black Bomber'), Red Leicester ('Red Devil'), smoked Cheddar ('Beechwood') and Cheddar with cranberries ('Bouncing Berry'). The business experiments with new recipes and unusual flavours to broaden its range.

A 200 g truckle (a small barrel-shaped cheese) of any variety costs £4.50. Most of the cheeses are also available as a 400 g truckle or a 3 kg wheel. The cheeses are encased in wax to preserve them. Each type of cheese has its own distinctive coloured wax and is labelled with the company's black and white label to ensure that the product is instantly recognisable on any deli counter.

The Snowdonia Cheese Company's cheeses are only sold through luxury grocers and delicatessens, but they have also become the cheese of choice in a number of upmarket restaurants. The business's cheeses can also be bought, either on their own or in speciality packs, through the company's online store.

Amongst other prizes, the Snowdonia Cheeses have won World Cheese awards, British Cheese awards and Great Taste awards. The Snowdonia Cheese Company shares news about its awards and success on social media, including Facebook and Twitter. After it emerged that HRH Prince William's favourite Welsh meal was a lamb burger topped with the business's Black Bomber cheese, the Snowdonia Cheese Company published the recipe on its website.

The Snowdonia Cheese Company's products are now stocked in more than 2,000 UK outlets, as well as shops in the USA, Canada and France.

Activity ?

1 Why might the Snowdonia Cheese Company offer a wide range of products?

2 How might the Snowdonia Cheese Company decide on their prices?

3 Why are awards important to a company like the Snowdonia Cheese Company?

Theme 2: Building the business

Your learning

In this topic you will learn about:

- product – the design mix, the product life cycle and the importance of differentiating a product or service
- price – pricing strategies and influences on pricing strategies
- promotion – promotion strategies for different market segments and the use of technology in promotion
- place – methods of distribution
- using the marketing mix to make business decisions – how each element of the marketing mix can influence other elements, using the marketing mix to build competitive advantage and how an integrated marketing mix can influence competition.

Product

Case study

Big Bobble Hats Ltd

Big Bobble Hats is a business selling a wide variety of colourful knitted bobble hats, particularly for skiers, snowboarders and golfers. The bobble hats are sold at sporting trade shows, fairs and through the business's online shop. All hats are 'one size fits all'. Customers also have the option of choosing their own pattern and colours when ordering on the website.

Activity

In pairs or small groups, discuss the following questions.

1 Using Big Bobble Hats as an example, what do you think makes a good product?
2 Why is the design of a product important?

Link it up

You have already learned about the marketing mix in Topic 1.4 *Making the business effective* and Topic 2.2 *Growing the business*.

Key term

Marketing mix: the four 'P's of marketing, which are product, price, promotion and place.

'Product' is the first element of the **marketing mix** and it refers to the thing or things sold by a business. The product might be a physical item such as a smartphone, a virtual item such as a smartphone app or a service such as a haircut.

The key to producing a successful product is to ensure that it provides customers with benefits that they value. For example, the benefits of a particular brand of screwdriver might be that it is strong and easy to use, has a comfortable grip and features interchangeable attachments for different types of screw. The benefits of a particular make of coat could be its style and durability.

The design mix

When developing a new product, a business will consider many features that will lead to that product either succeeding or failing. In particular, the business is likely to spend most of their time thinking about the three aspects that make up the design mix during their research and development activities:

- function
- **aesthetics**
- cost.

Function

Function is how well a product does its job. The function of a product can be very straightforward. For example, the function of a mug is to hold hot and cold drinks and to be easy to drink from. On the other hand, your laptop, or tablet, has a complex function, encompassing processing speed, storage space, weight and touchscreen technology.

Two examples of the same type of product may have very different functions. For example, the primary function of some cars is to be extremely fast, while the primary function of other cars may be fuel efficiency or passenger safety.

Another aspect of function is how easy a product is to use. For a service, its function might include how easy, fast or convenient the service is for someone to access and use. Many customers choose products or services based on their functionality – how well and how easily that product or service does what they expect it to do.

Improving any aspect of a product's functionality is one way in which a business can improve its competitiveness. This may also allow it to target specific groups of customers with specific needs.

Aesthetics

In the design mix, aesthetics refers to the look, feel and visual appeal of a product. In many cases, it is not enough for a product to just be functional: it must also be attractive and appeal to customers.

Aesthetics is extremely important for some products whereas it has little impact on other products. For example, when purchasing medicine, the aesthetics of the bottle will have limited influence on a customer's choice to buy that medicine. In comparison, the aesthetics of a bottle of perfume will have huge influence on a customer's choice to buy that perfume.

Often, aesthetics will be the most important element of the design mix for many customers, particularly when purchasing products such as sofas, watches or shoes. However, in the case of both the medicine and the perfume, the function of the product (that is, the remedy for illness or the smell of the perfume) may be more important than the aesthetics of the product's packaging.

Key term

Aesthetics: the visual attractiveness of something.

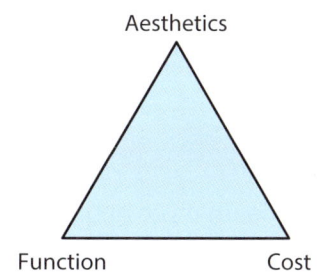

Figure 2.2.1 The three elements of the design mix are all linked. Changing one of these elements is likely to have an impact on the other two.

Link it up

You learned about the way in which a business may target specific groups of customers in the section 'Market segmentation' in Topic 1.2 *Spotting a business opportunity*.

Theme 2: Building the business

Link it up

You will learn more about costs, prices and pricing strategies in the section 'Price' in this topic.

Cost

Businesses not only have to design products that provide the right functions and are aesthetically pleasing, but that are also financially **viable**. This means producing the product for a cost that allows the business to make a profit.

Some businesses are able to design their products so that the cost of production is very low. This allows them to sell the product at a low price while still making a high profit margin. However, the disadvantage of low production costs is that there is often a trade-off between cost and function or aesthetics. For example, a business might decide to use cheaper materials in its products in order to lower the product's cost, but this could lower the durability of the product, therefore having a direct impact on the product's function. Alternatively, the cheaper materials might make the product uglier, therefore having a negative effect the product's aesthetics.

Balancing function, aesthetics and cost

When designing new products, all businesses have to consider the design mix and how they will balance the three aspects of function, aesthetics and cost. Improving any one of the three elements can have a detrimental impact on the other two. For example, the manufacturer of a hairdryer might improve the product's aesthetics by designing a uniquely shaped hairdryer. However, this aesthetic improvement might make the hairdryer's motor less efficient and therefore reduce the product's function, or the new shape may require a new production process and therefore raise costs.

Alternatively, a business might choose to accept the increased costs of additional features to improve the function or design features if it believes that the additional costs can be covered by the value that these features bring to the product. For example, Apple's iPhone® has many features that contribute to its function and an attractive design, meaning that it commands a high purchase price that can cover the costs of the improved function and aesthetics.

Activity ?

1 Look at the two razors. One is a disposable razor and one is a reusable razor. With a partner, discuss how the design mix for these two products is different. What factors would the manufacturers of these two products have considered when designing these razors?

2 Pick two products of your own choice. For each product, write down what you think is the most important element of its design mix. Try to give reasons for your choice.

The product life cycle

Another way in which a business can make product decisions is to use the product life cycle. The product life cycle plots the sales of a product through the four stages of its life:

- initial introduction
- growth
- maturity
- decline and discontinuation or extension.

The product life cycle can help a business to make decisions about its pricing, promotion, production levels and decisions about other products within its **product portfolio**.

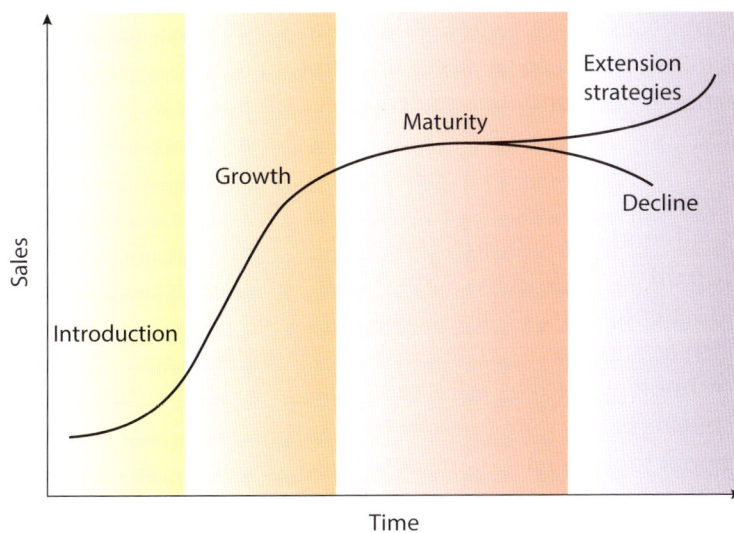

Figure 2.2.2 The stages of the product life cycle

The phases of the product life cycle

Introduction

The introduction phase covers the research, development and launch of a new product. During introduction, sales are low because product awareness is low and the brand's reputation is not very well known. The business will have invested money to develop the product and will not yet be making a profit on the product. At introduction, a business will need to do a lot of promotion to attract attention to the new product and may use special offers or a reduced price to attract customers.

Growth

If the product is successful during the introduction phase, it will enter the growth phase. During growth, the product becomes more and more popular and sales are likely to increase rapidly. During the growth phase, it is very important that the business is able to keep up with demand. Customer reviews and word of mouth may replace some forms of promotion. The business might choose to raise the price of the product if it believes that its popularity will maintain demand, even at a higher price.

Theme 2: Building the business

Exam tip

Give one benefit and then develop two linked explanations about that benefit, connecting the explanations to the benefit by using words and phrases such as 'therefore' and 'as a result'.

Did you know?

Loom bands are small colourful rubber bands that can be woven together to create many different styles of bracelet. During the craze for loom bands in 2013, loom bands were very popular, but sales then began to fall as the craze came to an end and their popularity declined.

Key terms

Economies of scale: a situation where average costs (of production, distribution and sales, for example) fall as a business increases the amount of product that it produces, distributes and sells.

Maximise: increase to the greatest possible amount or make the most of something.

Exam-style question

Explain **one** benefit to a business of using the product life cycle.

(3 marks)

Maturity

Once a product reaches the maturity phase, its growth has slowed down but sales will be at their peak. During maturity, the business is likely to receive repeat purchases from customers as there is a limit to the number of new customers that are interested in buying the product. A business will try to maintain sales at maturity for as long as possible and may use promotion techniques to remind its customers to purchase the product. For example, Cadbury uses short reminder advertisements on television, which do not necessarily promote one product but keep customers aware of the business's brand. As sales are high during maturity, the business is likely to experience **economies of scale** and should be able to **maximise** profitability.

Decline

Eventually, all products enter the decline phase. During decline, sales start to drop off as the product loses popularity. There are many reasons why a product enters the decline phase. For example, it might go out of fashion, such as shell suits in the 1990s, or be replaced by the introduction of a new technology, such as DVDs replacing VHS video tapes. During decline, a business will start to lower the product's price and use a variety of promotional tools to encourage customers to buy the product again. However, a business eventually has to decide to either discontinue the product or attempt an extension strategy.

Extension strategies

An extension strategy is any action that a business can take in order to lengthen the product life cycle and encourage growth in sales during the decline phase. The two simplest extension strategies that a business can deploy are:

- lowering prices
- increasing advertising.

A more complex extension strategy is totally rebranding the product. This might include modifying the product, giving it a new name and logo, and creating a new promotion campaign. Rebranding can have two different purposes. A rebrand can either stimulate new demand and interest in the original product or completely reposition the product in the market and target a totally different market segment, for example a different age group or gender.

Introducing new varieties is also an extension strategy. For example, Cadbury Dairy Milk is a long-established product that attracts new interest and sales by releasing new flavours such as Dairy Milk Oreo and Dairy Milk Daim.

The Ford Focus was first introduced to the UK in 1998. Using the internet, research the development of the Ford Focus over time. Using the results of your research, see how many extension strategies you can identify that Ford has used between 1998 and 2016 to extend the product life cycle of the Ford Focus.

The importance of differentiation

For a product to succeed in a competitive market, it must stand out from the other products on offer. To do this, it must be different from competing products or, even better, unique. Differentiation is the process of developing a distinctive or unique product.

A business may differentiate its products in a number of ways. It may:

- ensure that its product provides unique functions that are not provided by rival products
- give its product a unique style or design
- create and use a distinctive brand
- provide consistently excellent customer service
- ensure that its product is of a very high quality.

Differentiation benefits a business because it increases the competitiveness of that business. A differentiated product gives customers something that they cannot get from a rival product. This might be that the product's functions meet the needs of a particular target market, or that the product's brand is more recognisable or trusted. The particular characteristics offered by a differentiated product add value to the product, and this allows a business to charge a higher price for that product.

Key term

Unique selling point (USP): something that makes a product stand out from its competitors.

Exam tip

Differentiation is linked to the concept of the **unique selling point** (USP). What sorts of things could be a USP? Choose one of your ideas and explain it.

Exam-style question ⚪

Explain **one** way that a business might differentiate its products from those of its competitors.   **(3 marks)**

Theme 2: Building the business

Strengthen

S1 From memory, draw a fully labelled product life cycle.

S2 Identify two issues that a business must consider at each stage of the product life cycle.

S3 Why is differentiation important to a business?

Challenge

C1 List five pieces of advice that you would give a business that is developing a new product. Now prioritise your pieces of advice, starting with the most important at the top of the list.

C2 Explain the relationship between the design mix and the product life cycle.

Price

Case study

Lounge

Lounge is a fashionable coffee shop in Sheffield. It is located on a major high street, next to other bars and restaurants. The shop's décor gives it a relaxed but modern vibe. The business prides itself on the quality of its coffee, which is made from a blend supplied by an independent coffee company. The average price of a cup of coffee at Lounge is £4.25.

Activity   **?**

1 What factors do you think determine Lounge's decision to charge £4.25 for a cup of coffee?

2 What factors do you think determine how many cups of coffee are sold at Lounge?

In the marketing mix, 'price' refers to the amount charged by a business for its products and services. Price depends on a range of factors. Even two products that seem identical may have very different prices. For example, what factors do you think will determine the price you pay for:

• a sandwich at a motorway service station

• the price of a plane ticket to New York

• the latest Apple product?

The key factor that determines the price of any product is the perceived value that customers place on it – that is, what customers believe it is worth.

All businesses have to ask themselves, 'What is the right price to set for our product?' When you first start to think about this, you may think that a business should set its price as high as possible because a higher price generates more revenue, which increases the potential profit. However, if the business sets a low price, perhaps lower than its competitors, this would make its products more attractive to customers and therefore more competitive. This could increase sales even more, which would lead to more revenue and potential profit.

Pricing strategies

A pricing strategy is the way in which a business decides on the price of a product or service. The business will base its strategy on a number of factors in order to maximise sales revenue or volume. These factors might include popularity with customers, brand loyalty, and the other products or services the business sells. Two factors that all businesses will consider when setting price are:

- the volume of the product – how many of that product they can make and sell
- the product's profit margin, the difference between the price of the product and the cost of producing the product.

Businesses usually choose to adopt either a high-volume pricing strategy or a high-margin pricing strategy.

High-volume pricing strategy

A high-volume pricing strategy involves producing a lot of a product at a low cost. A business can do this because of the economies of scale that it achieves when making large quantities of the product. For example, a business producing high volumes of smoothies may be able to buy fruit and vegetables more cheaply by buying them in bulk than if they had to buy them in relatively small amounts.

A high-volume strategy is common for simple, standardised products, such as frozen pizzas sold in a supermarket. A high-volume strategy allows a business to reduce its production costs and set a low price for its product. Although this strategy results in a low margin, the business can still succeed because it is likely to sell large quantities of its product.

High-margin pricing strategy

Some businesses adopt a high-margin pricing strategy. With a high-margin strategy, a business attempts to maximise the difference between the production cost of each product and the price for which it can sell the product. This is known as adding value. Value can be added to a product in a number of ways, such as the product's quality or branding. Improving these factors may generate a premium product, for which customers are more willing to pay a premium price.

A high-margin strategy often results in low volumes. One reason for this is that a smaller proportion of customers are willing and able to pay such a high price, so there is no point in producing a lot of the product. A second reason for this is that producing a lot of the product may reduce a customer's impression that the product is very exclusive.

Link it up

You learned about added value in the section 'The role of business enterprise' in Topic 1.1 *Enterprise and entrepreneurship*.

Comparing high-volume and high-margin strategies

As you can see, either strategy can be effective for a business, depending on the product or service that it sells. Figure 2.2.3 shows how these two strategies relate to one another. Most businesses will set a price somewhere along the diagonal line.

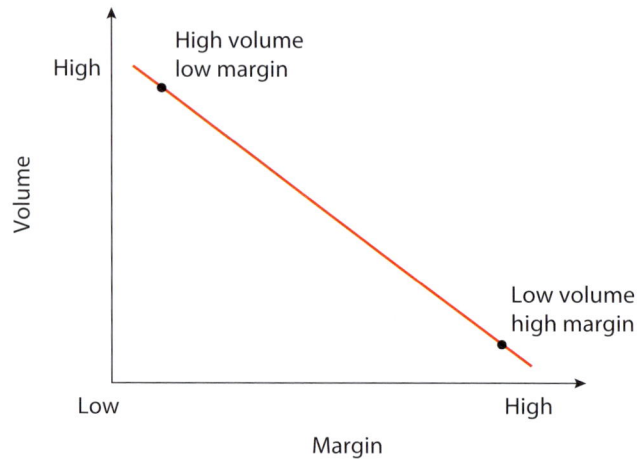

Figure 2.2.3 Pricing strategies

Exam-style question

Identify **one** factor that may influence the price of a product. **(1 mark)**

Activity ?

Draw a copy of Figure 2.2.3. Choose four different products that you are familiar with and try to place them somewhere along the line. Try to choose products that you believe operate at various points along the graph – for example, one high-volume low-margin product, one low-volume high-margin product and one or two products that fall between these points.

Influences on pricing strategies

A number of factors influence the price of a product. Where value is added, customers will be willing to pay a higher price. For example, some plumbing businesses offer an emergency service where they guarantee to be with the customer within the hour. This adds value to the service by making it faster and more convenient, and customers will value this service and be willing to pay a higher price. Similarly, a well-known and trusted brand name will act as a USP and add value to a product, and customers are more likely to pay a premium for this.

Technology

Modern technology plays a significant role in determining the price of products. It can also give a business flexibility in the way in which it sets its prices. For example, the taxi app Uber keeps an eye on demand for taxis in the local area by monitoring how many customers are searching for a taxi through the app. The price will be adjusted up or down, depending on whether the demand for taxis is high or low. If customers log in to the app to order a taxi at times of high demand, they will be told that the price will be higher. This ability to monitor demand and raise the price according to the level of demand encourages more taxi drivers to join Uber.

Another form of flexible pricing is in-product purchases. This strategy is common in products such as computer games, where the game itself is free to play, but gamers can make in-game purchases to enhance their characters or unlock new levels. The online game World of Warcraft offers players the opportunity to purchase virtual gold that they can spend within the game to buy virtual goods such as weapons, armour and potions.

Technology can also influence pricing by making it easier for customers to compare the prices charged by competing businesses. Carrying out a comparison using a search engine such as Google or Bing is easy for customers, making many industries more competitive. In addition, price comparison websites will perform a search and compare service for customers in many industries. For example, Trivago is a price comparison website that allows customers to search and compare hotels in destinations around the world, while MoneySuperMarket compares a range of products and services such as insurance and broadband. These websites make markets even more competitive, because customers have greater access to information that they can use to choose the best deals, which forces businesses' prices down.

Competition

The competitiveness of a market is directly linked to the supply of a product. If there are a lot of competitors in a market, customers have more choice when deciding where to shop, which means that they can shop around for the best deal. Where levels of competition are high, businesses generally have to set lower prices in order to compete unless their product has a USP or is obviously better than its competitors. This is often the case in busy town markets, where many sellers operate in close proximity to one another and to high street shops when selling products such as fruit and clothing.

If there are not many competitors in a market, customers have less choice and may be forced to purchase a product with a high price if they need it. You may notice that the price of petrol and diesel is higher at motorway service stations, because drivers are more willing to buy immediately rather than shop around for a cheaper alternative in a town off the motorway or at a later service station. In comparison, the price of fuel in a busy town may be much lower than on the motorway, because several service stations are competing in close proximity to one another, giving customers the opportunity to shop around.

Did you know?

Some businesses will set a price for a product that is below the cost of producing the product. This means that they will make a loss. These type of products known as 'loss leaders' and are used to entice customers to buy other products that are profitable.

Theme 2: Building the business

Link it up

You learned about segmentation in the section 'Market segmentation' in Topic 1.2 *Spotting a business opportunity*.

Key terms

Mass market: a large market where customers have similar needs and characteristics.

Generic: a characteristic relating to an entire group, not specific.

Niche market: a small market where customers have very specific needs and characteristics.

Discontinued: no longer produced and sold.

Exam-style question

Explain **one** reason why a product for a niche market might be sold for a high price.

(3 marks)

Exam tip

First of all, think of the characteristics of niche markets – maybe make yourself a list. Then choose one of these characteristics and use it in your answer.

Market segments

Businesses will often target different customers with a product at a different price. This is intended to meet the needs and characteristics of each particular market segment. For example, most car companies produce a range of models aimed at different types of customer, each of which has a different price, to meet customers' differing needs. Another example is the pricing of public transport. Bus and rail companies may offer lower-priced tickets for pensioners and students, who are likely to have low incomes, in order to encourage them to purchase a bus or train ticket.

Some products are sold in a **mass market**. A mass market is a large market with many customers who have similar needs. Products sold in a mass market include carbonated drinks such as Coca-Cola. Mass-market products generally have lower prices because the product is quite **generic** and customers have a wide choice of similar products from which to choose.

In comparison, other products are sold in a **niche market**. A niche market is a much smaller market than a mass market, and customers in a niche market have specific needs or interests. For example, Andybanjo Ltd is a UK company that specialises solely in banjos and provides customers with expert advice on this type of instrument. Businesses like Andybanjo Ltd that sell to a niche market are able to charge a higher price for their products. This is because they are meeting the specialist needs of their customers, and customers are more willing to pay a higher price for this.

Businesses are also likely to charge a high price for a brand new product. This is especially true in markets such as home electronics. For example, the latest 4K television will be very expensive when first launched, as there is a percentage of customers who are willing to pay a high price to be one of the first to own the product. These customers are known as 'first movers' or 'early adopters'. Over time, the product's price may fall as the novelty wears off and newer products are launched.

The product life cycle

As a product moves through the product life cycle, its visibility, popularity and demand will change. These changes will have a significant influence on its price. During the initial introduction phase, a business will try to establish a product and attract initial buyers. To do this, it is likely to set a low price. As the product grows in popularity, the price is likely to increase to something closer to its true value. Eventually, a stable price will be set as the product enters the maturity phase. During the decline phase, a product's popularity starts to fall. The business may use a number of extension strategies to regain interest and demand, and one of these strategies is to lower the price. If this strategy does not work, or the business decides that the product is no longer profitable, the product may be **discontinued**.

Activity ?

Consider the following statements, then think of an example of one product or service that could apply to each statement.

1 The business is happy to sell the product at a lower price than the amount that it costs to make.

2 The customers will accept a high price, even when they do not believe that the product or service is worth the price.

3 The business gives the product away for free for a limited time.

4 The business chooses to make and sell a product at a low margin.

5 The customer pays a low price for a product that they perceive to be worth more.

6 The business is happy to sell smaller amounts of its product.

For each statement, think of your own experiences when buying products and services from businesses you know.

Checkpoint

Now it is time to review your understanding of price.

Strengthen

S1 How might the volume of a product affect the pricing of that product?

S2 List three ways in which technology might affect the pricing decisions of a business.

S3 Explain the difference between a high-volume pricing strategy and a high-margin pricing strategy.

Challenge

C1 Describe what might happen to the price of a product if more competitors enter the market.

C2 Explain one scenario where a business might have to change the price of its products or services very suddenly.

C3 Using a real-life example, explain why a business might charge two separate prices for the same product.

Promotion

Case study

Land Rover

Land Rover manufactures and sells a range of sport utility vehicles (SUVs), including the Land Rover Defender and the Range Rover Evoque. Owners of a Land Rover are able to download a range of smartphone apps that allow them to track the location of their vehicle, track their journeys, read vehicle user guides and view Land Rover's *Onelife* magazine, a lifestyle magazine featuring articles on topics such as food, holidays and fitness.

Theme 2: Building the business

Promotion refers to the ways in which a business communicates its products and services to its customers. The most common form of promotion is advertising, which involves one-way communication through a medium such as television or radio. However, businesses may use other promotion techniques as well. In recent years, promotion has been enhanced by the use of technology, such as the internet and smartphones.

Promotion strategies

A promotion strategy is the group of techniques that a business uses to make customers and potential customers aware of and interested in its products and services. Promotion strategies include:

- advertising
- sponsorship
- product trials
- special offers
- branding.

Advertising

Advertising is when a business pays to put out an advertisement (advert) in order to communicate a message to customers and potential customers. Adverts may use a variety of techniques in order to grab customers' attention and gain their interest, such as colour, humour, imagery and **emotive language**.

Advertising is everywhere in the modern world. Often, an advert will have to compete with other businesses' adverts for customers' attention. In order to develop adverts that are effective, many large businesses employ specialist advertising agencies to design their advertising campaigns. Advertising is the most common form of promotion used around the world, and it uses a wide variety of **media**, as shown in Table 2.2.1.

Medium	Examples	% of total advertising spend in the UK in 2015
Television	• National channels such as BBC One and Channel 4. • Regional channels such as BBC Scotland and UTV in Northern Ireland. • Online channels such as BBC.	24%
Radio	• National radio stations. • Local radio stations. • Online or digital-only radio channels.	3%
Digital	• Website advertising. • Social media. • In-app advertising. • Email advertising. • Text messaging.	50%
Print	• National and local newspapers. • National and local magazines. • Brochures. • Event programmes.	16%
Roadside/outdoor	• Billboards and posters. • Advertising on transport, such as on buses, trains and the London Underground.	6%

Table 2.2.1 Different advertising media

An effective advert positioned in the right place at the right time can have a significant impact on customer awareness of a product and attitudes towards a business. One example of this was Barclaycard's 2008 television advert for its contactless card payment, featuring the slogan 'glide with us'. The advert showed a man riding through a city on a water slide. The man paid for products using his contactless debit card as he slid past payment machines at various locations throughout the city. The advert was fun, clever and entertaining, making customers feel good about the Barclaycard brand. In 2010, Barclaycard released a similar advert featuring a rollercoaster to launch the Barclaycard contactless app for smartphones.

Activity ?

Consider the following emotions:

• happiness

• anger

• shock.

In small groups, identify some real examples of adverts that you think have tried to make you feel these emotions. Discuss how and why each advert made you feel each emotion. What was the advert promoting? Do you think the advert worked?

Advertisements from brands such as Innocent that are creative and fun will help a brand to grab viewers' attention and make them remember the brand

Certain forms of advertising, especially television and print, can be very expensive. For example, a 30-second television advert during the American sporting event, the Super Bowl, will cost a business US $5 million, because the Super Bowl is the nation's most-watched sporting event. Apart from being expensive, it can also be very difficult to analyse the impact that advertising has on product sales, such as working out what impact each £1 spent on advertising has on generating sales revenue.

Exam tip

Try to identify at least two limitations of an extensive advertising campaign. For each limitation, try to develop your answer with linked consequences.

Exam-style question

Discuss the possible limitations of a business investing in an extensive advertising campaign. **(6 marks)**

The choice of advertising medium will depend on the size of the business, the nature of the market and the type of product. For example, only large businesses can afford to advertise their products on national television channels. In comparison, a regional business, such as an electrician in Worcestershire, may choose to advertise using local radio stations because it is much cheaper and is listened to by potential customers who live within reach of the business.

A business will choose a medium that allows it to access its target market. For example, sporting goods companies are likely to place adverts in sports magazines bought by active, health-conscious people such as *Cyclist*, *Runner's World* and *Trail*.

Sponsorship

Sponsorship is when a business supports an event, activity, person or organisation, either financially or by providing its products or services. For example, the official sponsors of the Rio 2016 Olympic Games included Bradesco (a Brazilian commercial bank) and Nissan (a global car manufacturer). These businesses provided products, facilities and services in exchange for the publicity that they received throughout the duration of the Games. Sponsorship may also happen on a personal level through celebrity endorsement, such as Nike's sponsorship deal with footballer Cristiano Ronaldo.

Sponsorship has many benefits for a business, such as encouraging positive consumer attitudes towards its brand and generating awareness of its products or services. As with advertising, sponsorship must be appropriate to the business and the nature of its product. Smaller businesses are more likely to sponsor local sporting teams or events to show their support of the local community.

Sponsorship can enhance a business's reputation by generating a positive association with an event, activity or celebrity

Product trials

A product trial is free access to or the giveaway of a product. Although this approach can be very expensive, it is an extremely effective method of encouraging potential customers to sample a new product. For this reason, product trials are often used for promoting a product that is entering the introduction phase of the product life cycle.

Examples of product trials include:

- small samples of shampoo or perfume distributed free inside relevant magazines
- samples of a new cheese or chocolate bar given away at supermarkets
- temporary free subscriptions to services like Sky or Netflix.

Special offers

Special offers, also referred to as **sales promotions**, are an effective promotion strategy that can be used to boost sales over a short period of time. Many businesses have special offers to entice customers into their shops, hoping that those customers will then purchase their other products. It is also used as a strategy to clear a business's **stock**. This is particularly important in industries such as fashion, where trends change by the season and old stock has to be cleared in order to make way for the new season's clothing.

> ### Key terms
>
> **Sales promotion:** a short-term special offer, usually in form of a discount, used by a business to attract customers to buy a product or service.
>
> **Stock:** the products held by a business in a shop or warehouse for sale to customers.

Special offers may take the form of discounts, such as 25 per cent off and buy-one-get-one free (BOGOF), or free upgrades to extra features or bonuses. For example, hotels may promote special offers such as a free breakfast or free access to spa facilities to a customer who books a room during quiet periods, such as midweek nights, when the hotel might not be able to fill its rooms.

Publicity

Publicity refers to any communication about a business that is created by the business, its customers or a third party. Publicity can be good or bad. For example, it could be an article in a newspaper, a product review from an organisation such as Which? or a protest staged by a **pressure group**. Good publicity can be extremely effective in generating interest in a business, as customers may be more likely to trust an independent source of information, such as an independent review of a product or service. However, publicity can also be dangerous for a business because it can come from someone outside of the business and this can make it difficult to influence the message that this publicity gives.

Some businesses use public relations (PR) experts or companies to deal with this. Large organisations may even employ a whole department of PR specialists to help influence and manage any publicity around the business and its products.

Many businesses, particularly hospitality businesses such as hotels and restaurants, receive online customer reviews through websites such as TripAdvisor. These websites allow customers to post detailed feedback and scores, which are then published for other potential customers to read. This customer-generated publicity can be good or bad, and some businesses spend a lot of time and effort responding appropriately to feedback in order to manage this publicity.

Branding

A brand is the personality or image of a product, which is generated through marketing activities. Brand personality helps consumers to identify with a product and associate a certain set of characteristics with that brand, such as quality, fun or sophistication. Developing a strong brand can help a business to generate customer loyalty, add value to its products and differentiate its products from those of its competitors.

Technology and promotion

Advances in digital technology have had a huge impact on how businesses promote themselves. In particular, new technologies have given many businesses the opportunity to have two-way communication with current and potential customers.

Targeted advertising on websites

Targeted advertising on websites, such as banner and side-bar adverts, is an effective way for businesses to get exposure to potential customers.

Key term

Pressure group: a group of people who join together to try to influence government policy or business policy for a particular cause.

Link it up

You learned about pressure groups and the impact of good and bad publicity in the section 'Ethics, the environment and business' in Topic 2.1 *Growing the business*.

Websites are able to track customers' searches and use this information to show adverts that are linked to those searches. By doing this, the adverts that are shown are relevant and more likely to interest the person visiting the website.

Social media and viral advertising

Social media platforms such as Facebook, Twitter, Instagram and Snapchat offer businesses the opportunity to advertise themselves to users. Businesses can also use these platforms as a user themselves in order to promote their products and services. For example, most businesses now have a Facebook page and a Twitter profile that they can use to communicate with customers.

Social media has also been instrumental in the growth of **viral advertising**. Viral advertising is when a message, video or image is distributed and shared among a lot of people on social networks. The original message may be created or sponsored by a business, but the distribution is done by people using social media platforms. Many popular adverts have been shared around the country or even around the world through social media, such as #ThisGirlCan by Sport England and other sports organisations. Viral advertising campaigns are often based on popular recent stories, so they do not usually last for very long.

Viral advertising can also be used to support a campaign or good cause. For example, a number of charities use viral advertising to generate interest in and donations to a good cause, such as the Ice Bucket Challenge, which raised more than US $98 million in aid of a neurological disease called ALS, and the No Make-up Selfie campaign, which raised more than £8 million for Cancer Research UK.

> **Key term**
>
> **Viral advertising:** advertising using social networking to increase sales or boost brand awareness.

Social media and viral advertising campaigns can generate global interest and exposure for a business, cause or brand

Apps

Software apps developed for smartphones and tablets offer another opportunity for businesses to promote their products and services. A business can advertise within an app, just like it would on a website, but it can also use apps creatively to engage with its customers as well. As you saw in the case study earlier, Land Rover uses apps in order to help and engage with its customers. Similarly, an app may give a customer access to a catalogue of products, allow them to book an appointment, show them the latest special offers or let them track their order. Some apps may also feature 'push' notifications, which is a message that pops up on an app user's mobile device.

Emails and e-newsletters

Many businesses collect contact details for their customers such as telephone numbers and email addresses. This allows them to build long-lasting relationships with these customers. For example, a business might send its customers regular communications about its latest deals. This sort of communication can be personalised, such as tailored offers, which could be more effective than a general advert on the side of a bus or a tweet. For example, a business may email a customer a special offer linked to their previous purchases, a reminder to renew a contract, or simply a birthday message with a discount.

A business might also use email to send e-newsletters to its customers. These e-newsletters can be used to communicate large amounts of information about the business's products and services. They can also be used to generate positive attitudes towards the brand, as in the case of the smoothie and juice business, Innocent Drinks.

The advantage of email promotion, as with other forms of digital promotion, is that it allows customers to access further information instantly by clicking through to the appropriate website. Thanks to **e-commerce** and **m-commerce**, customers can even go on to buy products and services instantly, all as a result of an email.

Activity ?

1 Consider each method of promotion listed in the following table and give it a score out of 10 for each of the categories shown. For example, if you think sponsorship has a very high cost you would give it 10, but if you thought it has a very low cost you would give it 1.

2 Discuss your scores with a partner.

	Advertising	Sponsorship	Viral marketing
Cost (overall cost of using the method)			
Reach (how many people are likely to see it)			
Control (how easily the business can control the message)			
Precision (how easily the business can target specific market segments)			

Table 2.2.2 Comparing different types of promotion

Checkpoint

Now it is time to review your understanding of promotion.

Strengthen

S1 List the five different types of media that a business could use for advertising.

S2 Describe the difference between sponsorship and sales promotions.

S3 Identify two ways in which a business could use technology to promote its products or services.

Challenge

C1 Using an example, explain how technology has changed the way in which businesses promote their products and services. You should compare this with traditional forms of promotion, such as posters and printed adverts in newspapers.

C2 Describe why a business might use a variety of methods when developing a promotion campaign to promote its products and services.

C3 Look again at the list you produced in response to S1. Choose one medium that you think would be most appropriate for your local greengrocer. Give a reason for your choice.

Place

Case study

SportShoes.com

SportShoes.com is an online retailer that specialises in sporting equipment, particularly sports shoes. It offers more than 12,000 products, including running shoes, clothing and hiking equipment. SportShoes.com stocks leading brands and features lots of expert advice on its website. Customers can talk to an expert via Live Chat, as well as reading articles and interacting with other runners through the site's MyRunspiration Community.

Activity ?

1 Why do you think SportShoes.com might have decided to only sell products via a website?

2 Why do you think SportShoes.com offers a Live Chat facility and posts articles about running and related topics on their website?

Link it up

In 'The competitive environment' in Topic 1.2 *Spotting a business opportunity*, you explored how businesses use their location to gain a competitive advantage.

Key terms

Retailing: selling products or services to customers – in this case, in a physical shop.

E-tailing: retailing to customers through the internet, such as through an e-commerce website.

'Place' refers to how a business gets its product to its customers. This includes the way in which customers access the product and how it is delivered. Place also refers to the physical location of a business, which can also be an extremely important aspect of the marketing mix and a way in which a business can add value to its products and services. For example, if a restaurant is positioned on the side of a mountain overlooking the sea, customers may pay a premium for their meal to experience the view offered by this restaurant's location.

A key decision that must be made when considering the 'place' element of the marketing mix is how customers will access the business's products or services. Specifically, a business will have to choose between **retailing**, **e-tailing** or a combination of both.

Retailing

Retailing is the traditional way in which products or services are distributed to customers. It involves selling products or services through a shop or other physical building that customers will visit in order to buy products or access a service such as a bank, hairdresser or dentist. Figure 2.2.4 shows two ways in which a business might use retailing to get its products to its customers.

Manufacturer sells products to a retailer → Customers visit retail store to buy products

Business has its own retail store/s that customers visit to buy products and services

Figure 2.2.4 The process of retailing

There are many benefits to retailing. For example, it allows customers to access face-to-face support from a business, such as asking questions and getting advice from sales assistants in the shop. It also gives customers the chance to trial, experience or try on a product or service before they buy it. This may encourage customers to buy the product because they can see or feel its qualities, and it also provides the shopping experience that many customers enjoy. In some cases, customers may think that it is essential to try the product before they buy it. Examples of this might include a new music system, where customers want to test the sound quality, or a piece of furniture, which a customer wants to check for comfort and suitability.

A physical location is central to many businesses that provide services or activities, such as an indoor crazy golf course. It is also very important to any business that adds value to its products through providing excellent customer service or high-street convenience, or that promotes its business through its location, such as a window display on a busy high street. Some customers consider that having a physical retail location is a sign of a business's long-established and trustworthy nature, especially in comparison with web-based businesses.

However, retailing also has disadvantages. One major downside is that owning or renting a physical shop can add expensive overhead costs such as rent or mortgage repayments to the business's finances. A disadvantage for manufacturers selling to an independent retailer is that they may have to reduce their profit margins, as the price will need to reflect the **markup** that the retailer will place on the product. For example, a jacket that costs £60 to make and sells for a retail price of £200 may be sold to a retailer for £130. This allows the manufacturer and the retailer to each make £70 profit on the jacket. However, if the manufacturer could sell the jacket directly, it could make a profit of £140.

> ### Key term
>
> **Markup:** the amount of money added to the cost price of a product or service to make the final retail price.

Activity ?

1 A burger van owner estimates that the cost of each cheeseburger that he sells is 75p. He sells each cheeseburger for £2.50. What is the percentage markup on each burger?

2 A new car costs the manufacturer £3,000 to build. The price paid for the new car by a customer is £12,000. What is the percentage markup on the car?

3 A pair of designer jeans has a markup of 500 per cent. What would be the unit cost of the pair of jeans if it is sold for £120?

Maths tip

If you are not sure how to approach a percentage calculation, work through a simple percentage calculation that you know the answer to – for example, 5 per cent of £100 = £5. Be sure that you understand how you came to this correct answer and then apply these steps to the calculation you are working on.

Theme 2: Building the business

Exam tip

Consider the alternatives to a manufacturer having its own retail stores. What benefits might it receive from having its own retail store in comparison with other options?

Exam-style question

Explain **one** reason why a manufacturer may want to open its own retail store.

(3 marks)

E-tailing

E-tailing is when products and services are sold directly to a customer through a website. This site may be accessed via a computer (e-commerce), or through a mobile device like a tablet or smartphone (m-commerce).

Businesses sell products and services to customers via e-commerce and distribute directly

A third-party website and/or distribution business may be used. E.g. Amazon

Figure 2.2.5 The process of e-tailing

Key benefits of e-tailing include:

- the business does not need to own or rent a physical building
- the business can access a national or international market that it could not enter otherwise
- small businesses can be started up much more easily if entrepreneurs do not have to establish their own retail stores or get their products stocked in other retailers' stores.

Amazon is the world's largest e-tailer. The business started in the 1990s by selling books online, but it has now expanded to sell a huge range of products. Notably, Amazon now acts as a **third-party platform** for other sellers, allowing many businesses to sell through its website. Amazon then takes a percentage of the sale price of each item, in the same way that a traditional retailer would add a markup on a product that it sells in its store. The advantage of this for the smaller business is that it allows it to sell to many more customers than it would be able to access on its own.

E-tailing has also allowed new markets to grow. For example, in recent years there has been a boom in the subscription box market, where customers receive a box filled with products such as fruit and vegetables, chocolates or cosmetics. Subscription box businesses include Birchbox, Graze and My Geek Box.

However, e-tailing also has its limitations. Customers can be worried about buying products online as they cannot check the product's quality before buying. Some people are also concerned that they may be purchasing products from fake websites. E-tailers also have to manage their own

Key term

Third-party platform: an e-commerce website or service that is run by an unrelated business.

distribution costs and this has to be factored in when considering their pricing strategies. In addition, having an e-commerce site is not enough to guarantee sales. Businesses need to undertake extensive digital marketing campaigns in order to ensure that people visit the site, which will also help it to feature higher up on the results of search engines such as Google.

Exam-style question

Explain **one** benefit a business may experience from e-tailing. **(3 marks)**

Exam tip

You need to state one benefit and develop two linked explanations of this benefit. Try thinking about the aspects of running a business that e-tailing makes simpler.

Activity ?

List as many high-street businesses as you can think of. Put the names of the businesses that you have identified into a table like the one below. For each business, find out whether it has a website and whether its website supports e-commerce (that is, whether it allows customers to buy products and services online).

Business	Website?	E-commerce?

1 Would any of the high-street businesses that do not offer e-commerce benefit from offering the option to buy products on their websites?

2 Do any of the businesses without e-commerce have online competition from e-tailers that sell similar products?

3 Would any of the businesses benefit from solely operating as an e-tailer? Explain your reasons.

Checkpoint

Now it is time for you to review your understanding of place.

Strengthen

S1 Describe why place is a key aspect of the marketing mix.

S2 Describe the differences between retailing and e-tailing. You may find it easier to create a table to do this.

Challenge

C1 You have been asked by your local business association to write a blog post or Facebook post about the choice between retailing and e-tailing. Write a short piece to help businesses decide whether they should use retailing, e-tailing or both strategies.

C2 Are there any products that you do not think could be sold via e-tailing? Why do you think this?

Using the marketing mix to make business decisions

The Greedy Greek

The Greedy Greek is a restaurant serving traditional Greek cuisine. It aims to offer quality food at affordable prices. The restaurant has a relaxed atmosphere, with simple décor and basic seating, and the owner prides herself on providing excellent service. The Greedy Greek also delivers food within the local area in order to compete against other takeaway restaurants. All deliveries come with a printed menu and vouchers for the customer's next order.

Activity

1 How does the Greedy Greek use the marketing mix effectively?
2 Which is the most important aspect of the marketing mix for the Greedy Greek?

Key term

Integrated marketing mix: a marketing mix that has a theme, with the elements all supporting each other.

Figure 2.2.6 The interconnected nature of the marketing mix

Although the marketing mix consists of four different elements, these elements should combine to form one joined-up marketing strategy that the business uses to meet the needs of its customers. For a business to be successful, the elements of its marketing mix should work together, rather than working against each other. A marketing mix that works together like this is known as an **integrated marketing mix**.

It can help to think about an integrated marketing mix as a cake. The four elements of the marketing mix are the ingredients for a business's marketing strategy. For the cake (the overall strategy) to work, all of the ingredients must be added in the right order and in the right amounts.

How elements of the marketing mix influence one another

A business must make decisions about each element of the marketing mix. However, the elements are interconnected, and this means that a decision made about one element of the mix can have a direct impact on other elements. The following examples show only some of the ways in which the elements interact with each other.

- **Product and price** – as a business develops its products, it will take into account the three aspects of the design mix (function, design and cost). As you have seen, these aspects are dependent on one another – for example, improving functionality may have a negative impact on the design features, whereas improving the design could lead to increased costs. A business must ensure that its products and services are profitable, so that any cost implications will directly affect its pricing strategy.

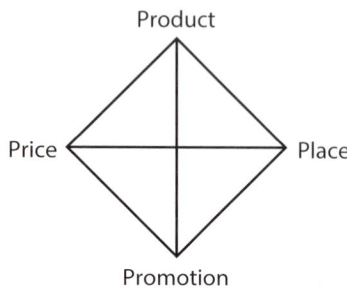

- **Price and promotion** – if a business is able to add value to a product through its design and features, it may be able to charge a premium price for that product. However, customers will only be willing to pay a premium price if they think that the product is worth this amount of money. This means that the promotion of the product, through advertising and other methods, must show customers that it is a premium product.

Watch an advert for any premium perfume, such as Chanel or Dior, or luxury watch brand, such as Rolex or Omega. Make a note of the ways in which the advert tells the customer that this is a premium product.

- **Promotion and place** – the purpose of promotion is to communicate a message to customers, create awareness of a product and make customers want to purchase the product. If a business is going to be promoted successfully, it must be very visible. This means that promotional requirements may determine the location of a business. For example, if a shop is hidden away in the basement of a large building, its location is not helping to promote its products.

- **Place and product** – if a business has decided that it is going to use e-tailing as its distribution method, it must design its product so that it is easy and cheap to post and will not get damaged on its way to the customer. For example, the boxes used by the snack subscription box service Graze are designed to slot easily through a letterbox.

Consider the following examples of global businesses. For each business, consider how the elements of the marketing mix interact with each other and answer the question that follows.

Starbucks

Starbucks is a global coffee chain that prides itself on providing excellent quality coffee and a laid-back, relaxing atmosphere in its stores. Starbucks aims to be a socially responsible business and it only buys its coffee from sustainable growers.

1 How might other elements of the marketing mix influence Starbucks's decisions about place?

Orla Kiely

Orla Kiely is an Irish designer who produces retro prints for use in her own range of products. Her brand covers products such as clothing, furniture and homeware goods. Famous for its distinctive patterns, the brand targets women between the ages of 20 and 40.

2 How might other elements of the marketing mix influence Orla Kiely's decisions about promotion?

Theme 2: Building the business

Exam tip

Try focusing on one element of the marketing mix. Consider how internal or external factors might influence the element that you have chosen.

Exam-style question

Explain **one** factor that may influence the marketing mix of a business.

(3 marks)

Can one element dominate the marketing mix?

As you have seen, the elements of the marketing mix are interrelated and influence each other. However, in the case of many businesses, one element can be more important than all of the others. This is usually due to the nature of the business. For example, a surf school in Cornwall may have a lease for a beach-side plot of land. The business's place may be a key factor in ensuring that the business gets noticed and can provide easy access to the beach for its target market. Promotion will help this business to succeed, but the place is the most important factor in its success.

In a similar way, a business may consider product to be the most important element in its marketing mix. An example of this would be a business like Arco, which produces safety equipment such as fireproof clothing, safety helmets and welding goggles. The priority for Arco's customers is safety, which is very closely tied to the quality of the product, meaning that product is more important than price or promotion. If the product was not of a high quality and did not keep people safe, customers would not buy it, no matter whether the business promoted its products a lot or set a low price.

Competitive advantage and the marketing mix

A competitive advantage is any advantage that a business has that makes its products and services more attractive to customers than those of its competitors. A business might find that its competitive advantage is its ability to offer a lower price, a unique feature or a prime location that its target market finds desirable.

A competitive advantage must be sustainable and difficult for a rival business to replicate. For example, the vacuum cleaner manufacturer Dyson holds design **patents** on many of its products. This gives Dyson a significant competitive advantage as it ensures that the business's products are unique.

The marketing mix offers businesses a number of ways in which they can achieve a competitive advantage. Using an integrated marketing mix can lead to business success, because it will drive home to potential customers what the strengths of a particular product or service are compared to others in the market. The following are some examples of the way in which elements of the marketing mix can create a competitive advantage.

- **Product** – the most obvious method of gaining a competitive advantage is to sell a product that is better than the competition. This might be achieved through the product's design, quality, functionality or customer service.
- **Promotion** – this can also be used to achieve a competitive advantage. If a business's advertising campaign is unique and memorable, it may go viral on social media and increase public awareness of the product enormously.

Key term

Patent: a legal protection of an invention, design or idea, meaning that it is illegal for another company to copy it.

Link it up

Look back at 'Promotion' earlier in Topic 2.2 for more information about viral marketing.

- **Product and promotion** – an extension of 'product' that can also be used to generate a competitive advantage is the product's brand image. A strong brand image may take a long time to establish, meaning that it is difficult for a rival business to copy. A strong brand image is also generated by promotion, as a major aspect of building a brand is the quality of the promotional activity carried out by the business.

- **Price** – some businesses can organise their production, procurement and logistics cheaply enough to ensure that their costs are lower than their competitors'. This means that the business can charge a lower price for the product, and therefore attract customers, while still achieving a high profit margin.

Link it up

You will learn more about organising production and logistics in Topic 2.3 *Making operational decisions*.

Exam tip

Think about the different ways in which a business might add value to its products or services and then choose one to focus on in your answer. These methods can often be a source of competitive advantage.

Exam-style question

Explain **one** way a business could achieve a competitive advantage.

(3 marks)

Checkpoint

Now it is time to review your understanding of using the marketing mix to make business decisions.

Strengthen

S1 Why are the four elements of the marketing mix interconnected?

S2 How might a pricing decision have an impact on a business's promotion?

Challenge

C1 Use a real-life example to describe why price is the most important element of the marketing mix.

C2 Choose one of the following elements: product, promotion or place. In no more than 250 words, write an argument explaining why you believe that your chosen element is the most important element of the marketing mix.

2.2 Making marketing decisions

1   Which **one** of the following is associated with the maturity phase of the product life cycle?   *(1 mark)*
    *Choose **one** answer.*

☐   A   Low sales   ☐   B   A slowdown in sales growth

☐   C   An increase in sales growth   ☐   D   A sharp fall in sales

2   Discuss the benefits a business might experience from selling its products through e-commerce.
    (6 marks)

Student answer

If a business sells its products through e-commerce, it might be able to sell the products for a lower price. This is because they will not need to run an expensive retail store so its costs will be lower and this saving could be passed on to their customers.

Another benefit is that the business might be able to target a much wider market, even a global market. This is because anyone can search and find products online, so potentially anyone could be a customer for the business. This will increase sales potential.

Verdict

This is a good answer. The student has identified two benefits: 'lower costs' and 'wider target market'. They have explained each benefit, showing cause and consequence. For example, in the first paragraph, the student has discussed how lower costs could be passed on to customers in the form of lower prices. They could have improved the answer by explaining that lower prices could increase potential sales.

Read the following extract carefully, then answer Questions 3, 4 and 5.

Shakeaway is the world's largest milkshake bar company. It offers more than 180 flavours in all kinds of blended combinations that can be customised by the customer. It also sells 14 'named shakes', which are set flavours with names such as Colin or Stella. A large serving of each named shake is priced at £5.15.

Over the years, Shakeaway has increased its product range to include healthy shakes, smoothies and frozen yoghurt desserts. Shakeaway also offers a mini taster cup, which it uses to provide free taster shakes to customers. These mini taster cups are promoted on social media sites such as Facebook and Instagram.

3   Outline **one** benefit for Shakeaway of offering a wide variety of flavours.   *(2 marks)*

Student answer

Shakeaway will benefit from a wide variety of flavours because it makes its business unique if it offers more milkshakes and smoothies than any of its competitors. As a result, they could attract a wider variety of people to their bars.

Verdict

This is a good answer. The student has given a benefit ('make its business unique') and developed a point in the form of a consequence ('attract a wider variety of people'). The answer also used the example of Shakeaway with reference to words from the extract, such as 'smoothies' and 'bars'.

4   Outline **one** issue Shakeaway will have to consider when offering free taster shakes.   **(2 marks)**

Student answer

Shakeaway will have to make sure that they have enough stock because if lots of people want the free taster shakes they might run out. They might also lose a lot of money if they give away too many.

Verdict

The student has identified a relevant issue 'have enough stock'. The student has then developed their answer with a consequence of running out of the taster shakes. However, the second mark will be awarded for a developed point in context and, apart from mentioning 'taster shakes', this has not been applied to Shakeaway.

5. Shakeaway are considering two options to increase profitability.

   Option 1: Increase advertising

   Option 2: Increase prices

   Justify which one of these options Shakeaway should choose.   **(9 marks)**

Student answer

If Shakeaway increase advertising, this might mean more people become aware of its milkshake bars. This means that more people may be convinced to visit the bars to buy a drink. It will also help Shakeaway promote its free taster shakes and this will encourage more people to visit knowing they can get a free drink. If they like the free taster, they may then buy more.

Increasing the price might help increase the profit margin on every drink so overall profits will go up if they can keep costs down. However, the price is already quite high at £5.15 so people might not be willing to pay a higher price, especially if it is much higher than other alternatives such as a can of Coca Cola.

Verdict

The student has discussed both options and explained how they might increase profits. The answer is also based in the context of Shakeaway, as the student has used information from the extract. The answer is also balanced, as the student has identified the limitations and benefits of increasing price. However, the student has not 'evaluated': they have not made a justified decision about which option should be chosen.

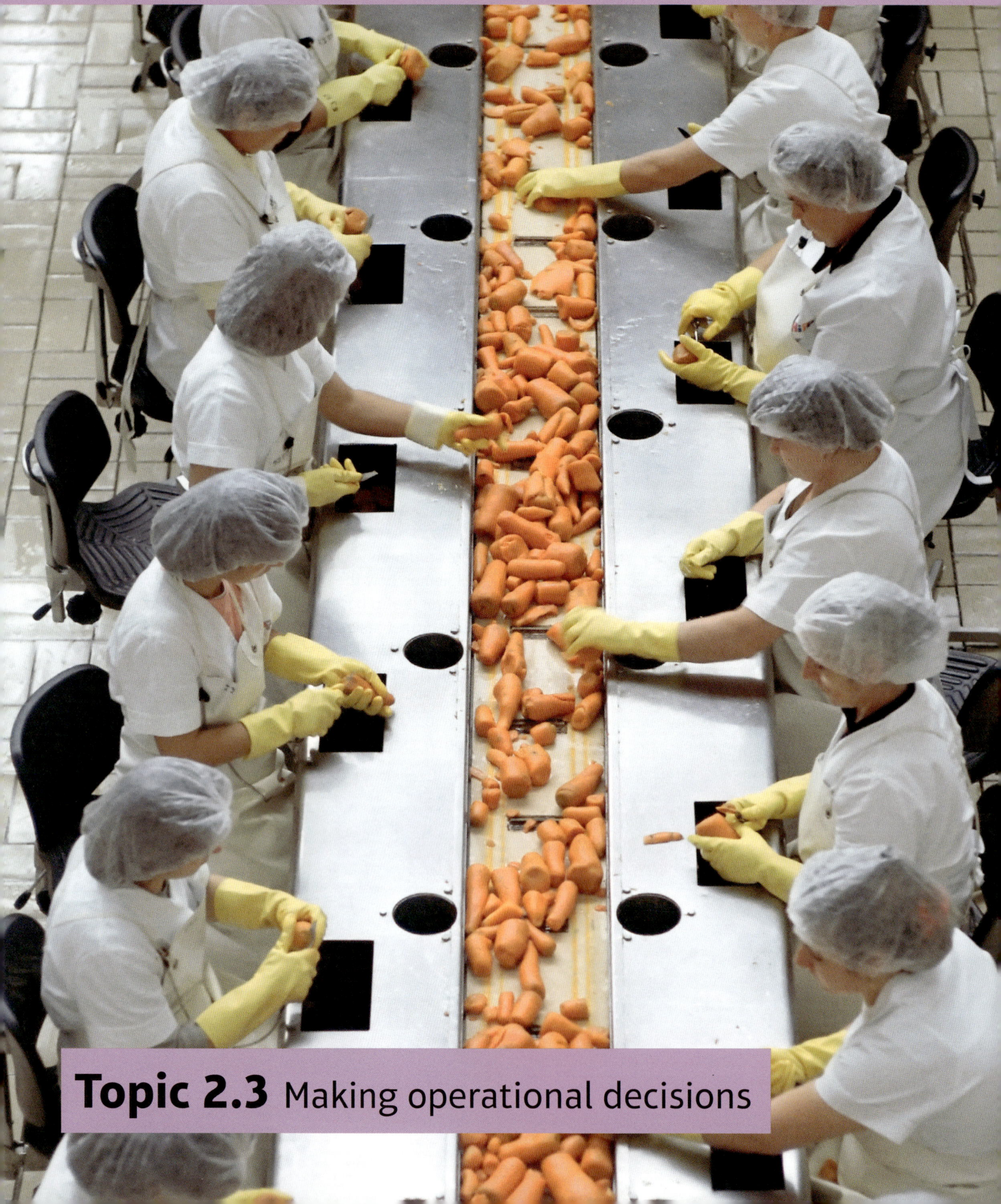

Topic 2.3 Making operational decisions

Topic overview

This topic focuses on how a business operates in order to meet the needs of its customers. You will examine the ways in which a business does this through the design, supply and quality of its products and services, as well as the way in which it manages the sales process.

Case study

PhotoBox

PhotoBox is an online photograph printing business. Customers can upload their photographs onto the business's platform in order to edit them and have them printed in a variety of sizes or into an album, as well as on a range of customisable products such as mugs and phone cases. As customers order customised products in a variety of sizes and in any quantity, each order fulfilled by PhotoBox is specifically tailored to each customer.

PhotoBox makes it easy for its customers to upload their photos from their computers, smartphones or social media profiles. Customers can then store their favourite photos in their account on the PhotoBox website, which also allows them to track the status of their order. For some of its products, PhotoBox also offers its customers a range of delivery options, including next day delivery for orders placed before midday.

The PhotoBox website automatically checks the resolution of each image before confirming the order. If an image is too small or the quality is too bad to be printed, the customer is informed of this. This ensures that customers will understand why a photo cannot be printed and only receive products that they will be totally satisfied with. The business prides itself on the quality of its products because 'every memory deserves to be cherished'.

The PhotoBox website also allows customers to leave feedback and review PhotoBox's products on a platform called Trust Pilot. In December 2016, the average customer satisfaction rating for PhotoBox was 8.5 out of 10. PhotoBox has also won a number of internet retailing awards. The business prides itself on the quality of its products because 'every memory deserves to be cherished'.

Activity ?

In pairs or small groups, discuss the following questions.

1 What issues do you think PhotoBox could face when fulfilling orders specifically tailored to each customer?

2 How important is technology to PhotoBox's business operations?

3 Why is a very good customer satisfaction rating important for a business like PhotoBox?

Theme 2: Building the business

Your learning

In this topic you will learn about:

- business operations – the purpose of business operations, different types of production process and the impact of technology on production
- working with suppliers – managing stock and the role of procurement
- managing quality – the concept of quality and its importance
- the sales process – the nature of the sales process and the importance to businesses of providing good customer service.

Business operations

Case study

A Suit That Fits

A Suit That Fits is a business that makes made-to-measure suits for individual customers. The business assigns each customer their own tailor, who takes measurements and helps the customer to design their own suit from a range of materials. Choices can include collar and cuff styles and embroidered initials. The suit is handmade and the service includes free fittings and adjustments before the customer collects their finished suit.

Activity ?

In small groups, discuss the following questions.

1 What level of skill does A Suit That Fits require its employees to have?

2 How do you think the way in which the business operates might have an impact on the number of suits that it can make?

3 How could a business like A Suit That Fits ensure it can provide customers with a lot of flexibility and customisation?

Understanding business operations

Business operations are the activities that allow a business to produce and deliver products and services to its customers. In its operations, a business uses resources such as labour (the skills and efforts of its workforce), capital (the money needed to run the business) and materials (the raw materials used in production, such as fabric or steel). A business's operations transform these inputs into its outputs – its products and services. This is shown in Figure 2.3.1.

Figure 2.3.1 Business operations transform inputs into outputs

For example, a sandwich shop uses the following inputs in its business operations to produce its products:

- labour – the employees who make the sandwiches
- capital – the rent paid for the shop and the money used to buy ingredients
- materials – the bread, fillings and packaging that are used to make the sandwiches.

When organising this transformation process, a business has to manage a number of issues.

- Productivity – a measure of the effectiveness with which a business produces its outputs (products and services). It is worked out by measuring the business's outputs (for example, the number of products made) divided by the business's inputs (for example, the number of hours worked by the workforce).
- Efficiency – how well a business limits the amount of waste that it produces. If a business can produce outputs while also reducing waste, such as damaged goods or wasted time, it will be more efficient and will have lower costs of production than less efficient competitors.
- Flexibility – a business's ability to change what it does to meet the needs of its customers, often in order to provide individual or **bespoke** products and services.
- Quality – how well a product or service does its job.

> ### Link it up
>
> Business operations are closely linked with what you learned about products and the design mix in the section 'Product' in Topic 2.2 *Making marketing decisions*.

> ### Key term
>
> **Bespoke:** designed and made for an individual customer.

> ### Activity ?
>
> 1 In small groups, identify some examples of businesses whose products or services are well-known for having one of the following characteristics:
>   **a** efficiency
>   **b** flexibility
>   **c** high quality.
> 2 How has each business achieved this characteristic?
> 3 What does this characteristic allow each business to do? For example, how does it affect the way in which they compete in their market?

> ### Link it up
>
> You have already learned about quality as a customer need in the section 'Customer needs' in Topic 1.2 *Spotting a business opportunity*. You will explore quality in more detail in 'Managing quality' later in this topic.

Production processes

Production processes or production methods refer to the different systems used by businesses to produce their products. The choice of production method will depend on the scale of production (how much of a product is being produced) and the characteristics of the product.

There are three main types of production process:

- job
- batch
- flow.

Job

Job production involves the production of one product (unit) at a time. Job production is used for making one-off bespoke products where each item is different. Job production normally requires a highly skilled workforce and a low level of **automation**, which means that this method of production is used to produce a product specific to an individual customer's needs and usually takes longer to produce every individual item than other production methods. Making one-off items means that the number of products produced is low. This means that every item produced has to make a high **profit margin**. This is why customised products are normally expensive.

Job production is common in the construction industry, because each construction project is customised to fit the environment and the preferences of the customer. For example, an extension to a customer's house is designed and built for that specific customer and is unlikely to be produced more than once.

The benefit of job production is that it is highly flexible. This means that the customer can be consulted about their requirements, so the product is more likely to meet the customer's requirements. It also means that job production is very good for building a positive relationship with customers as the business will communicate a lot with the customer and should produce something that perfectly meets the customer's individual needs.

Job production also has disadvantages. One disadvantage is that it requires highly trained employees who are skilled in a particular craft (such as dressmaking or painting), so these employees may be quite difficult to find. Such highly skilled employees may also demand higher wages or salaries than a low-skilled workforce. Finally, this kind of one-off creation of a product means that the business is unlikely to be able to achieve **economies of scale**. This is because the cost of the materials to make one unique product will be much higher than buying the same materials in bulk to make ten thousand products.

Batch

Batch production allows a business to produce products in relatively large production runs, with some of the work being done using automation. However, it also allows the business to be more flexible and vary the product being produced.

Even bespoke products that are unique to one individual customer might involve some aspects of batch production. For example, a wedding cake may be unique, but the cake mixture and icing might be made in larger batches and used to make and decorate a number of bespoke cakes.

Batch production has the advantage of allowing a business to be flexible because it can adjust the ingredients and materials in order to produce different varieties of its product. It also enables the business to get the benefit of reduced costs through production on a larger scale.

However, batch production does have disadvantages. For example, there is often **downtime** between batches where a business's rate of production falls.

Link it up

You learned about the high-margin and high-volume pricing strategies in the section 'Price' in Topic 2.2 *Making marketing decisions*.

Key terms

Automation: using machinery or robotics to do jobs instead of using people to do them.

Profit margin: the proportion of revenue left over after costs have been deducted.

Economies of scale: a situation where average costs (of production, distribution and sales, for example) fall as a business increases the amount of product that it produces, distributes and sells.

Downtime: time when a person or machine is not producing anything.

It is also difficult to anticipate demand when using batch production, which means that the business could experience wastage from overproducing its products or lose sales by failing to produce enough of a product.

Flow

Flow production takes place when a **standardised** product is produced on a large scale by a dedicated system. This normally involves a high degree of automation using machinery, robotics and computers. Flow production is also known as mass production. Flow production usually takes place in a factory or plant that is dedicated to making one single product. Products produced using flow production include televisions, tinned food and cars.

Flow production is used for products that are made and sold in large quantities, which means that a business using flow production can get the benefit of economies of scale and a low cost of production per product, which enables it to price its products more competitively. Higher levels of automation also mean that flow production involves more low-skilled workers, who are likely to be paid lower salaries than the skilled employees used in job production.

However, flow production has its downsides. The initial cost of the machinery and robotics required in many flow production facilities is very high and it can take a business a long time to pay back this money. Also, because flow production is dedicated to making a standardised product, it does not allow the business much flexibility in the variety of products that it can offer.

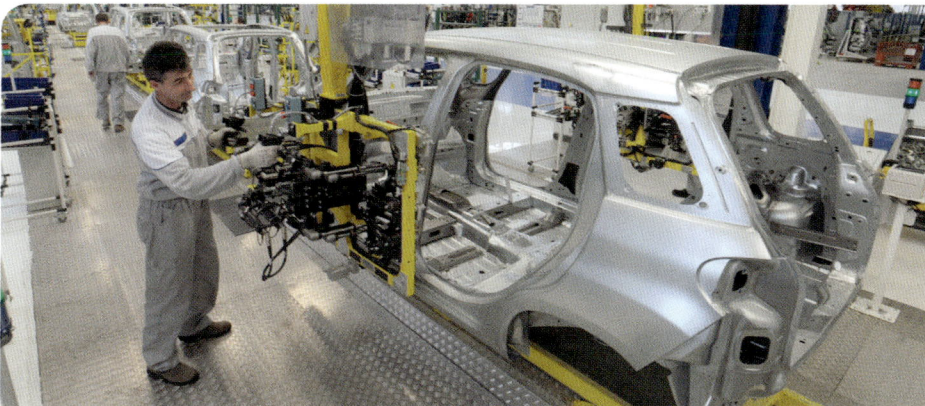

Flow production is used to produce large numbers of a single product

Exam-style question

Explain **one** benefit to a business of using a flow production process.

(3 marks)

Using a combination of production methods

In reality, a business may use job, batch and flow production in the production of one product. For example, some luxury car manufacturers will produce the body of a car using flow production, produce a variety of different components such as bumpers and trims using batch production, and finish the product off by using job production to personalise some features, such as printing the customer's name in the door sill or hand-stitching the leather seats.

Did you know?

Bread is a product that is normally produced in batches. In the UK, 328,000 tons of sliced bread is wasted every year.

Key term

Standardised: when every example of a product is exactly the same as the others.

Exam tip

Take a moment to reflect on what you know about the topic you are being asked about. For example, you know that flow production focuses on product standardisation and high-scale production. So what do you think this might allow a business to achieve when manufacturing its products?

Theme 2: Building the business

Activity ?

1 Look at the following products and decide which production method would be most appropriate for each one.
  a Pizza
  b Computers
  c Hand-painted pottery
  d Silk scarves
  e Smartphones
  f Doughnuts
  g A loft extension
2 Now think of two more products that would suit each of the three methods of production.

Key terms

Cost per unit: how much it costs to make each product or service, taking into consideration all of the variables.

Supply chain management (SCM): the management of the flow of goods and resources through the production process.

Link it up

You learned about cost per unit in the section 'Business revenues, costs and profits' in Topic 1.3 *Putting a business idea into practice*.

Although the three main methods of production are generally used when producing a physical product such as a car, they may also apply to the provision of a service. In general, most of the services that a business provides will fall into the category of job production. This is because a service is often specifically tailored to the needs of the customer. For example, a haircut is chosen by an individual customer for themselves and done for that customer. However, a business could standardise aspects of the service, such as the way in which customers pay, the process of consulting customers and follow-up satisfaction questionnaires.

The impact of technology on production

Technology such as manufacturing machinery and robotics is now widely used in many businesses' production processes. Using computers in the design and manufacturing process allows businesses to lower their **cost per unit**, while increasing their productivity, efficiency and the quality of their products.

Reducing costs

Computer-aided manufacturing (CAM) is commonly used in car production and other large-scale industries. CAM is very effective for manufacturing mass-produced products in a way that allows the business to gain economies of scale and reduce their production costs. Similarly, 3D printing now allows businesses to make products from plastics at very low costs. For example, businesses that produce medical implants can use 3D printing to make their products at a much lower cost than would have been possible using their traditional production process, meaning that these implants can also be sold at much lower prices than ever before.

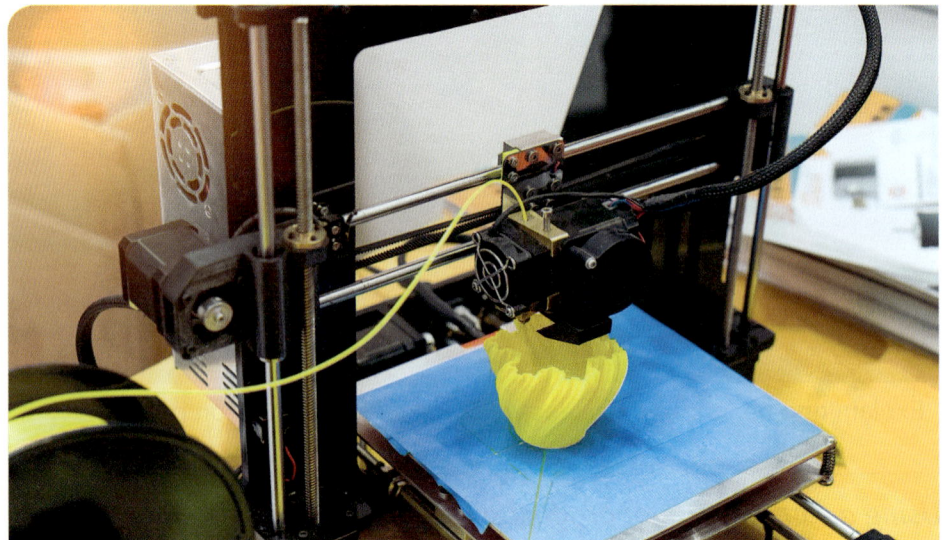

Can you think of any other potential advantages of 3D printing?

Improving productivity

Technology also helps a business to become more productive. For example, businesses often use a **supply chain management** (SCM) system that is integrated with the system used by their suppliers. This means that a business can easily co-ordinate the delivery of materials in time to meet customer demand. Another example of the way in which technology can make a business's production process more efficient is using barcode systems to monitor stock. This can help a business to prevent shortages of products or materials and avoid holding excess levels of stock, which prevents waste and maximises the business's productivity and profitability.

Improving quality

Technology can also help to improve the quality of a business's products or services. For example, a delivery company could improve its customer service by using GPS tracking to allow a customer to track the location of their order once it has been dispatched for delivery. This improves the quality of the business's customer service and improves the customer's experience of using the business. Similarly, communication technologies such as instant messenger allow mobile phone network providers to offer more customer support than they would be able to offer by only using the telephone.

Improving flexibility

A business can use technology to improve its flexibility, enabling it to improve the way in which it meets its customers' needs. A business could achieve this flexibility by being able to change the quantity of a product that it can make as well as the characteristics of each individual product. For example, an online bespoke curtain and blind business that operates an e-commerce site could offer its customers a wide range of options, such as producing curtains and blinds to their exact measurements and allowing them to choose from a wide range of fabrics. Similarly, in manufacturing, computer-based systems can cut, mould and shape many materials, allowing a business to offer customers a unique product at competitive prices.

Exam-style question ⚪

Discuss how a business might increase productivity by introducing new technology. **(6 marks)**

Exam tip ⚪

Wherever possible, try to give specific examples of businesses in your answers. This will show that you understand the concepts and ideas that you are discussing.

Activity ?

Choose a business and research the way in which it uses technology to:

a improve the quality of its products and services

b improve communication with its customers

c be more flexible in what it does

d be more efficient and increase its productivity.

Balancing cost, productivity, quality and flexibility

Technology can have a positive impact on a business's performance, increasing productivity, lowering costs and improving quality. However, introducing technology can also have negative aspects, as shown in Table 2.3.1.

Disadvantage	Description
Resistance to change	Some employees may not want to use new technology and may avoid using it.
Training costs	Employees need to be trained to use new technology. This costs money and takes up time that could be used more productively.
Cost of maintenance and updates	Technology used in production must be maintained and kept up to date to enable a business to compete with rival businesses.
Disruption	Introducing new technology can interrupt productivity while it is installed and while employees learn how to use it.
Excess information	New systems can make so much information available to employees that they cannot use it effectively. This can lead to wasted time.

Table 2.3.1 Disadvantages of introducing technology in a production process

As you have seen, technology can help a business achieve its operational objectives, including the need to balance the costs of production with productivity, quality and flexibility. However, the initial cost of introducing new technology can have a significant impact on a business's costs, so it must think carefully about the best time to invest in new technology.

Technology is a key part of production, particularly in flow production, and it can help a business to increase productivity and the scale of production. However, sometimes the use of technology can compromise the quality and flexibility of a business's products and services. For example, businesses can save money by operating online and reducing the need to employ sales staff in high street shops. However, this also removes the human interaction from the sales experience, and customers may value this interaction as part of a quality experience.

Checkpoint

Now it is time to review your understanding of business operations.

Strengthen

S1 Identify the three methods of production that a business might use.

S2 What are the benefits of batch production?

S3 Describe the impact that technology can have on production.

Challenge

C1 List the factors that may lead to a business choosing to adopt batch production over flow production.

C2 Using examples, discuss the issues that a business may face when introducing new technology to improve its productivity.

Working with suppliers

Case study

Spoilt for Choice

Spoilt for Choice is a sandwich shop in Lincoln that specialises in sandwiches and snacks made from local Lincolnshire produce. All the ingredients used in the sandwiches are organic and come from local growers and farms. Spoilt for Choice purchases its ingredients from 12 different suppliers, even though it could easily order similar ingredients from one or two large suppliers that sell ingredients sourced from all over the UK.

Activity

1 Why do you think using local Lincolnshire produce might be important to Spoilt for Choice?

2 Why might it be necessary for the business to use 12 different suppliers?

3 What issues do you think Spoilt for Choice might face when ordering ingredients from so many different suppliers?

The key to successful operations management is the **procurement** of stock from trusted and reliable suppliers. A good supplier will provide a business with products, raw materials or components in the right quantity, at the right time and of the right quality. If a supplier fails to do this, it can lead to:

- staff being unable to complete orders
- limited choice and variety for customers or no products at all
- loss of customers
- a poor reputation.

Suppliers are a crucial part of the business operations that enable a business to meet its customers' needs. As you learned in Topic 1.1, a business has to meet its customers' needs for quality, price, customer service and so on. However, a business can only meet its customers' needs if it can secure the same standards from its suppliers. For example, a business that receives low-quality raw materials from its suppliers can only produce low-quality products that may not meet its customers' needs. Similarly, a business that has unreliable suppliers that deliver stock late, or fail to deliver at all, is likely to give its customers an unreliable service.

Key term

Procurement: the process of managing a business's major purchases, from raw materials to delivery vans.

The role of procurement

Procurement is the process of a business sourcing and buying its stock, and it is a very important part of most businesses' operations. Even if a business makes its own products, it normally has to procure from another business the raw materials that it uses to make these products. The relationship between a business and its suppliers and the procurement decisions that the business makes can both have a huge impact on the performance of the business.

Relationships with suppliers

There are several factors that contribute to a business's relationship with its suppliers. These include:

- the cost of the materials or products being procured
- the delivery provided by the supplier, including the cost of delivery, the speed of delivery and the reliability of the delivery
- the quality of the materials or products that the business is procuring
- the availability of materials or products provided by the supplier
- the level of trust between the supplier and the business.

Cost is an important factor in procurement decisions, and a business should shop around to find the best deal. Businesses will often try to find the cheapest supplier as this will help the business to lower its **variable costs** and improve its profit margins. However, the cheapest supplier is not always the best. For example, the quality of its materials and products may be poor or its deliveries may not be reliable. This means that a business may be willing to pay higher costs for a supplier that it knows will be reliable, flexible and deliver high-quality stock.

The delivery offered by a supplier will have an impact on a business's procurement decisions. For example, a business may choose to use a supplier that offers cheap delivery. However, as with the cost of the materials or products themselves, this may have an impact on the quality of the delivery. This means that a business may pay more to ensure that a supplier provides fast, reliable delivery. Reliability is particularly important because it allows the business to guarantee that it will have the materials or products that it needs when customers want them.

Quality is a vital consideration when procuring materials or products. If a business knows that the stock it receives from a supplier is of a high quality, it knows that it is less likely to sell customers faulty products. This means that fewer products will be returned and customers are much more likely to be satisfied. On the other hand, if a supplier provides poor quality materials or products, customer satisfaction levels will fall and the business's reputation may suffer.

The availability of a supplier's stock is important to the businesses that it supplies. If a supplier cannot fulfil a business's order because it does not have enough of the materials or products that the business wants to buy, the business will be unable to meet its customers' needs and its reputation may suffer.

> ### Key term
>
> **Variable costs:** costs paid by a business that change depending on how many products or services the business sells.

All of this contributes to the relationship that a business has with its suppliers. If the business and supplier know that they can trust one another, both are likely to benefit from the relationship. The business knows that it is going to receive good quality products and materials when it needs them, and the supplier knows that the business is going to continue to make repeat purchases. This may even lead the supplier to offer the business favourable terms, such as lower prices and more flexible delivery or payment terms.

Some businesses draw up a contract with their suppliers known as a service-level agreement. This contract clearly states the level of service that the business expects its supplier to provide. This might include:

- a guaranteed timetable of regular deliveries
- the business's payment terms
- the level of quality required
- dispute settlement terms in case of any problems
- an agreement on quantities being ordered on a regular basis.

Because a service-level agreement sets everything out very clearly, this should help to create a positive working relationship between the business and supplier, because both sides know what is expected. Table 2.3.2 identifies some of the factors that a business may consider when drawing up a service-level agreement with its suppliers.

Issue	Questions to consider
Reliability	• Do the deliveries arrive on time? • Are the delivered orders correct? • Are there any faults with the materials or products?
Payment terms	• Does the supplier offer trade credit? • How and when do we need to pay?
Price	• Are the supplier's prices competitive? • What deals or discounts does the supplier offer for bulk purchases?
Capacity	• Can our suppliers meet our needs as our business expands? • Can the supplier be flexible if demand **fluctuates**?
Quality	• What level of quality do we need? • Does the level of quality provided meet our needs?

Table 2.3.2 Issues to consider when drawing up a service-level agreement

Exam-style question

Discuss the points that a small business owner should consider when choosing its suppliers. **(6 marks)**

Activity ?

You are planning on starting your own internet business. Your business will ship products to customers in a cardboard box that measures approximately 230 × 110 × 65 mm. You will also need to have these boxes printed with your business's logo and the product artwork.

1 Do some research to find two or three local businesses that could provide this service.

2 Imagine that your initial order is going to be for 1,000 boxes. Make a list of the key information that you would want to get from a supplier.

3 Compare the deal offered by the different businesses for this initial order.

4 If you were to choose one of these suppliers, which would you choose? Justify your decision.

Key term

Fluctuate: rise and fall in number or amount.

Exam tip

Remember to use appropriate business terminology about suppliers and supplier relationships in your answer. You could write down the terms that you want to use before answering the question.

The impact of logistics and supply decisions

Logistics is the organisation and transportation of goods. As you have learned, the logistics of getting materials and products from suppliers can affect a business's performance. The supply decisions that a business makes can have three main impacts on that business.

- **Costs** – for example, a well-organised logistics system can reduce transportation and packaging costs and limit the amount of stock that is lost or damaged.
- **Reputation** – for example, a business that manages its supply chain effectively may gain a reputation for providing a fast and efficient service.
- **Customer satisfaction** – for example, a business that can deliver a product or service in a fast, simple and flexible manner is likely to have the highest customer satisfaction ratings.

Managing stock

Stock is either the raw materials or ingredients that a business uses to make its products or the finished products that it has made or procured from a supplier. Stock can also include the raw materials, tools and ingredients that the business uses to deliver a service. For example, a beauty salon may stock a wide variety of hair and beauty products to provide its services.

You have already learned about how a business procures its stock from suppliers and how this can have an impact on costs, reputation and customer satisfaction. However, the way in which a business manages its stock once it has received it from a supplier is also very important.

A business that holds large quantities of stock is able to meet customer demand very easily. However, holding a lot of stock may also cost the business a lot of money. This can be because it will have to find space to store the stock, such as in a warehouse, and this can be expensive. This is because the money that it spends on stock that is not sold quickly cannot be used to cover other costs such as wages and rent.

Another stock management issue is that some materials or products are **perishable**, such as milk, or go out of fashion quite quickly, such as clothing. Businesses that sell these products have to be very careful that they do not keep too much stock, as it may go off or out of date if they cannot sell it in time.

An excess of stock is likely to cost the business a lot of money

Businesses can manage their stock in a number of ways. Two of the main methods used to manage stock are:

- bar gate stock graphs
- just-in-time stock control.

Bar gate stock graphs

A bar gate stock graph indicates the level of stock that a business is holding at any one time. These graphs can be used to make decisions about when new stock should be ordered and exactly how much stock a business should hold at any one time in order to meet its customers' needs. Figure 2.3.2 is a typical bar gate stock graph.

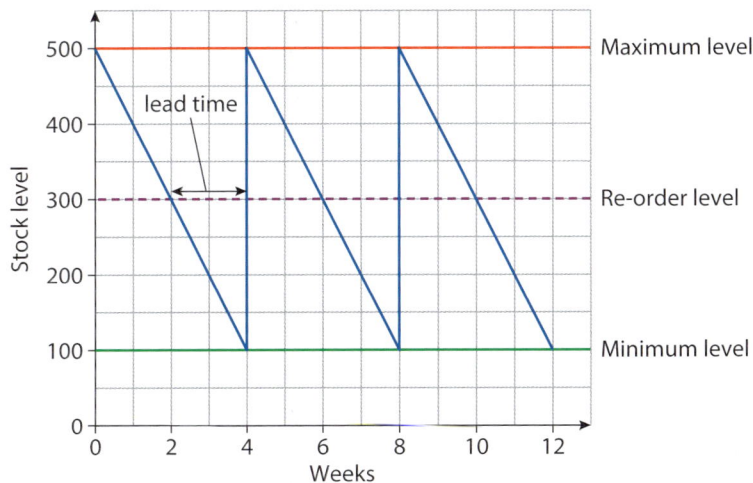

Figure 2.3.2 A typical bar gate stock graph

On a bar gate stock graph, the level of stock is represented on the vertical y-axis and the time period in weeks is represented on the horizontal x-axis. It shows four key pieces of information:

- the maximum stock level
- the minimum stock level
- the level of stock at which the business should order more stock
- the lead time.

Maximum stock level

Using Figure 2.3.2, you can see that this business has a maximum stock level of 500 units. This may be the limit of stock that it can physically hold in its warehouse. Alternatively, this could be the limit of stock that the business has set itself in order to avoid wasting stock and to ensure that it does not tie up too much cash in the amount of stock that it holds.

Minimum stock level

Bar gate stock graphs also show the business's minimum stock level, which is also known as the buffer stock level. The minimum stock level is the smallest amount of stock that the business can hold without running out of stock. Businesses set a minimum stock level in order to ensure that they have enough stock to meet customer demand and fulfil customers' orders.

> **Maths tip**
>
> Remember that the main 'zig-zag' line on a bar gate stock graph shows the level of stock held by the business. The horizontal lines represent important stock levels for that particular business.

Re-order level

The re-order level is the point at which the business orders more of that product. For example, in Figure 2.3.2, stock will be ordered when the level of stock falls below 300 units. In large supermarkets, stock levels are electronically recorded through the use of barcode readers, meaning that the stock-level figure for a product is automatically updated every time that product is bought by a customer and scanned using a barcode reader. When the supermarket stock management system recognises that the stock of that product has fallen below a certain level, new stock will automatically be ordered from the distribution centre.

Lead time

The lead time is the length of time between new stock being ordered and its delivery at the factory or shop. In Figure 2.3.2, you can see that the lead time for this business is two weeks (4 − 2 = 2 weeks). The lead time is a very important piece of information for a business. A long lead time will make it more difficult for a business to manage its stock. For example, most items shipped from China take around 6 weeks to reach the UK if transported by sea. In this case, a business in the UK must estimate its stock levels and place an order 6 weeks in advance to ensure that it has the stock when it needs it. In comparison, a short lead time makes it easier for a business to manage its stock. For example, a small greengrocer's business may be able to buy fruit and vegetables from its supplier the day before it wants to sell them in its shop.

Exam tip

In your exam, you may be asked to interpret a bar gate stock graph and use it to answer questions about a business. You will not be asked to draw one.

Exam-style question

Outline **one** piece of information shown on a bar gate stock graph. **(1 mark)**

Activity ?

Look at this bar gate stock graph, then answer the following questions.

1 What is the maximum stock level?

2 What is the buffer stock level?

3 Calculate the average weekly stock usage.

4 If the lead time is one week, calculate the re-order level.

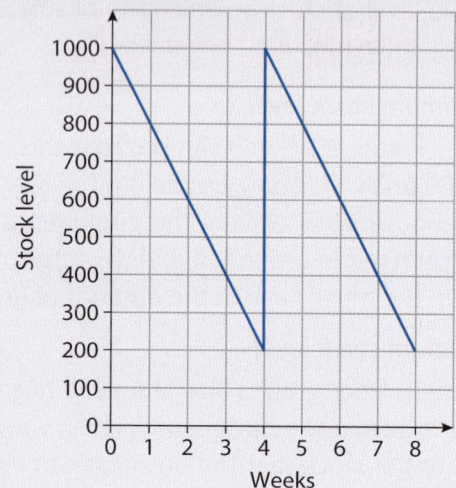

Just-in-time stock control

Some businesses may choose to procure stock only when they need it rather than holding stock in a warehouse. This method of stock control is called just-in-time stock control (JIT).

A business could choose to adopt just-in-time stock control in order to increase its efficiency and decrease its waste by receiving stock only at the point in the production process at which it is needed. However, this means that a business that uses just-in-time stock control has to be able to forecast customer demand very accurately. It also means that the business has to have a very good relationship with its suppliers, because any delivery delays could have a huge impact on the performance of the business.

Many large manufacturers that use hundreds of different components in their production processes choose to use just-in-time stock control. For example, if a customer orders a new car from a car manufacturer, the business's electronic supply system may automatically request the components that are needed from the suppliers. This sort of system can even ensure that the components only arrive precisely when they are needed. For example, the wheels for the new car should only arrive at the factory when the car is ready to have them put on.

The benefit of adopting just-in-time stock control is that it reduces the need for a business to hold expensive stock, meaning that the business has more cash available to cover other business costs and reducing the potential for stock to be damaged or misplaced. However, if the system fails, the business could be unable to fulfil its customers' orders, resulting in unhappy customers, a loss of business and damage to its reputation.

Did you know?

The global car manufacturer Toyota produces its cars using just-in-time stock management. A Toyota car can contain approximately 30,000 parts, which are supplied by more than 100 suppliers.

Exam tip

It might help you to think of an example when answering this question. However, you do not have to give an example for an 'explain' question. Just give one reason with two points of explanation that you can link together.

Exam-style question

Explain **one** reason why a business might use just-in-time stock control.

(3 marks)

Checkpoint

Now it is time to review your understanding of working with suppliers.

Strengthen

S1 Identify five things that a business may expect from a good supplier.

S2 What types of stock might a business hold? Give examples of each.

S3 Summarise the problems that a business might experience if it stores a lot of stock.

Challenge

C1 Using examples, explain two reasons why just-in-time stock control might not be suitable for a particular business or businesses.

C2 How do you think technology may be able to improve the way in which a business procures its stock?

Managing quality

Indigo Furniture

Indigo Furniture makes its furniture from European oak, Quebec pine and English leather that is tanned in Italy. The business still uses a water-powered mill that dates back to 1850 as its main workshop. Indigo's unusual chunky furniture is designed and handmade by a team of master craftsmen and every piece of its furniture has a 15-year guarantee.

Activity ?

1 What factors suggest that Indigo Furniture make high-quality products?
2 What do you think this level of quality allows Indigo Furniture to do with its prices?
3 How do you think this level of quality affects Indigo Furniture's ability to compete?

The concept of quality

Quality is usually defined as how well a product has been made, the purity of its ingredients or raw materials or how long it will last. A business's idea of quality should be defined by the customer, because a quality product or service is one that meets customer requirements.

Not all customers have the same needs, so their ideas of quality will vary. For example, one houseowner may be happy with a standard light bulb because it lights their room effectively, so they would see this as a quality product. However, another customer may want an energy-efficient light bulb that has a longer life expectancy than a standard light bulb, because this is their idea of a quality product. This means that you could define quality as meaning 'being fit for the customer's purpose'.

Activity ?

As a whole class group, choose ten different products that you can see in the room. These might be people's personal belongings or classroom furniture. Now complete the following tasks.

1 Working on your own, give each item a score out of 10 for quality, with 1 being very low quality and 10 being very high quality. If you can, you should hold and use the products before making your decision. Keep your scores to yourself.
2 Once the whole group has decided their scores, you should all share your scores for each product. Are they similar? Are there any big differences?
3 Discuss why you gave the scores you did and the factors that you think contributed to the product's quality. Did you all share the same opinion of quality?

For a product to be fit for the customer's purpose might just mean that the product does what it is supposed to do. For example, if a toaster toasts bread, it is fit for purpose. The components or materials used to make the product can also contribute towards its quality. For example, the quality of steel can vary, so a product made with high-quality steel is likely to be a high-quality product.

The quality of a product may also be influenced by the reputation of the product's brand. For example, a customer shopping for paint may choose to buy Farrow & Ball paint because of its brand reputation, rather than because they understand the actual quality of the paint compared to other brands. The quality of a product may have nothing to do with the actual materials, components or functionality of the product – instead, it has a lot do with the value that the customer thinks it has. Sometimes, customers may even judge that a product is high quality because it has a high price.

> ### Exam-style question ⬤
>
> Explain **one** factor that could reduce the quality of a product.   **(3 marks)**

A quality service is one that provides the level of value expected by a customer. This might be due to the way in which the business communicates with the customer through the sales process, because the quality of a service can be linked to customer service. For example, a customer visiting a five-star hotel would expect it to provide room service, valet parking and friendly, courteous employees.

There are two main ways in which the quality of a product or service can be assured:

- quality control
- quality assurance.

Quality control

Quality control is the process of checking the standard of a product's quality at the end of the production process. In a factory, this might be done by a supervisor who checks a certain number of products as they come off the production line. Quality control can also involve testing a product to ensure it meets a specific safety standard or to check that it does not break when it is used. Modern manufacturing businesses can use technology to test their products. For example, pottery can be inspected under ultraviolet (UV) lights to check whether there are any blemishes or cracks in the surface of the pottery.

For a service, quality control might involve an after-sales questionnaire or another way in which customers can provide feedback, so that the business can adjust its service in the future. Some businesses also use 'mystery shoppers' to check the quality of service provided to their customers. Alternatively, to get a more qualitative picture of its customer service, businesses may use a mystery shopper in order to understand what it is like to be a customer of their business. The mystery shopper will give feedback to the business about their experience, sometimes scoring sales employees on their customer service skills.

> ### Exam tip ⬤
>
> Remember that quality refers to how well a product does its job. What could prevent a product from doing this?

> ### Link it up ◥
>
> You will learn about the importance of the sales process to a business later in this topic.

Quality control is an important process as it can help a business to ensure that any faulty or sub-standard products are not sold to customers. However, quality control only stops a faulty product from reaching a customer, and the business will still have to repair or reproduce the product. This means that quality control does not help a business to reduce wastage. Instead, it only limits the number of faulty products that are actually sold to customers.

Businesses will check the quality of their products through quality control

Quality assurance

Quality assurance requires a business to take steps at every stage of the production process to ensure that it does not produce a faulty or sub-standard product, rather than producing some sub-standard products and only noticing the error at the end of the process.

Implementing quality assurance might mean that a business selects only the best possible suppliers who use or provide the best materials and carefully trains staff who are involved in the production process. As quality is the focus of every stage of the production process, it is far less likely that the product will need to be inspected using a quality control process at the end.

Quality assurance can be seen as a more advanced approach to achieving quality, as quality becomes the responsibility of everyone in the production process. However, implementing quality assurance can be very expensive and may mean that the business has to pass on these additional costs to its customers by charging higher prices. A business has to balance these additional costs against lower wastage and improved quality, depending on which is most important to that business and is most likely to give it a competitive advantage over its competitors.

The key differences between quality control and quality assurance are shown in Table 2.3.3.

Quality assurance	Quality control
Focused on improving the production process.	Focused on identifying defective products.
Establishes a good quality-management system.	Finds and eliminates problems.
Makes quality the responsibility of everyone in the production process.	Makes quality the responsibility of one person or one team in the production process.
Quality assurance is focused on the process.	Quality control is focused on the product.

Table 2.3.3 The differences between quality assurance and quality control

Exam-style question

Discuss the benefits to a business of using quality assurance. **(6 marks)**

Another way in which a business can guarantee that its products are high quality is by being accredited by a quality mark. A **quality mark** is recognition from a professional awarding body or government organisation that assesses the quality assurance processes used by a business. If the business achieves the standard set by the awarding body, it is permitted to use the quality mark logo on its products, packaging and promotional material. Quality marks include:

- **Kitemark** – awarded by the British Standards Institution, this is a quality mark given to products where safety is an important aspect of quality, such as bicycle helmets

- **Investors in People quality mark** – awarded to organisations that are committed to training and developing their employees and managing their staff well

- **CE mark** – given to products that comply with the essential requirements of European health, safety and environmental protection legislation.

Exam tip

Consider the difference between quality control and quality assurance. In particular, you may want to discuss how quality assurance may guarantee a higher standard of quality than quality control.

Key term

Quality mark: a standard of quality given to a business that is accredited by a professional body.

Activity

Consider the following industries:

a banking or the finance industry

b the restaurant and hospitality industry

c the children's toy industry.

For each industry, research the quality standards that exist within that industry. Once you have identified these standards, find two examples of businesses in each industry that carry the quality marks associated with their products and services.

The importance of quality

Quality is of great importance to businesses because it is a key consideration for customers purchasing a product or service. The level of quality perceived or experienced by the customer must match the value of the price they paid for it. A customer visiting a restaurant with an award for fine dining, like a Michelin star, may be willing to pay more than £200 for their meal if they believe that the quality of the food, the atmosphere of the restaurant and service provided by the staff justifies this price. However, if any of these factors do not meet the customer's quality expectations, they will not be happy to pay the same price. This means that, in order to achieve high quality, a business must understand its customer's needs and must be able to meet those needs with its products and services.

Quality can give businesses a **competitive advantage**. If a business is able to achieve a high level of quality while controlling its costs, this could provide it with a competitive advantage over its rivals.

Quality can also help a business to keep its costs under control. For example, consider a furniture manufacturer that finds that a lot of its furniture is failing its quality control checks. If it finds that this is because the furniture has been made from poor quality materials, it will have to spend a lot more money, either to ensure that it can repair and sell those products without making its customers unhappy or by scrapping those materials and finding another supplier.

> **Key term**
>
> **Competitive advantage:** an advantage a business has over its rivals that is unique and sustainable.

Checkpoint

Now it is time to review your understanding of managing quality.

Strengthen

S1 Summarise what factors may contribute towards the quality of a product or service.

S2 Summarise three differences between quality control and quality assurance.

S3 Why is quality important to a business?

Challenge

C1 Why might two people have a different opinion of a product's quality?

C2 Which is more important to a business: low prices or high quality?

The sales process

Case study

HSBC

The bank HSBC invests heavily in its UK-based customer service team. The call-centre process is designed to minimise waiting time, with employees aiming to answer calls within seconds. Employees are trained to deliver excellent service and all calls are monitored. After a call, customers receive a text message asking them for feedback about whether HSBC met their needs and expectations.

Activity ?

1 Why do you think HSBC invests so much in its call centre and customer service team?

2 Why is it important for a business to gather feedback from its customers?

3 Do you think that delivering excellent service always improves a business's profits?

The sales process

Operations management is not just about producing products and services. It also focuses on the process by which the business delivers the product to its customers. This includes the sales process outlined in Figure 2.3.3.

The sales process is represented as a circular process. This is because a business that manages the sales process well should receive customer loyalty and repeat purchases from its customers. The sales process may be different for different types of product, but it usually follows this model. In order for a business's sales process to succeed, a business must have effective processes, systems and procedures in place, as well as employing staff who are able to provide a personal friendly service.

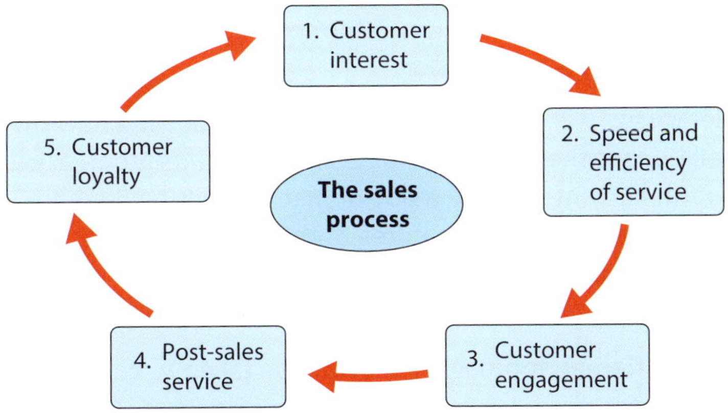

Figure 2.3.3 The sales process

Exam-style question ○

Explain **one** method that a business could use to attract the interest of a customer.   **(3 marks)**

Exam tip ○

Give one reason and develop that reason. The development of your answer could be an explanation of the cause or consequence of attracting the interest of a customer.

Activity ?

Consider the following examples of products.

a A pair of trainers

b A family skiing holiday

Describe how each stage of the sales process might differ between the two products.

Theme 2: Building the business

Link it up

You learned about marketing in Topic 2.2 *Making marketing decisions*.

Customer interest

At the first stage of the sales process, a business must make a customer interested in its product or service. This is often achieved through marketing. Marketing techniques that a business can use to get a customer's attention include:

- branding
- sponsorship
- advertising
- sales promotions and special offers.

Product knowledge

Another way in which a customer's interest can be attracted is through the product knowledge of a good sales employee. For example, a car salesperson may be able to talk knowledgably about the technical features of a new car and be able to give detailed answers to customers' questions. Sales staff with a high level of product knowledge are more likely to gain customers' interest and trust, both of which are very important in the sales process.

A high level of product knowledge may also add value to the product, especially where sales staff are in contact with customers throughout the sales process. For example, an architect with a high level of knowledge about structures, building regulations and construction techniques can help their customers to make better and more informed decisions about the design of their building or property extension.

A good salesperson will gain customer interest by showing how the product's features will benefit the customer. For example, a waterproof jacket may have underarm air vents and be made of machine-washable material. A salesperson will present these features to the customer as benefits: the coat will not be too hot in warmer weather and it will be easy to wash.

Sales approaches

There are two different approaches that can be taken to gain customer interest.

- **Hard approach** – sales employees actively approach and engage customers. They will do this in order to talk to them about the business's products in an attempt to encourage the customer to buy the product.
- **Soft approach** – sales employees make customers aware that they are available if the customer needs any information or support in making a purchase, but let the customer look through the products on their own.

Neither approach is necessarily better than the other. However, the suitability of each approach depends on the preferences of the customers and the nature of the product being sold.

Speed and efficiency of service

A speedy and efficient service is the next step in the sales process and it is vital for a business to get this right. Some customers may decide not to buy a product if it takes too long for that product to be made and delivered.

This means that it is important for a business to have a production facility that is flexible in order to meet customers' needs. Some businesses may offer a faster service by having their own delivery or installation teams. If similar products are sold by two different businesses for similar prices, a customer may choose which business to buy from based on the speed and convenience of the business's delivery service.

Efficiency is also important, as a complicated purchasing process can easily put customers off. Businesses that operate online (**e-tailers**) will try to make their websites as user-friendly as possible, meaning that customers have to take very few steps in order to place their order. If a business's website is difficult to use, customers are unlikely to buy from that business. Similarly, **retailers** also have to work hard to provide customers with an efficient service, such as reducing the length of queues at the till, installing self-service checkouts and ensuring that customers telephoning do not have to wait long to have their call answered.

Customer engagement

Customer engagement is the interaction between the business and the customer during the sales **transaction**. For some products, such as chocolate bars, this stage of the sales process may be less important because the customer has limited interaction with the business or salesperson. However, for some products, customer engagement is very high, with the customer interacting with the business on several different occasions. For example, the process of buying a house or a car could involve multiple interactions with an estate agent or car dealership throughout the sales process. Similarly, if the customer is buying a product that is highly customised, such as a tailor-made suit, customer engagement will also be a very important part of the sales process.

In situations where customer engagement is high, it is important for the business to have a highly skilled team of employees who are able to build positive relationships with customers and solve any customer problems. The level of service that a business provides throughout the sales process will have a significant impact on overall customer satisfaction.

Post-sales service and customer feedback

The post-sales service is the support given by a business to its customers after customers have bought the product or service. In many cases, this involves a customer needing support in using the product, such as a computer. It can also involve dealing with a complaint, where the product is faulty or does not meet the customer's expectations.

Other businesses treat the post-sales service as part of the product that they sell. For example, Barbour is a business that manufactures waxed coats and jackets. Customers can send their coat away to Barbour to be re-waxed or repaired in order to maintain their coat's waterproof features and condition. Similarly, jewellers and watchmakers may offer an annual clean or service for their products. Offering this sort of post-sales service

Link it up

In the section 'Place' in Topic 2.2 *Making marketing decisions*, you learned about the differences between e-tailing and retailing, including the factors that a business has to consider when selling its products through a website.

Key terms

E-tailing: retailing to customers through the internet, such as though an e-commerce website.

Retailing: selling products or services to customers – in this case, in a physical shop.

Transaction: the act of buying or selling something.

Activity

1 Choose two products or services that are sold by two different e-tailers. Visit these e-tailers' websites and give them a score out of 10 for each of the following features.

   a Appearance

   b Ease of use

   c Ability to complete a purchase (though you should not actually buy anything)

   d Availability of information

2 Explain which of the two websites you think is the best. How do you think this might affect the sales process of each business?

Customer engagement can be a very important part of the sales process

will cost the business money, but it may be worth the expense if it means that customers choose to buy from the business and then continue to buy from it.

Businesses often ask customers to give them feedback following a sale so that they know how to improve their sales process for the future. Businesses may use various approaches to collect feedback, such as online questionnaires and suggestion boxes in shops. This feedback may include information about how satisfied the customer was with the service and how the business could improve its products or services.

Customer loyalty

Businesses that manage the sales process effectively are more likely to gain a competitive advantage over their rivals. Satisfied customers who have a good experience with a business are also more likely to be loyal to that business's brand. This can encourage them to become a repeat customer. For many businesses, it is far better to retain existing customers than to attract new ones.

Did you know?

On average, a loyal customer is thought to be worth up to 10 times as much as their first purchase from a business.

Exam-style question

Outline **one** reason for a business to collect feedback from its customers.

(2 marks)

The importance of providing good customer service

Good customer service is a key operational factor that has to be managed by a business. It is very important for a business to meet and exceed customer expectations. Because customer expectations differ between different industries, a business must understand its customers and their expectations.

Many things can contribute to a business providing good customer service, and different customers can value different aspects of good customer service. The checklist in Figure 2.3.4 lists some of the aspects of customer service that contribute to the quality of customer service offered by a business.

- ☑ Is honest
- ☑ Meets legal standards
- ☑ Sells products that are free from defects
- ☑ Sets prices that reflect value and service
- ☐ Delivers on time
- ☑ Provides good communication throughout the sales process
- ☑ Has friendly and helpful employees
- ☐ Deals with problems quickly and properly
- ☑ Provides good after-sales service
- ☐ Exceeds customer expectations

Figure 2.3.4 The ways in which a business provides good customer service

A business may adopt a number of **quantitative metrics** to measure customer service. For example, a business may measure the length of time that it takes for sales employees to handle a sale, the number of enquiries handled and resolved by call-centre staff or the number of complaints in a given time period.

Alternatively, to get a more **qualitative** picture of its customer service, businesses may use a system such as a 'mystery shopper', where an employee acts as a customer in order to assess the quality of customer service provided. The mystery shopper gets first-hand experience of what it is like to be a customer of their business. They then give feedback to the business about their experience, sometimes scoring sales employees on their customer service skills.

The quality of a business's customer service can be used to help a business to **differentiate** its products and services from those offered by its rivals. Often, customers are willing to pay more for a product or service if they know that the business offers excellent customer service and employs knowledgeable and experienced staff who can answer questions and deal with problems quickly and effectively. This can help the business to retain customers, increase sales and maximise its profits.

Key terms

Quantitative: concerning the quantity or amount of something that can be measured in numbers.

Metric: a standard of measurement.

Qualitative: concerning the quality of something that cannot be measured in numbers.

Differentiate: show that something (in this case, a product) is different from similar things.

Activity ?

Below are examples of two services you could buy.

- A train journey to London
- An eye test at an opticians.

1 For each service, make a list of five or more things that you think would contribute to good customer service.

2 Rank the items of both lists in order of importance. Are the things in the same order for both services?

Link it up

You learned about product differentiation in the section 'Product' in Topic 2.2 *Making marketing decisions*.

Checkpoint

Now it is time to review your understanding of the sales process.

Strengthen

S1 List the different stages of the sales process.

S2 Describe why it is important for sales staff to have good product knowledge.

S3 Why is customer engagement more important for some products than others?

Challenge

C1 Can you think of an example in which customer service has little importance in the sales process?

C2 What do you think is the most important factor for a business to achieve good customer service?

C3 How do you think training its employees might enhance a business's sales process?

2.3 Making operational decisions

1   Which **one** of the following is not shown on a bar gate stock graph?   (1 mark)

    Select **one** answer.

    ☐ A Lead time

    ☐ B Reorder level

    ☐ C Minimum stock level

    ☐ D Break-even point

2   Explain **one** factor that a manufacturer may have to consider when choosing a production method.

    (3 marks)

Student answer

When deciding which production method to use, a manufacturer may consider the scale of production and the price it can sell each product for. If the business needs to make large quantities of a standardised product, they might choose to use a different method to a company who make small amounts of a product.

Verdict

The student identifies two relevant factors that may contribute to a business's choice of production method ('scale' and 'price'), even though they only need to give **one** factor. The student goes on to explain the reason why 'scale' affects the business's decision, but they do not show a connection between this and actual production methods, such as continuous flow production.

Read the following extract carefully, then answer Questions 3 and 4.

Blue Whale Spa is a British hot tub manufacturer with a manufacturing plant in China. Blue Whale Spa uses premium American suppliers for the electrical and mechanical components of its hot tubs. Its suppliers include Balboa, which is the industry leader in hot tub pumps. Blue Whale Spa focuses on producing competitively priced and high-quality products using the latest technology.

Blue Whale Spa directly handles every aspect of its hot tubs. It does its own research and designs, and manufactures its own hot tubs, installs them and provides its own post-sales service, including an annual service.

The business ensures that it provides the highest quality hot tubs by meeting and exceeding all European standards for quality and safety. Blue Whale Spa also offers all of its customers a 2-year warranty on electrical parts and 10-year warranty on the shell of their Blue Whale Spa hot tub.

3 Outline **one** reason why Blue Whale Spa may have chosen an industry-leading business to supply its hot tub parts.

(2 marks)

Student answer

Blue Whale Spa may have chosen an industry leader to supply its hot tub parts because they may be more reliable. Being an industry leader means that they are well established and successful, therefore less likely to have faulty pumps. As a result, this means that the parts that go into Blue Whale Spa hot tubs are more reliable and it is less likely that customers will have to claim on the 2-year warranty that Blue Whale Spa give all customers on electrical parts.

Verdict

This is an excellent answer. However, the student has written far too much for an 'outline' question. To gain both marks, one reason would need identifying with some development of the reason in the context of the Blue Whale Spa.

4 Evaluate the importance to Blue Whale Spa of providing excellent post-sales service. You should use the information provided as well as your knowledge of business.

(12 marks)

Student answer

A hot tub can be an expensive purchase and many customers will invest a lot of time engaging with a business in order to buy one. Customers would probably expect a hot tub to last over 10 years and for this it is important that they are looked after, like regular servicing which is part of Blue Whale Spa's post-sales service. Providing excellent post-sales service will ensure that customers are happy with their purchase because will have any problems resolved if their hot tub breaks down. If customers are happy then this could lead to them recommending Blue Whale Spa to friends and this might result in them selling other hot tubs.

Post-sales service is also a way to get a competitive advantage over competitors. If customers are happy with the service they received, they may be willing to post positive reviews online. When looking for a hot tub, customers may see these positive reviews and choose to buy a hot tub from them instead of other manufacturers. Especially if the designs, quality and prices are very similar.

Overall, post-sales service is very important for a business like Blue Whale Spa where the products they sell will need maintenance. Also providing excellent post-sales service is one way that they can differentiate their brand.

Verdict

This is a good answer. The student develops several reasons as to why post-sales service is important for Blue Whale Spa and refers to information from the extract. The student also gives a conclusion that makes a judgement based on the key points they have discussed. However, this answer is not balanced. The student needs to show an understanding of the disadvantages of post-sales service, such as the expense of providing it, or refer to some other factor that is also important to Blue Whale Spa's success.

Theme 2: Building a business

Topic 2.4 Making financial decisions

Topic overview

This topic considers the tools that a business can use to support its financial decision-making, including gross profit, net profit and the average rate of return, and the use and limitation of a range of financial information.

Case study

Whitbread

Whitbread is a large hospitality company that owns a range of well-known restaurant, hotel and coffee shop chains including Premier Inn and Costa Coffee. In 2016, Whitbread announced that its sales and profits had risen thanks to increased sales at Costa Coffee and Premier Inn. Its sales increased by 1.9 per cent, while its pre-tax profit rose by 5.4 per cent to £307 million.

The business believes that Costa Coffee still has potential to expand. However, exchange rates mean that the cost of coffee will rise. The business buys its coffee in US dollars, meaning that the weak pound will have an impact on the business's costs, although Whitbread is prepared for this.

Whitbread's chief executive, Alison Brittain, said that Costa Coffee's success is based on the fact that its products and service offer great value for money, and that the business would continue focus on that in the future.

Both Costa Coffee and Premier Inn were affected by the introduction of the National Living Wage. This is a new minimum wage for employees over the age of 25, which was introduced nationwide in 2016. At its launch, the National Living Wage was £7.20 per hour. This had a considerable impact on Whitbread's labour costs, particularly as Whitbread chose to introduce the new higher wage before it needed to, in October 2015.

By April 2017, the business plans to open another 230–250 Costa Coffee shops internationally and 3,700 new Premier Inn rooms in the UK.

Activity ?

In pairs or small groups, discuss the following questions.

1 Which is more important to Whitbread: its sales or pre-tax profit?
2 What strategies could Whitbread use to maximise its profits?
3 How might a business like Whitbread reinvest its profits?

Your learning

In this topic you will learn about:

- business calculations – the concept and calculation of gross profit and net profit, and the calculation and interpretation of the gross profit margin, the net profit margin and the average rate of return
- understanding business performance – the use and interpretation of quantitative business data to support, inform and justify business decisions, and the use and limitations of financial information.

Business calculations

Apple

In 2016, Apple's iPhone® sales started to decline. In October 2016, the business forecast that its profit margin would be smaller than previously expected, even though Christmas was approaching. It announced that it expected sales in China to improve, even though its revenue in China fell almost 30 per cent in the previous three months. Despite the launch of the improved iPhone 7, some people began to suggest that Apple had lost its technological advantage over its competitors.

Activity ?

1 What is the relationship between sales and profit?
2 How might Apple respond to the financial information in this case study?
3 What other information might Apple use to understand its overall business performance?

Link it up

In Topic 1.3 you explored the concept of profit in the section 'Business aims and objectives' and learned to calculate profit in the section 'Business revenues, costs and profits'.

Gross profit and net profit

As you have learned so far, profit is a key objective for most businesses and is an incentive for entrepreneurs to start new businesses. Profit is the financial reward for business owners and can be reinvested to promote business growth.

profit = total revenue – total costs

A business can increase its profits in two ways:

- increasing revenue
- lowering costs.

This principle is true of all businesses and is demonstrated in Figure 2.4.1. For example, in order to increase its revenue, a business could increase its advertising in order to attract more customers or introduce a special offer to boost its sales. Alternatively, it could lower its variable costs by negotiating better deals with its suppliers or cutting its fixed costs by reducing the number of employees.

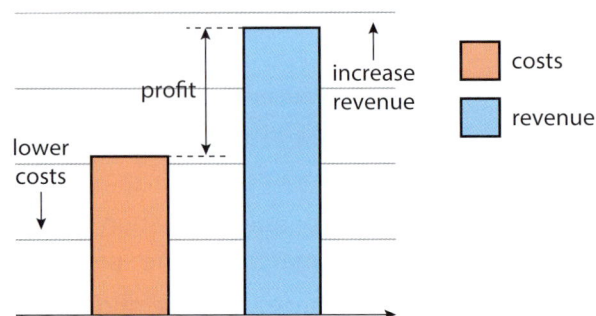

Figure 2.4.1 The two methods of increasing profit

However, in reality, these decisions are not simple and efforts to improve profitability can actually have disadvantages for other areas of the business. For example, if a business increases its advertising in an attempt to increase its revenue, a successful campaign may bring in sales that total many times the cost of advertising but an unsuccessful campaign is likely to cost more than the value of any extra revenue brought in. Similarly, a business that reduces the size of its workforce in order to lower its fixed costs could also lower its productivity, meaning that any gain made from lowering its costs would be cancelled out by lost revenue because of lower productivity.

In order to have a more precise understanding of its profits and performance, a business will calculate two different levels of profit: gross profit and net profit.

Gross profit

Gross profit is the profit that a business makes after deducting the costs associated with making and selling its products, or the costs associated with providing its services:

gross profit = sales revenue – cost of sales

This is demonstrated in Figure 2.4.2.

The **cost of sales** is the accumulated total of all costs used to create the product or service that has been sold. It is also known as the cost of goods. The cost of sales might include the cost of purchasing the goods that the business has sold. Alternatively, if the business makes its own goods, the cost of sales might include the direct costs of manufacturing and the wages of the employees who make the product. For example, in a small takeaway restaurant, the cost of sales includes the ingredients of the food, the packaging and the wages of the employees who make the food.

The owners of a business will calculate gross profit because it gives the business a good indication of how well it generates profit from its trading activities. In the case of the takeaway restaurant, a gross profit calculation would show how much profit the business is able to generate from selling its food.

> **Key term**
>
> **Cost of sales:** the direct costs of purchasing raw materials and manufacturing finished products.

Sales revenue

↓ minus

Cost of sales
(raw materials, packaging, direct wages)

↓ equals

Gross profit

Figure 2.4.2 The gross profit calculation

> **Exam-style question**
>
> Using the information below, calculate the gross profit for the business. You are advised to show your workings. **(2 marks)**
>
> - Total sales: 350 units
> - Total cost of sales: £27,000
> - Price per unit: £145

> **Exam tip**
>
> When answering a calculation question, start by writing down the formula you should use and then put in all the relevant figures. This should help you to avoid making simple mistakes.

> **Maths tip**
>
> You can use a calculator, but you should always show your workings.

Theme 2: Building the business

Net profit

Net profit is the amount of profit left over after all other indirect costs have been taken away from gross profit. These costs are also known as operating costs and include managers' salaries, the rent or mortgage paid for business's premises and interest on loans.

Net profit = gross profit — other operating expenses and interest

This is demonstrated in Figure 2.4.3.

Sales revenue
minus
Cost of sales
(raw materials, packaging, direct wages)
equals
Gross profit
minus
Operating costs
(salaries, rent, insurance, advertising)
equals
Net profit

Figure 2.4.3 The net profit calculation

Businesses consider net profit to be the most important measure of profitability because this is what is actually left over after all other expenses have been deducted. This means that it is the amount of money that can be returned to the owners or shareholders of a business or reinvested back into the business to stimulate growth.

A business will compare its gross profit and net profit over time in order to work out how well different areas of the business have performed. Gross profit enables the owners of a business to understand how much profit has been generated from its products or services, while net profit helps them to understand how well the business has managed the expenses or running of the business.

Using profit as a measure of performance

Calculating total revenue minus total costs gives you the total profit made in a given time period. Calculating gross profit and net profit gives you a more precise understanding of how that profit was generated. However, this is not necessarily the best way to measure the performance of a business.

Look at Table 2.4.1. This business has made more net profit in 2016 than in 2015, so it seems that the business has performed better in 2016. However, this table does not tell you how this profit compares to the revenue made in each year and how effectively the business has managed its costs.

Activity ?

Draw a table with two columns and eight rows. Label one column 'gross profit' and the other column 'net profit'. Now put the financial terms below into the table, separating them into the different columns by deciding which measure of profit they are used to calculate.

a Raw materials

b Salaries

c Rent

d Wages

e Distribution

f Tax

g Packaging

h Advertising

i Insurance

	2015	2016
Net profit	£2.7 million	£3 million

Table 2.4.1 Net profit of a business over 2 years

Now look at Table 2.4.2. Does it still look like the business has performed better in 2016? In 2015, the business generated 61p of net profit from every £1 of sales revenue. In comparison, in 2016, the business only generated 53p worth of net profit from every £1 of sales revenue. Although sales revenue and profit were higher in 2016, the business was more effective at generating profit from its sales in 2015.

	2015	**2016**
Net profit	£2.7 million	£3 million
Sales revenue	£4.4 million	£5.6 million

Table 2.4.2 Net profit and sales revenue of a business over two years

Exam-style question

Using the information below, calculate the net profit for the business. You are advised to show your workings. **(2 marks)**

- Interest on loans: £20,000
- Salaries: £400,000
- Other operating costs: £320,000
- Gross profit: £1,200,000

Exam tip

When answering a 'calculate' question, start by writing down the formula you should use and then put in all the relevant figures. The calculation may involve multiple steps.

Calculating and interpreting profit margins and average rate of return

As you have seen, a business's performance can be assessed using net profit and gross profit. However, other measures can also be used to evaluate a business's performance, including profit margins and the average rate of return.

Profit margins

The **profit margin** is the profit made as a proportion of sales revenue. By comparing gross profit and net profit to sales revenue, you can calculate two effective measures of performance:

- gross profit margin
- net profit margin.

Gross profit margin

Gross profit is the difference between sales revenue and the cost of sales. The gross profit margin (GPM) helps a business to measure its gross profit as a percentage of its sales:

$$\text{gross profit margin (\%)} = \frac{\text{gross profit}}{\text{sales revenue}} \times 100$$

The gross profit margin is calculated as a percentage. A business with a gross profit margin of 72 per cent means that, for every £1 of sales it makes, 72p is gross profit.

Key term

Profit margin: a measure of profitability calculated as a percentage of revenue.

Theme 2: Building the business

Net profit margin

Net profit is the difference between sales revenue and total costs. The net profit margin (NPM) helps a business to measure its net profit as a percentage of its sales:

$$\text{net profit margin (\%)} = \frac{\text{net profit}}{\text{sales revenue}} \times 100$$

The net profit margin is also calculated as a percentage. A business with a net profit margin of 12 per cent means that, for every £1 of sales it makes, 12p is net profit. Net profit is more important than gross profit because it is the calculation of the actual profit generated by the business.

These profit margins are often used together to identify whether a business is succeeding. For example, if the gross profit margin is increasing but the net profit margin is falling, then the business can identify that it is not controlling its operating costs. The gross profit margin and net profit margin are most effective as measures of performance when they are tracked over a period of time. This trend can then be used to indicate how well a business has performed from one year to the next.

Figure 2.4.4 shows the gross profit margin and net profit margin calculated for a business over a 5-year period. The business should be pleased that its gross profit margin is on an upward trend. This indicates that the profit generated from selling its products or services is rising and the business is able to control its direct costs. This might also suggest that the business has been able to increase revenue without having to incur additional direct costs. However, the business's net profit margin has remained consistent over the past 5 years. As you can see that the net profit margin has not improved between Year 4 and Year 5 in the same way as the gross profit margin has done, you could assume that the business's operating costs have risen. This means that this business might want to look for ways to cut back on its overheads.

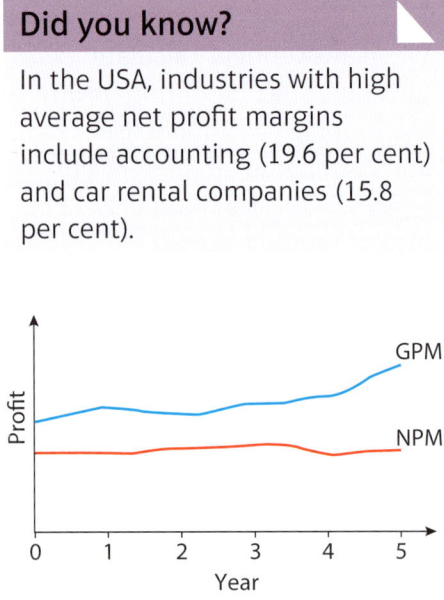

Figure 2.4.4 Comparing profit margins

Exam tip

You may find that you have been given additional information that is not required to calculate the correct answer. Make sure you highlight the information that you need before working out your answer. In this example, the figures from 2016 are not needed to answer this question.

Exam-style question

Using the information in Table 2.4.3, calculate the business's net profit margin for 2015. You are advised to show your workings. **(2 marks)**

	2015	**2016**
Gross profit	£2.9 million	£3.1 million
Sales revenue	£4.7 million	£5.35 million
Indirect costs	£1.1 million	£2.4 million
Net profit	£1.8 million	£700,000

Table 2.4.3

Activity ?

Identify two large public limited companies that operate in the same industry and use their websites to find their most recent sets of financial accounts. This information may be in their annual report.

1 Using these accounts, find out the businesses':

   a sales revenue / turnover

   b gross profit

   c net profit (may be shown as operating profit, pre-tax profit or profit after tax)

2 Using this information, calculate the gross profit margin and net profit margin for each business.

3 Based on this information, decide which of the two companies performed best over the past year.

4 Are you surprised by the results? Can you think of any reasons why one business might have performed better than the other?

5 What other information might you need in order to make a judgement on the success of these two businesses?

Average rate of return

When making investment decisions, the owners of a business will consider the potential profit that an investment will make for the business. As a business can invest money in a variety of ways, such as in a new advertising campaign or in a new piece of machinery, its owners use the average rate of return to compare the potential profitability of different investments.

The average rate of return is the average annual amount of income generated over the life of an investment. This rate is calculated by averaging all of the business's expected cash flows and dividing this average by the number of years that the investment is expected to last:

$$\text{average rate of return (\%)} = \frac{\text{average annual profit (total profit} \div \text{number of years)}}{\text{cost of investment}} \times 100$$

For example, an investment in a new factory is expected to generate returns of £22,000 in Year 1, £32,000 in Year 2 and £36,000 in Year 3. The average of this amount is calculated by:

$$\frac{\text{total profit}}{\text{number of years}} = \text{average annual profit}$$

$$\frac{£22,000 + £32,000 + £36,000}{3} = £30,000$$

The initial investment was £300,000, so the average rate of return is calculated by:

$$\frac{\text{average annual profit}}{\text{cost of investment}} \times 100$$

$$\frac{£30,000}{£300,000 \text{ investment}} \times 100 = 10\%$$

Using this method allows a business to compare the expected return on different investment decisions.

Table 2.4.4 compares two different investment decisions for a manufacturing business.

Option 1: Purchase a new piece of machinery.

Option 2: Extending the factory.

Year	Net cash flow (£)	
	Option A: New machinery	**Option B: Extend factory**
0	(£600,000)	(£1 million)
1	£200,000	£300,000
2	£300,000	£300,000
3	£200,000	£300,000
4	£100,000	£300,000
5	£50,000	£300,000
6	£20,000	£200,000

Table 2.4.4 Potential investment forecasts for a manufacturing business

The average rate of return for Option A can be calculated by:

average annual profit =

$$\frac{200,000 + 300,000 + 200,000 + 100,000 + 50,000 + 20,000}{6} = £145,000$$

average rate of return (%) =

$$\frac{£145,000}{£600,000} \times 100 = \textbf{24.2\%}$$

The average rate of return for Option B can be calculated by:

average annual profit =

$$\frac{300,000 + 300,000 + 300,000 + 300,000 + 300,000 + 200,000}{6} = £283,333$$

average rate of return (%) =

$$\frac{£283,333}{£1,000,000} \times 100 = \textbf{28.3\%}$$

Link it up

As you learned in the section 'Business revenues, costs and profits' in Topic 1.3 *Putting a business idea into practice*.

Using the average rate of return, the business can identify that it would be more profitable to invest in extending its factory because, on average, this investment should generate 4.1 per cent more every year as a percentage of the initial investment. However, the business also has to consider the fact that the initial investment of extending the factory is £400,000 more expensive than investing in the new piece of machinery.

You can see that the average rate of return is a useful financial measure for a business to use. However, one of its limitations is that it does not account for the time value of money. **Inflation** generally means that the value of £1 today will be worth more than £1 in 2 years' time, which means that businesses would prefer to receive cash inflows from their investment sooner rather than later. Cash flows in later periods are worth less than cash flows in more recent periods, and the average rate of return does not take this fact into account.

Key term

Inflation: the general increase in prices over time.

Case study

Land Rover

In 2016, Land Rover announced that it would launch a new version of the Land Rover Discovery. Before making the decision to launch a new product, Land Rover will have forecast the average rate of return over the lifespan of the new model.

Activity ?

In small groups, discuss what other information you think a car manufacturer might consider when making decisions about investing in the design and production of a new vehicle. Try to identify at least five pieces of information that the business is likely to consider.

Exam-style question ⬤

Using the information in Figure 2.4.5, calculate the total net cash flow for Investment A and for Investment B. You are advised to show your workings. **(3 marks)**

Exam tip ⬤

When you are asked to interpret charts and graphs, it is useful to use space in your answer booklet to calculate your workings. For example, in your answer to this question, you could add up the annual net cash flows totals represented by Investments A and B over the 5-year period.

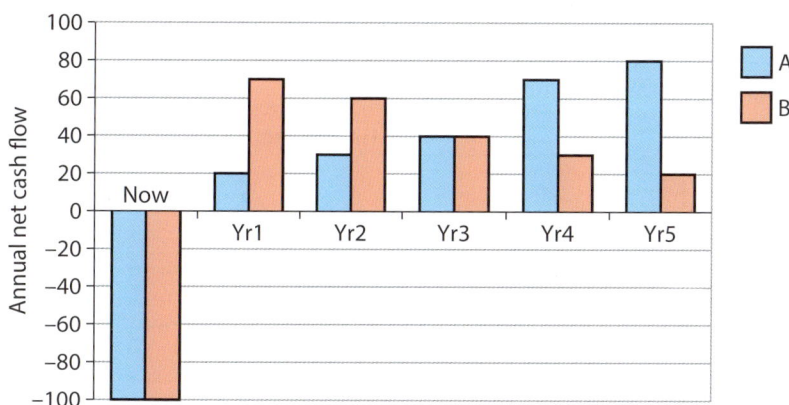

Figure 2.4.5 Net cash flow of investments A and B

Link it up

You learned how to calculate net cash flow in the section 'Cash and cash flow' in Topic 1.3 *Putting a business idea into practice*.

net cash flow = cash inflows − cash outflows in a given period

Theme 2: Building the business

Understanding business performance

Case study

Vintage Collection

Vintage Collection manufactures hand-made luxury teddy bears, mainly for toy enthusiasts and collectors. The bears are produced in small batches and handmade to a high standard of quality. The average production run of each design is 3,000 units. However, sometimes fewer than 500 units of a particular design are made. Retail prices for each bear range from £60 to £120.

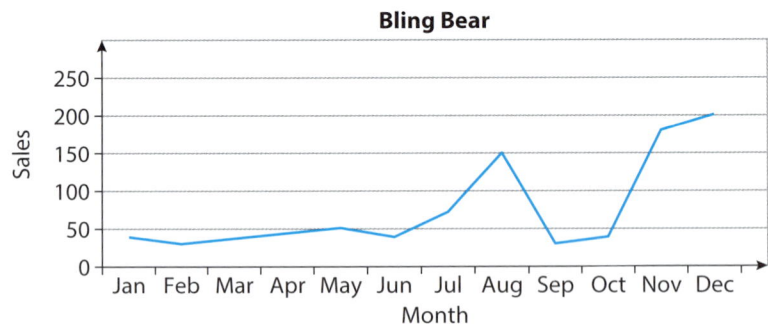

Figure 2.4.6 Annual sales figures for 'Bling Bear'

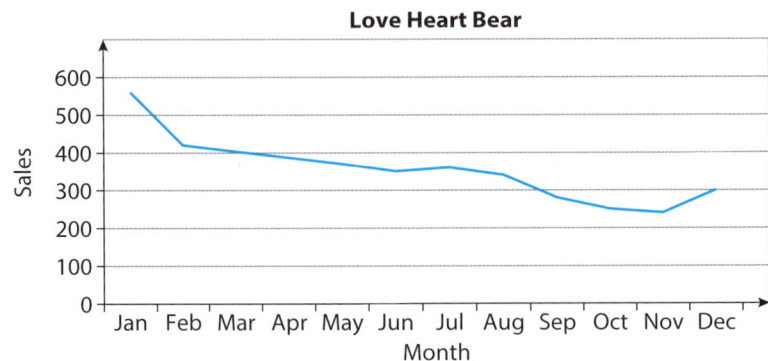

Figure 2.4.7 Annual sales figures for 'Love Heart Bear'

You have learned about some different types of financial data and how a business uses this data in calculations to judge its performance and to make business decisions. However, businesses use a wide variety of information in order to make and justify decisions. These include:

- information from graphs and charts
- market data
- marketing data
- financial data.

This data is quantitative data, meaning that it is data that can be measured in numbers, such as the quantity of something.

These forms of data may come from the business's own financial accounts, from market research into its customers, from government departments such as the Office for National Statistics (ONS) or from information published by rival businesses.

Using and interpreting graphs and charts

A graph is a visual representation of numerical data, often plotted on two axes. Figures 2.4.6 and 2.4.7 are examples of graphs that plot sales over time. A chart is an easy-to-interpret visual representation that is designed to show differences in information. A common type of chart is a pie chart.

Graphs and charts are widely used by businesses because they help to present information in a way that makes it easier to understand and interpret. For example, displaying information visually on a graph can make it easier to interpret trends over time or to compare one data set to another, such as comparing the sales figures of two rival businesses or the sales figures of a business over a number of years. Plotting sales revenue on a graph can also help to identify seasonal trends and variations.

Figure 2.4.8 compares a business's sales data over two years. It shows that the sales data from August 2016 onwards is not available, but the business will be able to estimate likely sales using historical data. Because performance in 2016 has generally been higher than in 2015, the business might also anticipate that its December sales could exceed 369 if this trend continues.

Theme 2: Building the business

In the section 'Business revenues, costs and profits' in Topic 1.3 *Putting a business idea into practice*, you learned about break-even diagrams. A break-even diagram is a way of presenting business information on revenue, costs and profit in order to make decisions.

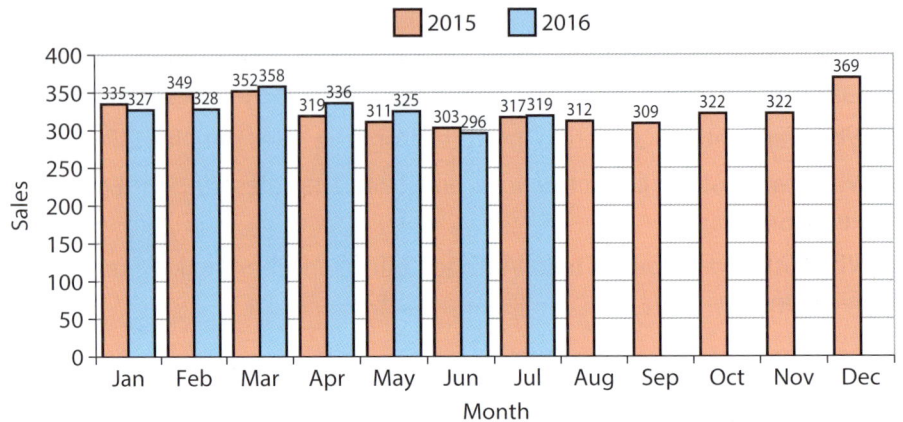

Figure 2.4.8 A 2-year comparison of sales data

When interpreting charts and graphs, make sure that you understand what is measured on each axis and what each data series represents. A single graph may include several data ranges, which could be represented by different bars or lines. It is important that you understand the information before you can begin to interpret it.

Using Figure 2.4.9, calculate the total profit made by the business between January and June. You are advised to show your workings.

(2 marks)

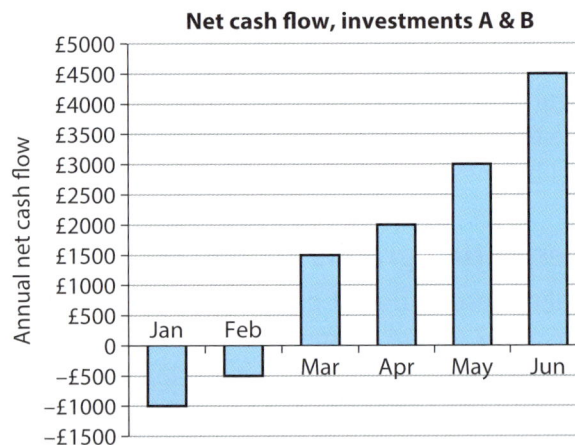

Figure 2.4.9 Monthly profits for a coffee shop (January to June)

Charts can be used to represent different things. For example, a pie chart shows the different parts of a whole, such as Figure 2.4.10, which represents the UK car industry and the market share of each car manufacturer as a percentage. The chart makes it easy to interpret the relative success of different companies and where direct rivalries might exist.

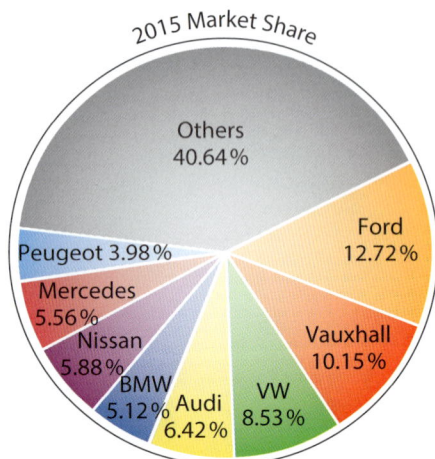

Figure 2.4.10 The 2015 market share of each leading car manufacturer in the UK

Similar data could also be presented for different types of car. For example, although Audi is only the fourth largest seller of cars in the UK, it might dominate a particular segment of the market, such as saloon cars. This could be shown in a pie chart.

Graphs are also particularly useful in demonstrating the relationship between two **variables**. For example, a scatter graph could show the relationship between the amount of money that a business spends on advertising and the business's sales revenue. If these two variables have a strong positive correlation, then a business might decide that spending money on a new marketing campaign is likely to generate higher sales. On the other hand, managers of a business might look at other ways to boost sales if these two variables have a weak correlation.

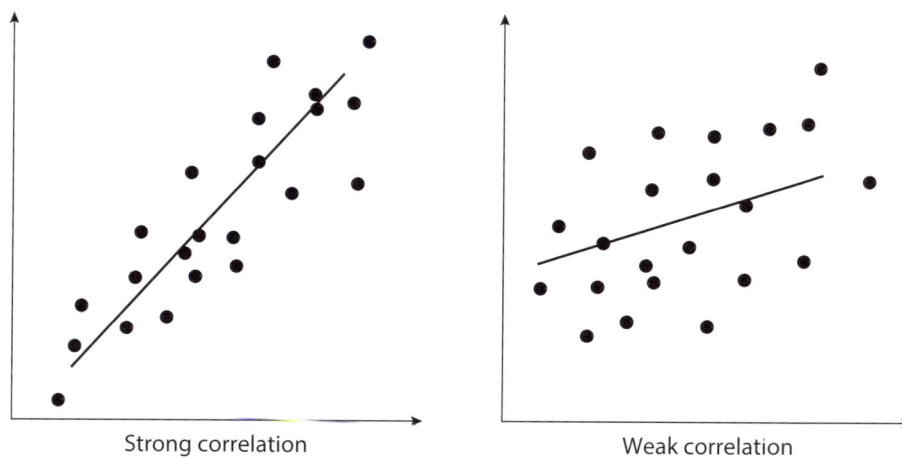

Strong correlation

Weak correlation

Figure 2.4.11 Two scatter graphs showing strong and weak positive correlations

Many businesses now use infographics as well as charts and graphs. An **infographic** is a visual representation of information in a way that makes the information interesting and easy to absorb.

> **Key terms**
>
> **Variable:** a quantity used in a calculation or some measurable piece of information.
>
> **Infographic:** a graphic representation of information to make it interesting and easy to understand.

Activity ?

Find two examples of interesting infographics produced by a business or an industry body, then answer the following questions.

1 Do you think these examples are good or bad ways of presenting data? Why do you think this?

2 Who do you think would use these infographics in the business or industry?

3 Compared with graphs and charts, what do you think are the advantages and disadvantages of infographics?

Theme 2: Building the business

Using and interpreting market data

Market data is data relating to the characteristics of the market in which a business operates. This might be the general market in a country or countries, including **demographic** information such as population change, average income, migration and unemployment rates.

Market data can also refer to markets for specific products, such as cosmetics or food. This kind of market data can include information on market size (for example, the number of products sold or the total revenue in that market), the number of competitors in the market and average price data.

Market data can help inform a business about new opportunities and areas of potential growth. A business will then use this information to make decisions and justify them. For example, it could use market data to decide the location of its next store or to make decisions about the quantity of a product that it produces.

Activity ?

Look at the information presented in Figures 2.4.12 and 2.4.13, then answer the following questions. Figure 2.4.12 is a chart that represents the proportion of the population across different age groups, forecasting up to the year 2039. Figure 2.4.13 is a graph that represents the average weekly earnings growth rates for workers across the UK.

1 List three facts that could be interpreted from the chart and three facts from the graph.

2 How could a business use the market data contained in these charts?

3 Explain one decision that a hotel chain might make based on the information presented in Figures 2.4.12 and 2.4.13.

	Population aged 0 to 15 (%)	Population aged 16 to 64 (%)	Population aged 65 and over (%)
1974	25.2	61.0	13.8
1984	21.0	64.1	14.9
1994	20.7	63.4	15.8
2004	19.5	64.5	15.9
2014	18.8	63.5	17.7
2024	19.0	61.1	19.9
2034	18.1	58.5	23.3
2039	17.8	57.9	24.3

Figure 2.4.12 A table showing the age distribution of the UK population

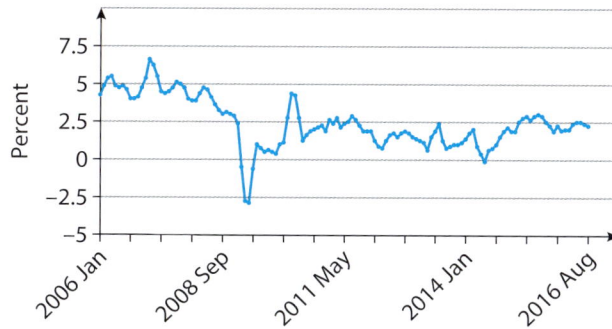

Figure 2.4.13 A graph showing the average weekly earnings growth rates for UK workers

Using and interpreting data for marketing

Marketing data is information about a business's own products and services and its marketing activity. For example, a business may collect customer satisfaction ratings or product reviews in order to assess the success of its products and the attitudes of its customers. However, although customer satisfaction ratings can easily be quantified and turned into statistics, customer attitudes and opinions are often collected as **qualitative data**. If a business finds that its customer ratings are low, suggesting that customers are not satisfied with their service, it might use qualitative marketing data to inform and justify its decision to invest in customer service training. Another example of marketing data is the number of customer visits to a specific page on the business's website. A business will use this data to evaluate the success of its website and inform decisions about any future website design.

> **Key term**
>
> **Qualitative data:** concerning the quality of something that cannot be measured in numbers.

> **Exam-style question**
>
> Explain how a business could use marketing data to make decisions about its products and services. **(3 marks)**

> **Exam tip**
>
> What information might help a business to make decisions about its products or services?

Using and interpreting financial data

Financial data includes a business's sales revenue, costs and profits. Every year, limited companies must produce a set of financial accounts that contain this financial information. Financial data can also include information such as wage rates, tax rates, interest rates and exchange rates. These may be external factors that the business cannot control, but they will directly influence the business's decisions and performance. For example, an increase in interest rates may influence how the owners of a business choose to raise new capital to invest in the business's growth.

You have already learned about the ways in which businesses can use the information in financial reports to carry out analysis, such as by calculating gross profit margin and net profit margin. This allows the owners of the business to understand the business's performance in the previous year and make informed decisions about the business's future.

However, financial information does have some significant limitations.

Britain's biggest supermarket Tesco has revealed half-year profits dropped by more than a quarter, as it still struggles to grow market share amid the bitter industry price war. The supermarket price war has come at the expense of profits with Tesco revealing a group pre-tax profit of £71 million, down 28.3 per cent on the same period last year. Despite the drop, Tesco's group like-for-like sales were up 1 per cent in the half-year to 27 August.

Figure 2.4.14 An extract from a newspaper article about Tesco

Time delay

One of the key limitations of financial information is that it can only be used and interpreted after it has happened, when it is already out of date. For example, read the extract from the newspaper article in Figure 2.4.14 and decide what this information tells you about Tesco's current financial position.

All of the information in the article refers to information that is at least 2 months out of date. This means that, while financial information can be used to give an indication of how a business has performed in the past, it is relatively limited in telling us what is likely to happen in the future.

Help in decision-making

Because it concerns the past, historical financial information can only give businesses a very small amount of help in making decisions at the present moment. For example, if a business sees an increase in like-for-like monthly sales revenue of 9 per cent compared to the previous year, this might suggest that the business is performing well. However, it gives managers very little help if they are struggling with an increase in direct costs or if a new competitor enters the market.

In addition, a single year's financial data is not very useful if it cannot be compared with at least 3 years' worth of financial data. Without a lot of data to compare against, a business cannot tell whether an increase or decrease in sales is a trend or a one-off. Similarly, a business's financial accounts will not tell them much unless they know about trends in the market or how other similar businesses have performed over the same period of time.

Differences in interpretation

Financial information and statistics can be interpreted very differently by looking at it in different ways. For example, a 9 per cent rise in sales revenue might seem very positive. However, it looks less positive if you also know that the market has grown by 20 per cent in the last year or that the business's net profit margin fell by 1 per cent

Statistics can also be expressed differently to produce different interpretations. For example, '90 per cent of customers were happy with the service they received' is the same as 'One in every ten customers would not recommend the business to a friend'. However, while the first seems positive the second seems negative.

Non-financial aims and objectives

Another limitation of financial information is that it only shows the financial position of a business. Although financial success is very important to most businesses, it is not the only indicator of success. Many businesses will use alternative performance indicators to judge their overall success, such as their social responsibility and environmental impact. For example, The Body Shop is a British cosmetics business that aims to be the world's most ethical and truly sustainable global business. The Body Shop values its financial success, but net profit margins will have limited bearing on this aim.

Link it up

You learned about non-financial aims and objectives in the section 'Business aims and objectives' in Topic 1.3 *Putting a business idea into practice*.

Qualitative factors

Financial information, such as revenue, return on investment and cash flow, is quantitative, which means that it is easy to measure. However, there are also qualitative factors in assessing a business's success. For example, a business's profits may increase in the short term if it reduces its production costs. However, if its products start to become unreliable and have to be recalled, this will have a huge impact on the business's reputation and long-term success.

In 2016, Samsung recalled its Galaxy Note 7 smartphones after the devices were reported to have caught fire, and this loss of reputation is a qualitative factor that will not necessarily be captured in the business's financial information. Often, non-financial information, such as a business's reputation, employee morale and brand loyalty, are better indicators of the long-term success of a business than its short-term financial performance.

Exam-style question

Explain **one** limitation of a manager using financial information to make business decisions. **(3 marks)**

Exam tip

When you are asked about business data, it is always worth considering the use of quantitative data versus qualitative data.

Activity ?

Look at the following statements about a business's financial position and identify one limitation for each statement. Think about what other information you might need in order to fully understand the information given.

a The business achieved annual sales revenue of £1.5 million.

b Market share grew by 3 per cent.

c Gross profit increased by 12 per cent.

d The business was able to reduce indirect costs by 10 per cent.

e Product sales (units) are up 16 per cent compared to the same month last year.

Checkpoint

Now it is time to review your understanding of business performance.

Strengthen

S1 What sort of information can be shown in a graph or chart?

S2 How could a business use market data to make business decisions?

S3 Give one limitation of financial information.

Challenge

C1 Describe a reason for why businesses may prefer quantitative data rather than qualitative data.

C2 Using examples, explain why statistics can sometimes be misleading.

2.4 Making financial decisions

1 Which **one** of the following is not used to calculate gross profit? **(1 mark)**

Select **one** answer.

- [ ] A Sales revenue
- [ ] B Rent
- [ ] C Raw materials
- [ ] D Wages

2 Discuss the issues that a business may face when trying to interpret financial data. **(6 marks)**

Student answer

One of the problems with interpreting financial data is that for it to be meaningful the owners of a business should consider them over a number of years. For example, looking at the profits of a business over a three-year period might show a trend. A trend is more important than a single year's data because anything can happen in one particular year to skew the information.

Verdict

The student has identified an important issue, which has been clearly explained using appropriate examples. To improve this answer, the student could discuss a second issue, such as the need to compare financial data with market trends or rival businesses' results.

Read the following extract carefully, then answer Questions 3 and 4.

Benicos is a successful clothes retailer.

Benicos's success has resulted from its 'low cost' strategy. This is where cheap clothes are made, usually in low cost locations such as China and India, and then imported to the UK. Despite European Union (EU) import protection controls, Benicos can still sell the clothes at very low prices. With consumer confidence low, there has been an increased demand for clothes which offer 'good value for money'. This has allowed Benicos to increase its profits.

However, despite Benicos's success, the business has been criticised for its very low prices. Critics of Benicos's ethics have repeatedly stated that if a T-shirt is priced at £2, questions have to be asked about why it can be produced so cheaply. Benicos says it has a strict ethical policy. Despite these worries, by the end of 2015, Benicos's profits had risen by 2% to £673 million.

3   Calculate Benicos' profit in 2014. You are advised to show your workings.   (2 marks)

Student answer

673 million = 100% of 2014 profit + 2%

673/102 = 6.59 (1% of 2014 profit)

× 100 = **£659 million profit in 2014**

Verdict

The question asks the student to use the information in the case study to work out a percentage decrease. The 2015 profit figure of £673 million is 102% of the 2014 profit figure. The student has then used this information to calculate the 2014 profit of £659 million. The answer is correct and the student has clearly shown their workings.

4   Evaluate the importance of Benicos being able to keep the cost of its products low in order to maximise net profit.   (12 marks)

Student answer

Benicos is a business that operates at the cheap end of the market. It attracts its customers by selling its products at very low prices, for example some of its T-shirts are sold as low as £2. For Benicos to be able to maintain profits it must be able to keep its costs very low. Benicos also has to sell high quantities in order to make a large profit. Selling large quantities of its clothing also helps it keep costs low by economies of scale.

On the other hand, there are other ways to maximise net profit. For example, Benicos could find ways to cut back on salaries and advertising costs as this would reduce the indirect costs and not affect the wages of employees who are making the clothes or the price they pay for the cotton. This might be a good idea as Benicos face a lot of criticism and questions over the conditions for workers in its factories and its ethical practices.

Overall, there are a number of methods that Benicos could use to ensure its products are produced at a low cost and the best option may depend on a number of factors. For example, the quality of the products and the impact of its production facilities on its ethical reputation. Keeping costs low is important when trying to increase net profit, but Benicos could also use strategies that might increase sales revenue. For example, Benicos could use marketing techniques to improve its brand image.

Verdict

At first glance this seems like a very accomplished answer. The student has shown really good knowledge of how a business like Benicos could keep its costs low. However, the student has misinterpreted the actual question. Instead of evaluating the importance of keeping costs low, the student has discussed and evaluated how Benicos could keep costs low. It is always important to read the question carefully, highlighting key words to ensure you know exactly what the question is asking.

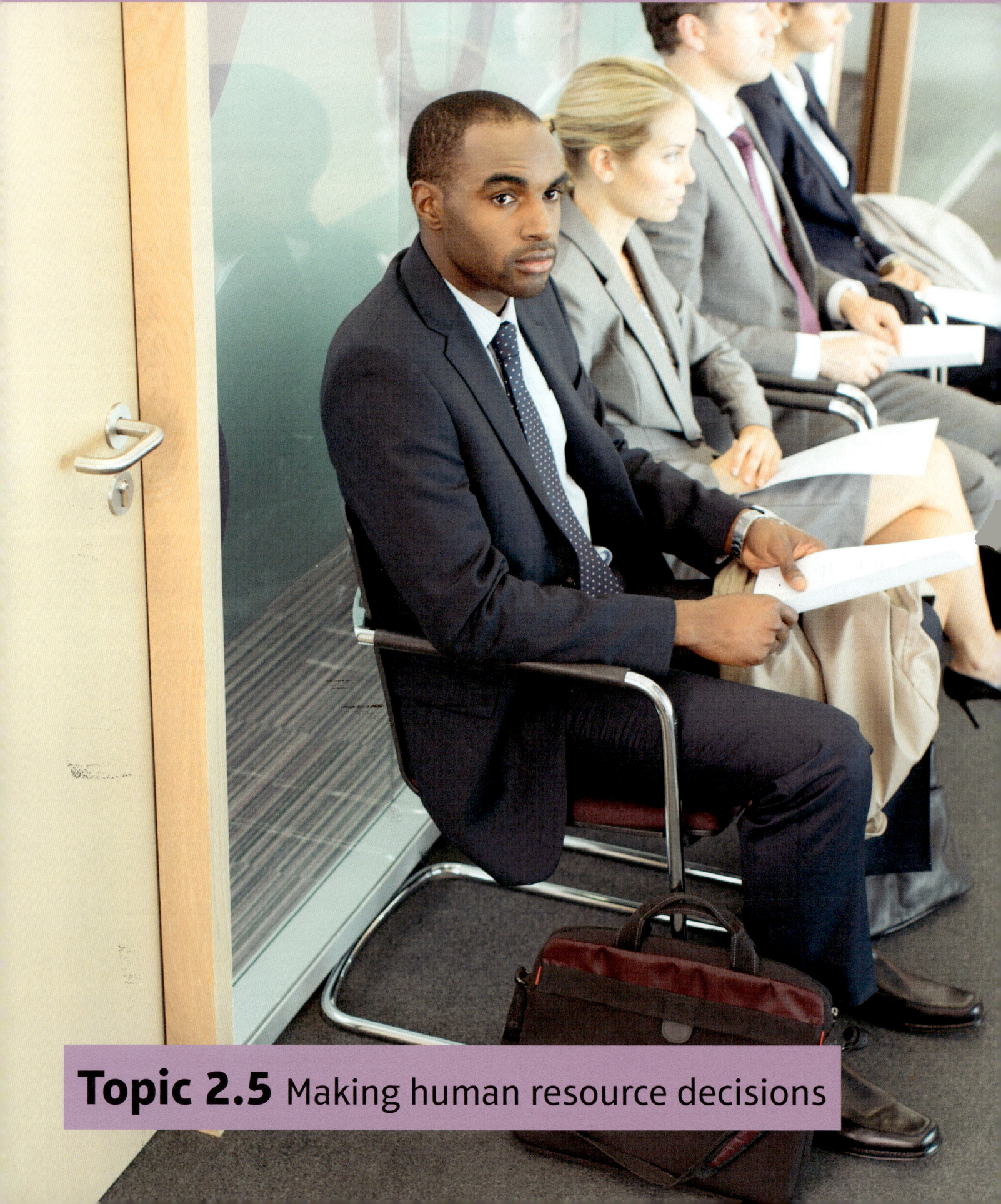

Topic overview

This topic will help you learn about the decisions that growing businesses must make about organisational structure, recruitment, training and motivation. You will learn about the ways in which these decisions can influence business activity.

Case study

Lush

Lush is a business that produces and sells toiletries and cosmetics. Its products include shower gels and soaps handmade from ethically sourced ingredients. From its beginnings in Dorset, Lush has expanded to become a global business, with shops in the United States of America, Hungary, Mexico and the United Arab Emirates.

Lush prides itself on developing its employees. This includes recruiting the right staff, training them and keeping them motivated by offering them challenging and interesting work. It also believes in the importance of paying its employees fairly, such as paying the voluntary minimum wage for London-based employees called the London Living Wage.

Lush has a strong commitment to its social responsibilities, so it gives a significant amount of money to charity, buys ethical ingredients for its products and sets up projects in the countries and communities of their suppliers, which are often found in developing nations like Ghana and Laos. This is designed to ensure that suppliers get to share in Lush's success as well as to give Lush's employees further job satisfaction by knowing that they work for an ethical company.

In 2016, Lush was voted one of the top 50 best companies to work for in the UK, based on its own employees' assessment of their job satisfaction.

Activity

1 What has Lush done to ensure that its employees are motivated and enjoy their work ?

2 What are the advantages to Lush of having a strong commitment to social responsibilities? How does this commitment benefit Lush's employees?

3 Do you agree with the idea that employees are a business's most important asset? Justify your opinion.

Your learning

In this topic you will learn about:

- organisational structures – different organisational structures and when each are appropriate, the importance of effective communication and different ways of working
- effective recruitment – different job roles and responsibilities, and how businesses recruit people
- effective training and development – how and why businesses train and develop employees
- motivation – the importance of motivation in the workplace and how businesses motivate employees.

Organisational structures

Key term

Layers: in an organisational structure, this means the levels of job roles in the business, from the highest-paid directors to the most junior members of staff.

Case study

Potters Resort

Potters Resort is a holiday resort in Norfolk run by a family-owned private company, Potters Leisure. The business is run by the managing director and owner, John Potter. It employs more than 500 members of staff, including staff members at various levels within the structure, such as directors, managers, team leaders and employees.

Activity

Why might an employee benefit from working for a business that has a structure with a lot of **layers**? Discuss your thoughts with a partner or in a small group.

Different organisational structures

All businesses have an organisational form, which defines how staff members work with one another, how decisions are made and how employees are managed.

There are different types of organisational structure. The type of structure that a business chooses to use depends on the type of business and the way in which it needs to make decisions. A business has to make two decisions about its organisational structure.

- Will it be hierarchical or flat?
- Will it be centralised or decentralised?

The organisational structure will affect a number of factors, such as the number of employees that managers need to look after, employees' chances of being promoted and the speed of decision-making.

Hierarchical

Hierarchical organisations are known as 'tall' organisations because they have lots of layers of management. You could think of a hierarchical organisation as being like a ladder.

Managers have a number of employees to look after, but in a hierarchical business they are likely to have a small **span of control**, meaning that they may only manage three or four employees. An employee is likely to be paid more if they are higher up a hierarchical organisational structure, and the number of employees at each level will get smaller as the levels get higher.

Decisions have to be made through the layers of the organisation. For example, an employee may seek permission to do something from their manager. The manager may then have to seek permission from their manager, who may then have to seek permission from their manager.

Hierarchical structures can have benefits. For example, they provide lots of opportunities for employees to seek promotion and the chance to earn more money. However, they also come with disadvantages. For example, the need to seek permission up through the layers of the organisation can make decision-making very slow as communication takes longer.

> ### Key term
>
> **Span of control:** the number of employees that are managed by a manager. If a person manages three employees, their span of control is three.

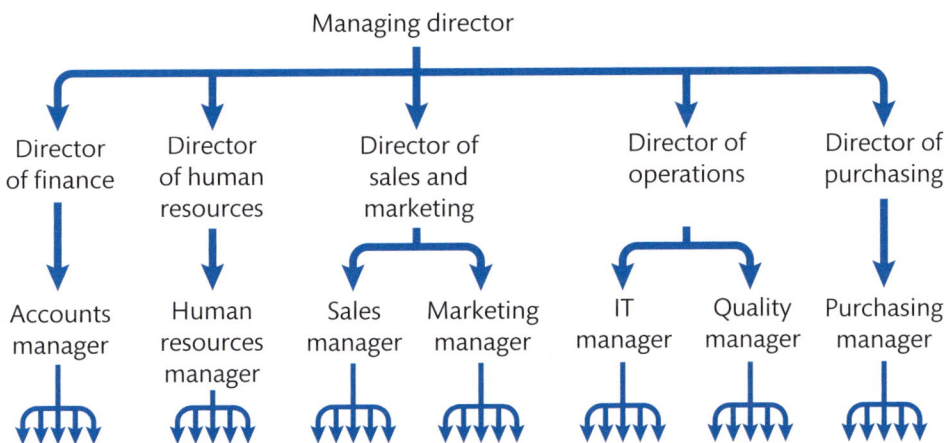

Figure 2.5.1 A hierarchical organisational structure

Flat

A flat structure is one with very few levels of management. Managers often have a wide span of control, meaning that they look after a larger number of employees than managers in hierarchical structures.

Communication and decision-making in flat structures are often quicker and more efficient than in hierarchical structures because there are fewer layers of management to go through. However, because managers have a wider span of control, they have more employees to look after. This means that managers' workloads can become very large, making it difficult for them to ensure that all employees are supported and working to the best of their ability. Flat structures can also be limiting as they do not offer employees many opportunities for promotion.

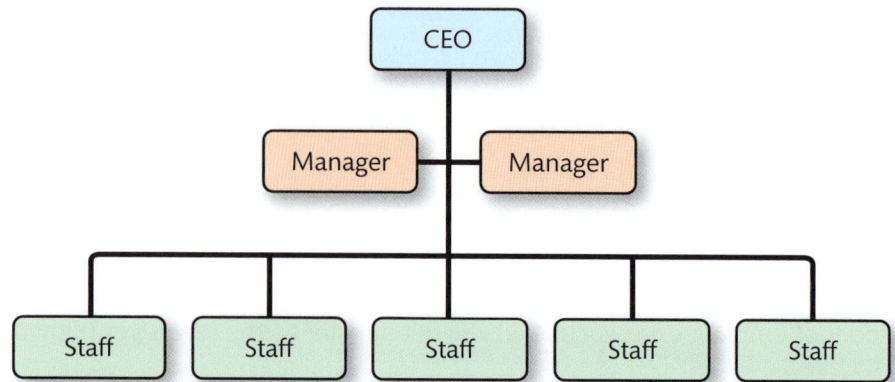

Figure 2.5.2 A flat organisational structure

Exam-style question

Explain **one** advantage to a business of having a flat organisational structure.

(3 marks)

Centralised

A centralised structure means that decisions are made at the 'centre' of the organisation. Decisions need to be approved by the highest levels of management before they can be implemented. In a global business, this may mean that all decisions are made in one country, even when those decisions affect the business's branches in other countries.

The benefits of centralised structures are that:

- the business and its activities are very focused
- the vision of the organisation is clear
- the performance of employees is tracked and managed
- there are high levels of control
- the **accountability** of all members of staff in the business is clear.

Decentralised

Decentralised structures are the opposite of centralised. This means that decisions are made locally or at a lower level. For example, in a chain of high street retail shops, decisions could be made by the manager of each shop around the country, rather than centrally by senior management.

Some of the benefits of having a decentralised structure include the following.

- Senior managers can focus on the bigger picture or strategic concerns for the business because managers at lower levels have been given the power to make decisions locally.
- Local managers can be more creative in their thinking and respond to the local needs of their customers rather than having to seek permission or following the same processes as every other store around the country (or the world).

- Fewer mistakes are made and the business operates more efficiently, as managers close to where the work is being completed can make changes to improve it.
- Local managers, and employees, feel more empowered and responsible for their work, rather than simply doing as they are told from the centre of the business.

Although decentralised structures may seem to be less expensive to run, because there are fewer layers of management, they may require managers and employees to be more highly trained. This is because managers need to be able to make good decisions and clearly communicate what is going well to the rest of the business. If they do not, the business may take too many contradictory decisions. This can confuse staff and customers, and it can also cost a lot more money.

Whether a business is centralised or decentralised can have a huge influence on the way in which it responds to change. Businesses that need to respond quickly and locally to changes in different areas of the country, or world, often need to use decentralised decision-making. For example, global retailers such as Walmart (Asda) allow their managers in different countries to vary the products that are offered according to country requirements. However, this requires them to trust the employees making those decisions.

Activity ?

1 Find a partner. Each of you should choose one of the following organisational structures: flat, hierarchical, centralised or decentralised. Explain your chosen organisational structure to your partner. You may want to draw a diagram or use an example to help explain the structure.

2 Working in pairs or small groups, find out more information about a large business or organisation that is based in your area. Find out about its organisational structure and why it is structured like that.

The importance of effective communication

Communication is affected by the type of organisational structure that a business chooses to use. Most businesses start small and then grow. This means that they are usually flat at the beginning, with all decisions being made by a small number of people, but then as they grow they usually add on more layers of management and start to become hierarchical.

Communication takes place in lots of different ways. Communication can be spoken, such as:

- having conversations in offices
- discussing things in meetings
- talking to colleagues on the telephone
- using digital methods such as Skype, Google Hangout or video conferencing.

Theme 2: Building the business

Many organisations use video conferencing to communicate

Communication can also take place in writing, such as:

- letters sent by post
- printed reports or posters
- digitally using email, instant messenger facilities, texting and social media.

As a business grows, communication can become a problem for three main reasons:

1 The business communicates too little.

2 The business communicates too much.

3 Other information or activities act as barriers and get in the way of communication.

It is important that businesses use the right amount of communication and the right methods of communication to make sure their businesses operate efficiently and effectively.

Activity ?

In small groups, discuss the advantages and disadvantages of using digital communication methods such as instant messenger, then complete the following tasks.

1 Create a table or diagram showing the advantages and disadvantages of digital communication to a small business with a flat organisational structure.

2 Create a second table or diagram showing the advantages and disadvantages of digital communication to a large decentralised global business that operates in several countries.

3 How do the two tables or diagrams compare? What do you notice about communication in different types of business with different organisational structures?

The impact of insufficient communication

Insufficient communication means not enough communication. Insufficient communication leads to managers and employees being unaware of what is happening in the rest of the business, and this can lead to mistakes and inefficiency. This can lead to financial difficulties and could have potentially fatal consequences.

The impact of excessive communication

Excessive communication means too much communication. Excessive communication can be as bad as not having enough communication. If managers and employees receive too many different communications and instructions, they are unlikely to be able to do their jobs efficiently because of the time needed to read through all of it. This could mean that their output will be slower or completely reduced. Excessive communication also includes having too many meetings, emails and forms.

Email overload is a real problem for many businesses. In some industries, email overload has been found to lead to employees suffering from stress or not being able to complete their work. In 2012, a survey by McKinsey Global Institute found that employees spend on average 28 per cent of each week at work reading or replying to emails. Excessive communication through too many emails can mean that staff are unable to get on with their work.

Some businesses also require employees and managers to fill out lots of forms, and this is another type of excessive communication. If a business asks an employee to fill out too many forms, this can take up a lot of time and serves no purpose unless the information is needed by another part of the business. It is very important that a business is clear about the purpose of its communications, including gathering information from its employees.

Barriers to effective communication

Barriers to effective communication are all the things that stop communications from reaching their intended audience.

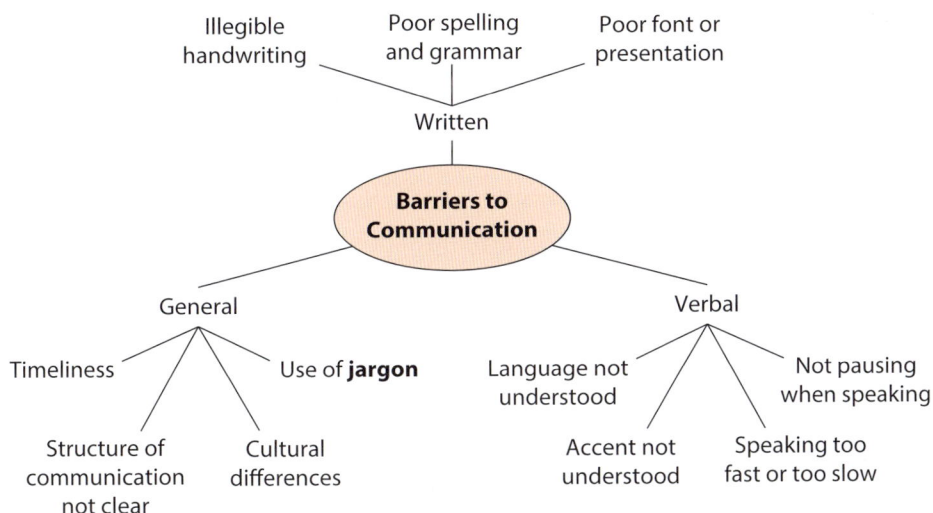

Figure 2.5.3 Common barriers to communication

Did you know?

In 2003, NASA's Space Shuttle Columbia broke apart on re-entry into the Earth's atmosphere, killing all seven crew members. NASA identified 'organisational silence' or poor communication as one of the factors that caused the crash, because problems identified by employees were not communicated to more senior managers.

Key term

Jargon: technical or obscure words or terms used by a particular group of people that may not be understood by everyone.

Activity **?**

Look at Figure 2.5.3. For each of the barriers that it lists, write down one possible impact on a small retail business. Now rank your list of barriers in order of impact, with the barrier that has the biggest impact on the business at the top.

Exam tip ●

Read all of the possible answers, even if the correct answers look obvious.

Exam-style question ●

Which **two** of the following are disadvantages of excessive communication? **(2 marks)**

Select **two** answers.

- [ ] **A** Improved productivity
- [ ] **B** Staff not being able to do their jobs
- [ ] **C** Decisions being made very quickly
- [ ] **D** Important information being lost or ignored
- [ ] **E** Staff working efficiently at their desks

Different ways of working

Not all businesses work in the same way. Like organisational structure and communication, the way in which a business works can have a big impact on its success. Ways of working include the type of hours worked by staff, the type of contracts used and the technology that is used to conduct the business's activities.

Hours

Hours refers to the number of hours worked by an employee every week. A full-time employee usually works 35 hours or more every week, while a part-time employee will usually work less than this.

Businesses do not always need to have employees working full-time. Part-time employees may work two or three days a week or do shorter hours every day, such as in the mornings or evenings. It is illegal for a business to treat part-time employees less favourably than full-time employees. This means that part-time employees have to be paid the same rates, receive the same benefits and have the same career or promotion opportunities as full-time staff.

Some employers offer jobs that fit around school holidays. This means that an employee with children works full-time during their children's school terms but does not work during the school holidays. These employees would be classed as part-time employees because if their hours are spread out across a year, they do fewer than full-time hours over a full year.

Some businesses also offer flexible hours, and there are many different types of flexible working hours. Some employers offer annualised hours, meaning that an employee is given a specified number of hours to work during a given year and can work more hours in some weeks or months than in other weeks or months. Employees can also be asked to work flexible hours by being given a zero hours contract. This means that an employee does not know how many hours they will be asked to work for the business in any week or month.

Flexible hours can be good for businesses and employees. They can help a business to cover temporary gaps in staff numbers due to sickness or holiday and can give employees a lot of flexibility in their working life. However, employers need to be careful that flexible working contracts are fair and treat workers legally.

Activity ?

1 In pairs, discuss the advantages of flexible working for employees.

2 Do some research into zero hours contracts. What do you think are the advantages and disadvantages to the following businesses of using zero hours contracts?

   a a holiday park

   b a restaurant

   c an events company.

Did you know?

The Advisory, Conciliation and Arbitration Service (ACAS) is an organisation that gives free impartial advice to employees and employers about employment relations and workplace law.

Contracts

A contract is a written agreement between two people or organisations. In this instance, a contract is a written agreement between an employee and an employer. There are three main types of employment contracts.

- **Permanent contract** – an employee will be employed by a business on an ongoing basis.
- **Temporary contract** – an employee will be employed for a fixed amount of time. For example, a business may hire someone on a temporary basis to cover for an employee on parental leave.
- **Freelance contract** – a business has asked a **freelancer** to work for them, usually on a particular project. The freelancer is not employed by the business but is self-employed and paid by the business for the work that they do.

Key term

Freelancer: someone who is self-employed and contracted by businesses to work for them.

Activity ?

In small groups, do some research into the advantages and disadvantages:

a to a person of working as a freelancer

b to a business of using freelancers.

Share your ideas with the rest of the group.

Exam tip

A good answer will include at least two benefits for a business and will give detail for each. You gain more marks if you include business terminology in your answer and link together the different points in your argument.

Exam-style question

Discuss the benefits to a business of having employees working on flexible hours contracts. **(6 marks)**

The impact of technology on ways of working

Technology has had a big impact on the way in which people work and the type of work that they do. You have already learned about communication and the way in which people and businesses can communicate with each other through email, instant messenger services and social media platforms.

Using technology can improve the **efficiency** of employees and businesses because there are fewer barriers to communication and it makes it possible to make decisions very quickly, even in a global business. Thanks to the internet and other advances in digital technology, businesses can employ people working in different countries and in different time zones who can communicate with one another using technology. Meetings do not need to take place in person anymore as they can take place over the internet, using VoIP (Voice over Internet Protocol) applications such as Skype or Google Hangout or smartphone applications such as FaceTime or WhatsApp.

Exam tip

A good answer will include only one disadvantage but will give two points explaining why this is a disadvantage.

Exam-style question

Explain **one** disadvantage to an employee of using technology in the workplace.

(3 marks)

Advances in technology have made it possible to work remotely rather than from an office. Working remotely means working for a business from somewhere that is not that business's main site or office. Usually, this means working from home. Remote working has many benefits for employers and employees, as shown in Table 2.5.1.

Benefits for employers	Benefits for employees
• Lower costs due to less travel requirement and reduced workspace requirements	• Reduced time spent travelling to and from work
• Lower sickness rates as staff are less likely to take time off	• More flexible times to start and end of workdays
• Happier staff because they can work more flexibly, meaning that they are less likely to leave the business	• Less chance of being prevented from getting on with work by conversations or meetings with colleagues

Table 2.5.1 The benefits of remote working for employers and employees

Did you know?

According to the Centre for the Protection of National Infrastructure, in 2012, 20 per cent of the British workforce carried out some form of remote working. That number is likely to have risen since then.

Activity ?

In pairs, research the disadvantages of working remotely. Produce a poster that shows your findings.

Checkpoint

Now it is time to review your understanding of organisational structures.

Strengthen

S1 List three disadvantages to a business of having excessive communication in a business.

S2 Describe two benefits of a business operating using a flat structure.

S3 Describe the difference between a permanent and temporary contract, giving an example of each.

Challenge

C1 A large business operating in your local area has asked you to write a short report that discusses the benefits to a large organisation of having a decentralised structure.

C2 Consider the following statement: 'technology makes a workplace more efficient'. Do you agree or disagree? Justify your opinion.

C3 In pairs or small groups, find two businesses that use remote working. Write an explanation of the impact of remote working on each business and the sector that it operates within.

Effective recruitment

Case study

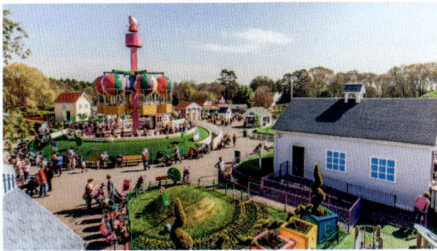

Paultons Park

Paultons Park is a large award-winning theme park in the New Forest. Each year, Paultons recruits new staff for the busy tourist season between Easter and October and for the busy Christmas period.

Paultons needs a wide range of employees to staff its rides, catering facilities, entertainments and animal attractions.

Activity ?

1 Find the Paultons Park recruitment website by typing 'Paultons Park recruitment' into a search engine and find out what roles are available.

2 Compare and contrast the different roles, looking at the:

   a responsibilities

   b method of recruitment

   c type of person that Paultons would like to hire.

All businesses want to employ the best possible people. This requires effective recruitment, which will attract the right applicants and identify the most suitable candidates.

Theme 2: Building the business

Key terms

Roles: these are the different jobs within a business. For example, roles at a restaurant might include head chef, chef, kitchen assistant and so on.

Responsibilities: these are the things that someone is required to do in order to fulfil their role in a business. For example, at a restaurant, a responsibility of the role of head chef might be to create the restaurant's menu.

There are two main stages of recruitment:

- the business needs to be clear about the different **roles** that it needs to fill and the **responsibilities** of those roles
- the business needs to develop the documents and processes that are used in job applications and the selection process.

Different roles and responsibilities

All of the roles within a business or organisation will have different responsibilities. Roles at different layers of a business will be paid different wages and will have different responsibilities. Usually, roles at higher levels in the organisational structure will have more responsibilities, but will be better paid.

Key job roles

The names of roles will vary depending on the business, but most businesses employ people in the same sorts of roles. Roles that are commonly seen in many businesses are:

- director
- senior managers
- supervisors and team leaders
- operational and support staff.

Directors

The people at the top of a business's organisational structure are the directors. They are usually the highest-paid employees in the business, but have a lot of responsibilities. Their biggest responsibility is to make sure that the business is run correctly and that decisions are made in the best interests of the business, its employees and its customers. Directors are also responsible for ensuring that the business's accounts are made available to government departments and agencies, and that taxes and employee benefits, such as pension contributions, are paid.

In some businesses, the directors are the owners of the business, as they have invested their own money into starting up and expanding the business. In other businesses, directors are hired to run the business and may not have invested money in it. Larger businesses will employ a number of directors who all have particular functions, such as a Director of Marketing or a Director of Human Resources. Some businesses also use non-executive directors, who give advice to the business, but do not work for it on a day-to-day basis.

A business may pay its directors a salary or they may be paid a share of the business's profits, depending on whether or not they own part of the business.

Activity ?

1. The Institute of Directors (IoD) supports and guides directors of businesses. In pairs, use the IoD's website to find out more about what directors of businesses do. Once you have done this, share your findings with another pair.

2. In a group of four, now discuss the view that a business is only as good as its directors. Give examples where possible.

Senior managers

The managers at the highest level of management in a business are known as the senior managers. They usually form a team called the senior management team. They are responsible for ensuring that all the other layers of management work well together. The number of senior managers in an organisation depends on the size of the organisation and the number of layers below them in the organisational structure.

Senior managers are usually responsible for setting the business's strategy, including its aims, objectives and targets. These aims, objectives and targets can either be short term (over the next year or 2 years) or longer term (in the next 3 to 5 years).

> ### Activity ?
>
> In small groups discuss the following questions.
> 1 What is the purpose of a senior management team in a business?
> 2 How important is good communication between the senior managers in a business and the layers of managers and staff below them?
> 3 What do you think would be the impact on the business of having a lot more men than women in senior management roles? Do you think there would be any disadvantages?

Supervisors and team leaders

Supervisors and team leaders are the managers who are in charge of the business's staff. They ensure that employees work effectively and are completing their work on a day-to-day basis.

The responsibilities of a supervisor or team leader depend on the type of business they work for. For example, in a restaurant, the head waiter or waitress acts as a team leader. They may train new waiters or waitresses and observe their staff taking orders and waiting on tables, as well as waiting on tables themselves. In other businesses, team leaders and supervisors do not do the same sort of work as the staff that they manage. Instead, they may organise staffing and tell staff what hours they will work.

The role of a supervisor or a team leader will depend on the number of staff members that they manage. Their responsibilities will also affect the level of their wages.

Operational and support staff

Operational staff are the employees who are employed within the business to carry out the operations of that business. For example, in a college, the operational staff are the teachers providing education to students in the classroom. Their responsibilities will depend on the nature of the business, but in a factory setting they would usually include manufacturing products, or, in a call centre, they could involve selling services to customers.

Support staff are the employees who are employed within the business to carry out duties that are not directly associated with operations, but are necessary to make the business's operations possible.

> ### Did you know?
>
> In 2014, a report found that only about 20 per cent of senior managers in British businesses were women. However, in other countries, that percentage was even lower. For example, in Portugal and Russia, fewer than 5 per cent of senior managers were women.

For example, in a college, financial support staff will ensure that the college can go on teaching students by paying teachers' wages and authorising purchases of equipment such as textbooks and classroom furniture. Other examples of support staff include human resources, marketing and information technology (IT) teams.

Activity ?

Team leaders or supervisors are given targets and instructions by senior managers to work with the staff.

1 List three ways in which you think team leaders work differently to senior managers.
2 What kinds of pressure might a team leader face compared to those faced by a senior manager?

How businesses recruit people

When a business adopts an organisational structure and creates the roles within that structure, it also needs to consider how it will actually attract people to work for it. This is the process of recruitment.

It is important for a business to make sure that its recruitment process is fair, legal and ethical. Businesses must obey the Equality Act 2010, and fair treatment is particularly important in the recruitment process as discrimination in recruitment can have a big impact on candidates' lives. The Equality Act 2010 means that it is illegal to discriminate against a person due to their age, sex, religion or other protected characteristics.

Recruitment documents

There are four main documents that are often used in the recruitment process:
- the person specification
- the job description
- the application form
- the curriculum vitae (CV).

Person specification and job description

When a business decides to recruit a new employee, it writes a person specification and a job description. These documents are often written at the same time because they are linked together.

- **Person specification** – the type of person that is required for the role. This includes any essential or desirable qualifications that are needed, work experience and personal attributes that a candidate needs in order to fulfil the job.
- **Job description** – the job itself. This includes the duties and responsibilities of the person doing the job.

Producing detailed job descriptions and person specifications is very important for businesses, in order to make sure that they have the right roles advertised and that the best people for the job will notice the advert and apply.

Activity ?

Using a variety of job sites, such as Monster, Reed and Fish4jobs, find some job descriptions and person specifications for the role of 'finance assistant' and use them to answer the following questions.

1 Explain the difference between a job description and a person specification.

2 Compare the job descriptions for the different finance assistant roles you have found. Are they all the same? Note the differences.

3 Compare the person specifications for the different finance assistant roles you have found. Are they all the same? Note the differences.

Exam-style questions

Which **one** of the following documents outlines the qualifications and experience needed by a candidate for a particular role? **(1 mark)**

Select **one** answer.

- [ ] **A** Curriculum vitae
- [ ] **B** Application form
- [ ] **C** Job description
- [ ] **D** Person specification

Exam tip

Read the instructions carefully. This question is only asking for **one** answer.

Key term

Salary band: a range of possible salaries for the role being advertised. For example, a role may be advertised as having a 'Band 1' salary, where Band 1 covers salaries between £15,000 and £20,000. The band will be part of a larger salary scale.

Job descriptions vary from business to business, but they all contain the same essential information, which is outlined in Table 2.5.2. This ensures that potential employees can easily find this information in the description. It will also help them to work out whether they have the necessary skills and decide whether or not they want to apply for the job. Businesses should review and update their job descriptions regularly, as roles can change and develop over time.

Title	This tells applicants the title of the job and gives them an idea of the likely level of responsibility. For example, 'finance assistant' is a title.
Department	This tells applicants the department or team that they would work for. For example, a finance assistant role is likely to be within the finance department. If the business is a large business, this section will also say which location the role is based at.
Terms of employment	This gives applicants an outline of what the job will involve. Many businesses also include the **salary band** or actual salary and the hours to be worked in this section of the job description.
Responsibilities	This tells applicants what they would do on a day-to-day basis.
Responsible to	This gives applicants details about the person who would be their manager.
Written by and date	This information is usually given, though it is not likely to be useful to the applicant.

Table 2.5.2 Elements of a job description

Person specifications are used alongside job descriptions. They list all of the attributes that a person applying for a particular job should or might have. These requirements are usually split into two categories: essential and desirable.

- **Essential requirements** – things that a candidate must have. Without these, a candidate will not even be considered for the role. For example, the role of hair stylist is likely to have an essential requirement of a qualification in hairdressing.

- **Desirable requirements** – things that a candidate may not have, but that may be helpful when fulfilling the role. If there is a very high number of applicants for a role, the business is likely to interview only applicants who have some or all of the desirable requirements, as well as the essential requirements.

Most person specifications contain some or all of the sections listed in Table 2.5.3.

Qualifications	This tells applicants which qualifications are essential for the post. For example, it may require GCSE Maths and GCSE English at Grade 4 or above. It may also list desirable qualifications such as an A level, a BTEC or a degree, depending on the level of the post.
Experience	This tells applicants what kind of experience they need to have. This experience could be essential or desirable. For example, a role as a waiter or waitress in a restaurant could require the essential condition of 1 year's experience waiting tables and the desirable requirement of being trained to provide silver service.
Knowledge and understanding	This tells applicants what sort of knowledge they would need to do the job. This is likely to be less specific than sections about qualifications or experience. For example, a candidate may need 'a knowledge of finance'. The detail of the knowledge required will depend on the level of the role.
Skills	This tells applicants what skills they should have before applying for the role. It may also list desirable skills that they may be able to learn on the job. For example, an essential skill for a finance assistant might be an ability to use spreadsheet software, whereas a desirable skill for the same task could be an ability to use a specific accounting software package.
Character and attitudes	This tells applicants about the business and its culture or ways of working. For example, if the business prides itself on its friendly customer service, it may require candidates with a good sense of humour. This can help applicants work out whether they will fit in and feel comfortable working in the business.

Table 2.5.3 Sections often included in a person specification

Exam-style question

Which **two** of the following are not included in a job description?

(2 marks)

Select **two** answers.

- ☐ **A** Previous experience required to fulfil the role
- ☐ **B** Knowledge and understanding required to fulfil the role
- ☐ **C** Job title
- ☐ **D** Department in which the employee will work
- ☐ **E** Hours of work

Exam tip

Sometimes it can help to identify the incorrect answers. In this case, you could think about all the things that you know are found in a job description and compare your list with the possible answers.

Application forms

When a business is recruiting for a role, applicants need to be able to contact it in order to give it their details. One of the most common ways to apply for a job is using an application form (see Figure 2.5.4).

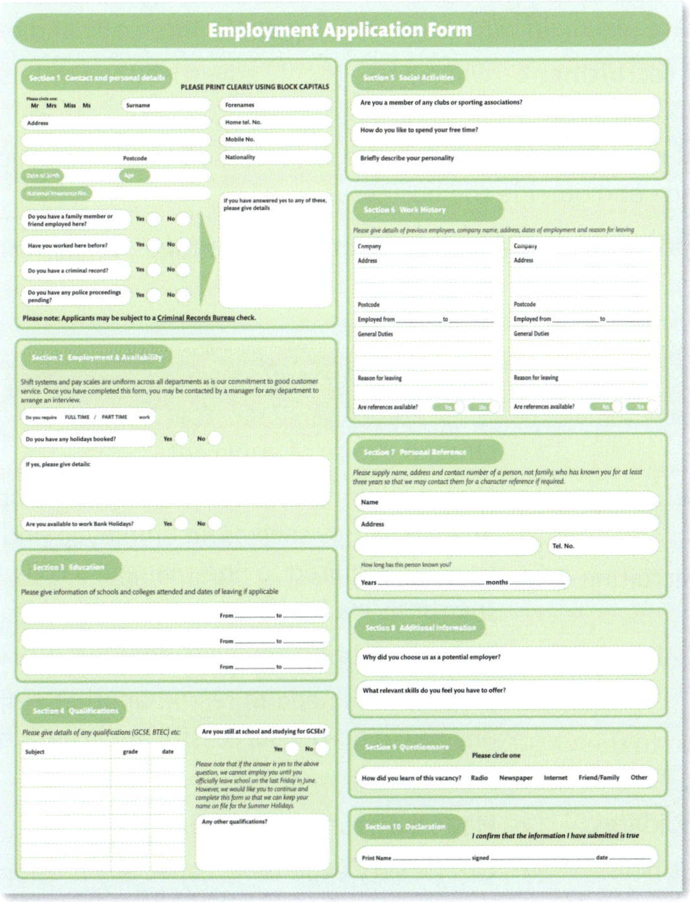

Employment Application Form

Section 1 Contact and personal details

PLEASE PRINT CLEARLY USING BLOCK CAPITALS

Please circle one: Mr Mrs Miss Ms

Surname

Forenames

Address

Home tel. No.

Mobile No.

Postcode

Nationality

Date of birth

Age

National Insurance No.

Do you have a family member or friend employed here? Yes No

Have you worked here before? Yes No

Do you have a criminal record? Yes No

Do you have any police proceedings pending? Yes No

If you have answered yes to any of these, please give details

Please note: Applicants may be subject to a Criminal Records Bureau check.

Section 2 Employment & Availability

Shift systems and pay scales are uniform across all departments as is our commitment to good customer service. Once you have completed this form, you may be contacted by a manager for any department to arrange an interview.

Do you require FULL TIME / PART TIME work

Do you have any holidays booked? Yes No

If yes, please give details:

Are you available to work Bank Holidays? Yes No

Section 3 Education

Please give information of schools and colleges attended and dates of leaving if applicable

From .... to ....

From .... to ....

From .... to ....

Section 4 Qualifications

Please give details of any qualifications (GCSE, BTEC) etc:

Subject	grade	date

Are you still at school and studying for GCSEs? Yes No

Please note that if the answer is yes to the above question, we cannot employ you until you officially leave school on the last Friday in June. However, we would like you to continue and complete this form so that we can keep your name on file for the Summer Holidays.

Any other qualifications?

Section 5 Social Activities

Are you a member of any clubs or sporting associations?

How do you like to spend your free time?

Briefly describe your personality

Section 6 Work History

Please give details of previous employers, company name, address, dates of employment and reason for leaving

Company

Address

Postcode

Employed from .... to ....

General Duties

Reason for leaving

Are references available?

Company

Address

Postcode

Employed from .... to ....

General Duties

Reason for leaving

Are references available?

Section 7 Personal Reference

Please supply name, address and contact number of a person, not family, who has known you for at least three years so that we may contact them for a character reference if required.

Name

Address

Tel. No.

How long has this person known you?

Years .... months ....

Section 8 Additional Information

Why did you choose us as a potential employer?

What relevant skills do you feel you have to offer?

Section 9 Questionnaire

Please circle one

How did you learn of this vacancy? Radio Newspaper Internet Friend/Family Other

Section 10 Declaration

I confirm that the information I have submitted is true

Print Name .... signed .... date ....

Figure 2.5.4 Application forms are commonly used by many businesses when recruiting for a role

Application forms can be very useful for businesses to use because they make sure that all applicants fill in the same information that is needed to choose between them. It also provides this information in the same format or style for all applicants, so it makes it easier to compare applicants.

Curriculum vitae (CV)

A CV is a document that lists a person's experience and qualifications. CVs can be used to give an employer an overview of the qualifications and experience of potential employees. They are usually sent in by an applicant with a covering letter, which is a brief letter explaining why they are applying for the role.

Requesting CVs, rather than requiring applicants to fill out an application form, may encourage more people to apply, as it is often easier for the applicant. However, it usually means that the business will need more time to sort through the applications in order to select the right applicants for the next stage of the process. A CV and covering letter format can also make it easier for a candidate to hide any gaps in their employment history.

Recruitment methods

When recruiting for a role, a business also has to consider how to advertise the job vacancy, assess the applicants and select the right person for the role. There are two main ways of advertising a role: internally and externally.

- **Internal recruitment** – when a role is only advertised to the business's existing employees.
- **External recruitment** – when a role is advertised to potential applicants both inside and outside the business.

Both methods have their advantages and disadvantages, as shown in Table 2.5.4.

Activity ?

In pairs, discuss why you think it might be important for an employer to find out why an applicant has gaps in their employment history.

Recruitment method	Advantages	Disadvantages
Internal	• Fast recruitment process. • Easy to advertise (could even be advertised just through email). • Cheaper than advertising and recruiting externally. • Could offer job as a promotion for an existing employee. • All candidates are already known to the business.	• Limited choice of applicants. • May cause problems among existing employees due to change, such as an employee finding that they are required to line-manage a colleague at the same level, which may be awkward. • Unlikely to bring any new ideas into the business. • Business will need to recruit another employee anyway to do the successful applicant's previous job.
External	• Higher number of potential candidates. • May bring new skills into the business. • May bring new ideas into the business.	• May take a long time to find the right candidate. • Can be very expensive, especially if using a recruitment agency. • The candidate may turn out not to be as good as they seemed at interview.

Table 2.5.4 The advantages and disadvantages of recruiting internally and externally

The methods used during the recruitment process may differ depending on whether the job is advertised internally or externally. For example, an internal applicant may only need to email the recruiting manager to apply, whereas this may be inappropriate for an external applicant. Some recruitment methods are shown in Table 2.5.5.

Method	Description	Suitable for internal process?	Suitable for external process?
Interview	One or more people (interviewers) ask candidates questions to find out about why they want the job, their experience and their suitability.	✓	✓
Test	Candidates are given a scenario and/or questions and either must pass a minimum standard to be hired or can be compared to other candidates.	✓	✓
Application form	Applicants fill in a form with information such as their experience and qualifications, which allows recruiting managers to compare them to find the most suitable applicant.	✗	✓
Tour of the facilities	Candidates are shown around the business to understand what it is like to work there and ask any questions.	✗	✓
Role play	Candidates are given a scenario to act out so that their behaviours can be assessed, such as selling something to someone else playing a customer.	✓	✓
Group discussion	Candidates are given a topic to discuss and are observed during the discussion.	✓	✓
Presentation	Candidates are asked to give a presentation that they have prepared, usually using visual aids or handouts, and that is marked to assess their performance.	✓	✓

Table 2.5.5 Different methods of recruitment

If a business finds it difficult to fill a vacancy, it may use a recruitment agency to find applicants. This can be an expensive way to fill a vacant role, but it is usually very effective.

Checkpoint

Now it is time to review your understanding of effective recruitment.

Strengthen

S1 Describe the difference between the role of a senior manager and the role of a supervisor or team leader.

S2 Describe two or three responsibilities of a team leader working in a retail store.

S3 Describe three elements that you would expect to find in an application form and explain why businesses need this information from applicants.

Challenge

C1 Consider the following statement: 'support staff are never as important as operational staff'. Do you agree or disagree with this statement? Justify your opinion using examples.

C2 Examine why a business might prefer to use a CV rather than an application form when recruiting. Explain your thinking in your answer.

C3 Choose a large business that operates in your local area. Create a leaflet for this business's human resources (HR) department explaining the benefits and drawbacks of internal and external recruitment methods.

Effective training and development

Case study

Christie Intruder Alarms (CIA)

CIA is a family-run security business based in southern England. The business designs, installs and maintains security systems, such as burglar alarms, CCTV and fire alarms. CIA employs more than 200 employees in Hampshire. The business is committed to training and developing its staff. For example, 85 per cent of its senior management team started their careers with CIA as junior employees, showing how training and development can help employees to achieve their full potential.

Activity

1 In a small group, produce a poster to encourage businesses to train and develop their employees. Include a mind map of the different methods businesses could use to train and develop their employees.

2 If you have a part-time job or have done any work experience or volunteering, think about the methods that were used with you to train you and develop your skills.

It is important for a business to recruit the right employees, but businesses also have to make sure that those employees are trained and developed. This will ensure that they can work as well and as efficiently as possible, and it will make staff feel valued because the business is investing in them and their knowledge and skills. Training and development will also mean that employees are more likely to be able to continue carrying out their roles effectively when the needs of the business change or when technology is updated.

How businesses train and develop employees

There are lots of different methods that can be used to train and develop employees. These methods can be grouped into two different categories: formal training and informal training.

Formal and informal training

Formal training is structured training, such as taking a course or gaining a qualification. For example, an employee could be required to complete an apprenticeship or qualification as part of their training, such as a proofreading qualification for a secretary. Some other examples are shown in Figure 2.5.5.

Figure 2.5.5 Formal training methods

Informal training is less structured or is delivered by a colleague and takes place as and when required. For example, a new employee could watch another employee complete a particular task or have a chat with a colleague about how to carry out a role in their workplace. Some other examples are shown in Figure 2.5.6.

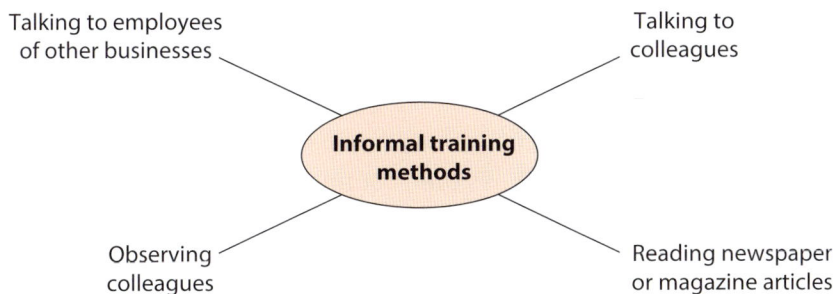

Figure 2.5.6 Informal training methods

Formal and informal learning may take place because an employee is told that they must do some training. For example, an employee may have to complete health and safety training before they can start doing their job.

Alternatively, training and development can happen because the employee chooses to do some formal or informal learning by themselves. For example, a team leader in a retail store may choose to take a management qualification to improve the way in which they manage the employees in their store.

Self-learning

If a person teaches themselves something without being supervised by a teacher or tutor, this is known as self-learning. They may do this by reading, watching videos or doing research to answer any questions they have about their role or responsibilities.

Businesses can encourage self-learning to ensure that employees increase their skills and gain additional knowledge. This can be useful for the business, as it means that its employees are more knowledgeable, but it is also useful for the employee because those skills could help them to get another job in the future. Self-learning does not have to mean learning alone. For example, a group of employees could get together to set up a self-learning group, and use this to help each other to learn.

Activity ?

Think about a time when you tried to teach yourself something and answer the following questions.

1 What did you find difficult about self-learning?
2 What did you find easy about self-learning?
3 Produce a table showing what you found easy and what you found difficult, then compare your answers with someone else in your class.
4 What do you think are the advantages and disadvantages to businesses of encouraging employees to self-learn?

Exam tip

A good answer will include only one disadvantage but will give two points explaining why this is a disadvantage.

Exam-style question

Explain **one** disadvantage to a business of asking employees to undertake self-learning in order to improve their skills in the workplace. **(3 marks)**

Ongoing training

Employees often have to be trained when they first take on a role. Ongoing training is training that employees then continue to do throughout their time in that role. It is very important for all employees to do some ongoing training, as it ensures that everyone stays up to date and is able to contribute to the success of the business. If employees are trained to understand what they have to do to fulfil their roles and to do their jobs well and efficiently, the business is likely to have higher levels of **productivity**.

Key term

Productivity: the measurement of how much work a business is able to complete. Higher levels of productivity mean that employees are completing more work.

Target setting and performance reviews

In order to make the most of ongoing training and development, employees should have targets to aim for and should have their progress and performance reviewed regularly. Often, employees set targets for themselves with input from their manager. For example, an employee may identify a number of skills that they would like to gain or improve, and their manager will help them to decide which of those skills are most important for them in their role and what training they should do.

Performance reviews are meetings that managers have with employees to discuss the employee's performance in their role, the progress that they have made in developing their skills and knowledge, and any training that they have completed. In many businesses, performance reviews take place once a year.

Ongoing training is usually linked to employees' targets and performance reviews, because training should improve employees' performance and productivity. For example, an employee may undertake training to improve the quality of the work that they do or the service that they offer to a customer, or they may undertake training in order to learn how to do work that they were not able to do before. Setting employees' targets to include training also means that employees are more likely to make sure that they complete the training before their next review, particularly if their targets are linked to their pay or benefits.

Reasons why businesses train and develop employees

There are many reasons why businesses decide to train and develop their employees. One of the main legal reasons is to obey **legislation**. Some other reasons are shown in Figure 2.5.7.

Figure 2.5.7 Reasons for a business to train and develop its employees

In particular, businesses will use training and development to **motivate** their employees and to ensure that their employees can use any new technology that has been introduced.

Link it up

You learned about the impact of legislation on businesses in Topic 1.5 *Understanding external influences on business*. You will learn more about motivation in the section 'Motivation' later in this topic.

Did you know?

Ongoing training does not just apply to businesses. It also applies to other organisations, such as charities. For example, Scout leaders and volunteers have to undertake ongoing safety training to ensure that the young people they work with are kept safe.

Activity ?

Alone or in pairs, think about targets that you have been set during your time at school. These could be exams, or they could be personal targets such as improving your knowledge of or skills in a particular subject.

1 Which targets do you think you achieved successfully?

2 Have there been any targets that you have been unable to achieve?

3 When do you know if you have been successful in achieving a target?

4 How do you think employee training targets could be used to improve the performance of a business?

Key terms

Legislation: the laws that a country must comply with.

Motivation: reasons for behaving in a particular way. In business, motivation usually refers to the reasons that an employee has for working well and increasing their productivity.

Theme 2: Building the business

Training, motivation and retention

As you have already learned, ongoing training often makes employees feel valued, as the business they work for is willing to invest in their development. This means that they are more likely to be happy in their work, more interested in contributing to the business and its success and more willing to work hard in order to progress in their career.

This means that training can be used to motivate employees to work hard and stay with the company. If employees are happy and feel that their employer cares for them, they are more likely to want to keep working for that business or be **retained**.

A business may look at its employee retention rate to see how well it is doing at motivating its employees. To calculate the retention rate, a business works out how many employees have left in a specified amount of time (for example, a year). It then works out the number of employees who have continued to work for the business in that same period of time as a percentage of the whole. This percentage is the retention rate:

$$\text{retention rate} = \frac{\text{number of employees who continued to be employed during specified time period}}{\text{total number of employees}} \times 100$$

If 95 per cent of employees have been retained in a year, this is a good sign because most employees have chosen to stay with the business. If 20 per cent of employees have been retained in a year, this is likely to be a bad sign because it means that 80 per cent of employees have chosen to leave the business in that year.

The type of business and the industry in which it operates will have an impact on employee retention. For example, a theme park that uses seasonal staff on temporary contracts (such as students or teenagers who work during their holidays) is likely to have a much lower retention rate than a business that only hires full-time staff.

> **Key term**
>
> **Retain:** keep something or someone.

> **Maths tip**
>
> Remember that per cent means per 100. The retention rate shows you how many employees in 100 employees continued to work for the business.

> **Activity**   **?**
>
> 1 In pairs, discuss which of the following businesses are likely to have the highest and lowest employee retention rates and rank them from highest to lowest:
>
>   **a** a fast-food restaurant
>
>   **b** a school or college
>
>   **c** a bank
>
>   **d** a supermarket.
>
> 2 Share your ranked list with the rest of your class. Did you all agree? If you disagree with another group's decision, what are your reasons for disagreeing?
>
> 3 If 5 out of 125 employees leave a business in a given year, what is that business's employee retention rate?

Retraining to use new technology

Continual advances in technology is another reason why businesses continue to train and develop their staff. As new technology emerges and starts to be used by businesses, staff need to be trained in how to use new technology or retrained to use a system or device that now has new functions.

Keeping employees' technological knowledge up to date means that a business can adopt the latest technology without having to put its employees through too much training all at once. It also means that the business is up to date and is therefore likely to be more efficient and provide its customers with the best service possible.

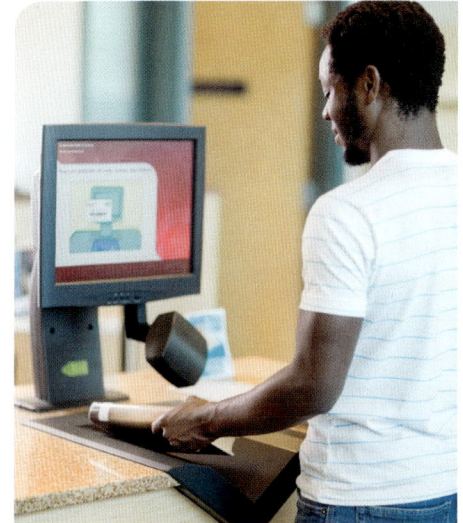

Keeping up to date with technology is very important in order to make sure that employees offer the best possible service and productivity levels

Did you know?

The first apps for smartphones were only created after the launch of the iPhone in 2007 and the introduction of Apple's App Store in 2008. Since then, the number of apps available has increased enormously and continues to grow.

Exam-style question

Explain **one** reason why a business should train and develop its employees. **(3 marks)**

Exam tip

Include one reason, but remember to give and explain two points about this reason. Giving more reasons will not get you any additional marks.

Checkpoint

Now it is time to review your understanding of effective training and development.

Strengthen

S1 List three different formal methods of training that can be used by a business.

S2 Why might an employee choose to self-learn?

S3 Describe one reason why a business would choose to train and develop its employees.

Challenge

C1 Describe the benefits to an employer and to an employee of regular performance reviews.

C2 Consider the following statement: 'training always leads to increased employee motivation'. Do you agree or disagree? Give reasons for your opinion.

C3 If a business sees that its sales and revenue are decreasing, it might want to reduce its costs. What do you think might be the disadvantages to a business of cutting the amount of money spent on training and developing its employees?

Theme 2: Building the business

Motivation

Case study

Archant

Archant is a newspaper, magazine and media business. The business is committed to investing in its employees' development, in particular running the Archant Sales Academy to train and develop its sales staff. Archant encourages employees to stay with them for a long time by offering a long-service award. In reviews, employees say that they are happy and enjoy working as part of the business.

Activity

1 Identify the different ways in which Archant tries to motivate its employees.

2 Choose a company that operates in your area and do some research to find out how it motivates its employees. Does it offer higher levels of money or other benefits? What makes people want to work there?

3 Compare your findings with Archant. What do the two companies have in common? What are their differences? Where would you prefer to work?

Employee motivation refers to an employee's reasons to work hard for their employer. Businesses can try to increase employees' motivation to encourage them to work harder.

Different forms of motivation work on different people. For example, some employees will work harder if they are rewarded by being paid more money, whereas other employees are motivated by the satisfaction of doing a good job, by feeling valued by their employer or by being part of a supportive and productive team.

Exam tip

When you are asked to define a term, you just have to give a sentence about what the term means. You do not have to give a detailed explanation.

Exam-style question

Define the term 'motivation'. **(1 mark)**

Importance of motivation in the workplace

It is very important for businesses to consider how they motivate their employees at work. Highly motivated employees are more likely to be happy at work and work harder for their employer. Some of the benefits of having highly motivated employees are:

- employee attendance at work is higher because employee absence due to illness or stress is reduced

- the reputation of the business improves because employees will be proud of the business and will tell other people about it

- employees' productivity and work output during the working day is higher, so costs are lower because the business needs to pay less overtime

- employees stay at the business a long time, avoiding the cost of having to recruit a lot of new employees
- there are more ideas for improving the business, because employees feel valued and want to contribute to the business and so will make suggestions to improve the business and its products or services
- employees communicate better with each other and complete their tasks efficiently because they all want the business to succeed.

These benefits will make a business more efficient, meaning that it is likely to make higher profits than less efficient competitors. In this way, employee motivation can have a huge impact on the performance of a business. For example, if attendance is low because motivation is low and employees feel stressed, the business's costs will increase because they have to pay other staff to cover the extra work through overtime, as well as paying sick pay to the absent employees.

Highly motivated employees are very good spokespeople for their employer. They are more likely to tell their friends and acquaintances about their job or about the products and services that the business offers. This will improve or maintain the business's reputation, meaning that other people will hear about that business and want to buy from it or work for it. If a business can attract a lot of potential employees when it is recruiting because of its reputation, it will have a broader range of candidates to choose from and is more likely to find the best people for the job.

On the other hand, if an employer has a bad reputation, people may not want to work for it. This makes it more difficult for the business to retain employees and to recruit people to replace the employees who leave. Losing a lot of employees and having to recruit replacements also costs a lot of money, as it means that the business has to train a lot of new employees and may lose knowledge or skills when employees leave.

> ### Link it up
>
> You explored different aspects of costs and profits in Topic 1.3 *Putting a business idea into practice* and Topic 2.4 *Making financial decisions.*

> ### Did you know?
>
> A website called Glassdoor allows employees to post anonymous reviews of their employer. Applicants for a job vacancy at that business can use Glassdoor reviews to see whether the business's employees are motivated and decide whether they want to work there.

> ### Exam-style question
>
> Which **two** of the following may indicate low levels of employee motivation? **(2 marks)**
>
> Select **two** answers.
>
> - ☐ **A** High absence rates
> - ☐ **B** High productivity
> - ☐ **C** Employees leaving the business
> - ☐ **D** Good company reputation
> - ☐ **E** High levels of communication amongst managers and employees

> ### Exam tip
>
> Remember to read the instructions carefully. You should choose two answers in order to complete this question.

How businesses motivate employees

Different businesses have different ways of motivating employees, but methods of motivation generally fall into two groups: financial methods and non-financial methods.

Some employees are highly motivated by money whereas others are motivated by non-financial methods

Financial methods

Financial methods of motivation focus on giving employees more money, usually by increasing their salaries or by offering them payments for doing extra work. Many businesses use financial methods to motivate their employees, and some people believe that the best way, or the only way, to motivate employees is by offering them more money. However, not everyone agrees with this.

There are five key financial methods of motivation:

- remuneration
- bonuses
- commission
- promotion
- fringe benefits.

Remuneration

Remuneration means the money that is paid to an employee for working. If an employer wants to attract good employees and motivate them in the workplace, it needs to make sure that they are paying those employees enough money to satisfy them. Even employees who are not mainly motivated by money still need to be paid well enough to feel satisfied.

Employees could be remunerated with a wage (usually paid weekly) for the hours that they work. If these employees work any additional hours, they may receive overtime pay. Alternatively employees could be remunerated with a salary, which is a fixed monthly amount that is paid into their bank account. They may also be paid for any additional hours they work, but are more likely to be given time off in return for those hours instead of payment.

Activity ?

Do some research into the National Minimum Wage and the National Living Wage. How do you think they could affect motivation at work? Try to give examples of these wage rates in different types of employment or different businesses.

Bonuses and commission

In some industries or businesses, employees receive bonuses. A bonus is an additional amount of money paid to an employee if they achieve a target or high level of performance. Bonuses are common in industries such as banking or in businesses that are focused on sales, such as selling cars. For example, if a car salesperson sells a certain number of cars, they will receive a bonus of an amount of money on top of their wage or salary in return.

Commission works in a similar way to bonuses. Commission is an extra amount of money paid to an employee, usually if they make a certain number of sales. In some industries, such as finance, an employee is given an amount of money for each product or service that they sell.

Link it up

You explored different aspects of sales in Topic 2.3 *Making operational decisions.*

Did you know?

In 2013, a survey found that London bankers' bonuses had increased by more than 29 per cent. However, 41 per cent of the bankers surveyed thought that their bonus was not high enough.

The amount of commission earned by the employee may be a percentage. For example, they could be paid 10 per cent of the value of the service or product that they sell. Commission can also be paid as a set amount of money per sale. For example, a financial consultant could be paid £250 for every mortgage or insurance product that they sell to a customer.

Using bonuses and commission to motivate employees can result in higher levels of productivity and sales. The benefit is that the rewards are only paid if the business achieves those higher levels of performance, whereas an increased salary will be paid to an employee regardless of how well the employee or the business performs. If a business chooses to use these forms of motivation, they also need to make sure that employees understand clearly what they need to achieve in order to get their bonuses. This means that the system needs to be transparent and easily understood by everyone.

However, using these forms of motivation can encourage employees to put pressure on customers to achieve sales. This could have a negative impact on customers and result in unhappy customers, negative media coverage and a poor reputation. If a business chooses to use bonuses and commission to motivate employees, it must train them to operate ethically, rather than pressurising customers to buy a product that they do not need.

Promotion

A promotion is when an employee is given a more senior role in a business or organisation. A business can offer promotion as a financial method of motivation, because a promotion usually comes with an increased salary. As you learned in the section 'Operational structures', this is because a role at the next level within the business's structure is likely to come with increased responsibilities. If an employee wants to earn more money, they may aim to be promoted.

Fringe benefits

Fringe benefits are other benefits offered by a business that financially benefit employees. The benefits offered by an employer will vary depending on the industry. In some industries, employees may receive shares in the company. In other industries, employers may offer their employees:

- a company car
- meal vouchers for lunch
- free health insurance
- company contributions to their pension plan
- free travel or parking
- free gym membership
- corporate parties or entertainment, such as having a box at a football club
- accommodation
- free or subsidised childcare
- vouchers for shops or other services.

> **Activity**   **?**
>
> 1 In small groups, discuss the advantages of being paid on commission or being paid a bonus. Would you like to be paid in this way? Are there any disadvantages for the employee?
>
> 2 Create a mind map to summarise the points that you discussed.

Fringe benefits can be used to motivate employees at work

Employers can give their employees lots of different fringe benefits, but they need to be careful that these benefits do not result in the business or employee needing to pay additional tax. If they do lead to additional tax, the employer or employee must declare the amount of benefit that they have received to the government.

Link it up

You learned about taxation in the section 'The economy and business' in Topic 1.5 *Understanding external influences on business*.

Exam tip

Read the question and every answer carefully before making your choice, as the correct answer or answers may not be as obvious as you first think.

Exam-style question

Which **two** of the following are examples of fringe benefits for employees?   **(2 marks)**

Select **two** answers.

- [ ] **A**   Bonus
- [ ] **B**   Job rotation
- [ ] **C**   Promotion
- [ ] **D**   Free health insurance
- [ ] **E**   Gym membership

Non-financial methods

Businesses do not have to use money to motivate their employees. Some people believe that money can only satisfy employees in the short term and think that it is better to motivate employees in other non-financial ways. Many non-financial methods that a business can use to motivate staff focus on the employees' role and responsibilities:

- job rotation
- job enrichment
- **autonomy**.

Key term

Autonomy: independence or the freedom to make your own decisions.

The advantage of non-financial methods is that they can improve employee motivation and productivity levels but do not cost much, and may cost nothing, to implement unlike financial methods.

Job rotation

If an employee does the same job for a long time, day after day, it can become boring and they may lose motivation. Some businesses avoid this by implementing a job rotation scheme. This gives employees the chance to move around or 'rotate' within the business and do different jobs. As long as the job is at the same level as the employee's current role and can be performed without much additional training, an employee can do something different and increase their motivation. For example, an IT business may move its employees from one project to another, while in a factory an employee might move to a different stage in the production process.

The employee benefits from job rotation by doing something different and learning new skills, which may benefit them in the future if they seek a promotion or apply for a job with a different business. Job rotation also benefits the business because:

* employees learn how to do more than one job
* employees gain a better understanding of the work that happens in other parts of the business
* employees develop a network of contacts around the business, improving communication between different departments
* employees gain additional skills and knowledge about the business that can increase their productivity when they return to their previous role.

Job enrichment

Job enrichment is the process of adding more interesting elements to an employee's role in order to improve their motivation. This includes encouraging employees to take greater levels of responsibility for their work, increasing the type of activities that they complete and allowing them to influence and shape the role that they fulfil.

Roles can be enriched by:

* reducing or removing any negative elements, such as repetitive tasks or tasks that could be done differently
* giving employees the opportunity to develop additional skills
* giving employees additional responsibilities
* adding extra tasks to a role
* giving employees more flexibility to choose how they do a job
* giving more feedback to employees.

However, a business must not add too much additional responsibility to a role. This can overwhelm an employee, leading to stress and decreased motivation. It could also change the employee's role so much that their pay would have to increase in line with their extra duties or responsibilities, as an employee could be left feeling very demotivated if they feel they are doing too much work for the amount that they are paid.

Theme 2: Building the business

Exam-style question

Discuss the advantages to a business of motivating employees through job enrichment. **(6 marks)**

Autonomy

Autonomy is having the independence to make your own decisions. At work, this means allowing an employee to organise, control and influence their work and the way in which they complete their work. This can be used to motivate employees, as they will feel more in control of their work and be able to complete work without being checked constantly by a manager or supervisor. Autonomy can be offered to individual employees but can also be given to a team, which then starts to manage itself and its own workload.

Having employees that can work autonomously is a great benefit to a business, because it means that employees:

- are more motivated because they have greater **job satisfaction**
- take a greater interest in their own work and do it to a higher standard
- can set their own schedules and organise their own work, rather than needing a manager to do it for them
- suggest and make improvements to the way in which the business works and share their ideas with colleagues.

Happy, motivated and satisfied employees usually produce better work, so the business's customers get better products, services or customer service, and this then leads to higher levels of sales and profits.

If a business decides to give its employees more control over their work or ways of working, it is important that this is done gradually and carefully, in order to ensure that employees are still working effectively and doing the jobs that they need to do. It is particularly important that there is good communication between different groups of employees, as well as between employees and their managers.

Activity ?

You have been asked to produce a poster about non-financial methods of motivation for a local business. Your poster should show the differences between job rotation, job enrichment and increased autonomy and explain the benefits of each for the employer and the employee.

Checkpoint

Now it is time to review your understanding of motivation.

Strengthen

S1 Describe two reasons why a business needs to motivate its employees.

S2 Describe the difference between financial methods and non-financial methods of motivation, giving examples of each.

S3 List three ways in which an employee's role can be enriched.

Challenge

C1 Consider a marketing and advertising business that has low levels of employee retention. What would the impact of a low retention rate be? Identify three ways in which the business could improve its retention rate.

C2 Consider the following statement: 'job rotation always motivates employees more successfully than bonuses'. Do you agree or disagree with this statement? What are your reasons for your opinion?

2.5 Making human resource decisions

1 Which **two** of the following are typical features of a hierarchical organisational structure? Select **two** answers.

(2 marks)

☐ A Has many layers of management

☐ B Enables fast, efficient decision-making

☐ C May be described as flat

☐ D Managers have large numbers of employees to look after

☐ E Does not provide many promotion opportunities for employees

2 Explain **one** advantage to a business of using an application form when recruiting new staff.

(3 marks)

Student answer

The advantage to the business of using an application form is that all the information is given in the same way. This means that it is easy to compare different candidates for the job and makes the process of choosing which candidate is best easier for the business.

Verdict

This is a very good answer. It gives one chosen advantage, as asked (information being given in the same way). It then goes on to describe two points in detail about why it is best for the business (makes it easier to compare candidates and makes it easier to choose the best candidate).

3 Explain **one** disadvantage to a business of only using internal recruitment.

(3 marks)

Student answer

Internal recruitment is when a business only advertises to its employees and does not advertise outside of the business. The drawbacks of doing this are that the number of candidates could be small, that there may not be the right people and people may be unhappy with who is chosen.

Verdict

This answer is okay but could be improved. The student shows that they know what internal recruitment is and have given one drawback (the number of candidates could be small). However, they have not given enough detail about that one disadvantage but have listed some more disadvantages instead.

Read the following extract carefully, then answer Questions 4, 5 and 6.

> The Parravani family has been making ice cream in Norfolk and Suffolk since 1898. The family produces ice cream and sorbets in the small market a town of Beccles in Suffolk and has a range of more than 40 different flavours. Parravani's supplies ice cream to restaurants and local shops. It also continues to have its own ice cream vans that service local areas and go to events in East Anglia.
>
> In 2012, the family moved the factory as the business was expanding. The new premises started making sorbets, cakes and patisserie items and had offices for support staff to work from. Staff have a range of different roles including working in manufacturing, distribution, retail and support. They are employed on different contracts that include temporary contracts for the summer.

4   Define the term 'support staff as detailed in the case study.   (1 mark)

Student answer

Support staff are those staff that are not directly involved in the operations of the business, for example finance.

Verdict

This is a good answer. It gives a clear definition and includes an example.

5   Outline **one** advantage for Parravani's of having staff on temporary contracts.   (2 marks)

Student answer

Parravani's can employ staff only when they need them. For example, in the summer when ice cream sales are higher, they can employ staff to cover the higher level of sales.

Verdict

This is a very good answer. The student gives an advantage (staff only being employed when they are needed) and briefly explains the advantage by linking this to the fact that ice cream sales are higher in summer.

Parravani's is considering two options to increase the motivation of employees making the ice cream in the factory.

Option 1: Financial methods

Option 2: Non-financial methods

6   Justify which **one** of these two options Parravani's should choose.   (9 marks)

Student answer

Parravani's should choose financial methods because this means that staff would get more money. Giving them more money would mean that staff would be happier because they would have more money to spend on their families. If staff were given a bonus for how much ice cream they made, this would mean they would produce more ice cream to get more pay.

Verdict

This is not a very good answer and would not get many marks. The student shows that they understand financial methods by giving the answer of a bonus. They also show some limited understanding of motivation by mentioning 'being happy'. However, the student should be clearer about what is meant by 'motivation' and 'financial rewards' and they should focus more on the benefits for Parravani's, using the information in the extract where possible.

Index

Index

Acknowedgements

Edexcel GCSE (9-1) Business

The publisher would like to thank the following for their kind permission to reproduce their photographs:

(Key: b-bottom; c-centre; l-left; r-right; t-top)

123RF.com: Andrey Tirahov 74br, wavebreakmediamicro 215tr; **Alamy Stock Photo:** Actionstock 168br, Agnieszka Olek / caia image 151tl, Ammentorp Photography 19, AndySmyStock 48cr, Chris Putnam 3tl, Clynt Garnham Food & Drink 161cl, Cultura RM 39bl, Doug Houghton Images 243cl, Francesca Moore 14br, Frederick Kippe 254, GARY DOAK 282tl, Huntstock / Disability Images 131tr, Janine Wiedel Photolibrary 116tr, Mark Richardson 174, Mark Sinclair 70tl, Martin Plöb / INSADCO Photography 66c, Michael Rosenfeld / Maximilian S / RGB Ventures / SuperStock 206, , Newscast Online 153c, PhotoEdit 159tc, Radius Images 2/ , Steve Vidler 218br, TAR-TASS Photo Agency 193bl, Westmacott 265cl, Xinhua 191cl; **Bake Me Happy:** 65c; **Childbase Partnership:** 21cl; **Courtesy of the Ford Motor Company:** 181tl; **FareShare:** 118br; **Fotolia.com:** DURIS Guillaume 207tr, georgejmclittle 8tr, 38tr, jandruk 110, Liv Friis-larsen 200tc, Maridav 196tc, Monkey Business 46br, 60, 230tl, 260tr, NorGal 142br, pikselstock 34tr, svetavo / Fotolia 178br, Tyler Olson 279tr, UBER Images 234, Zsolt Biczó 178bc; **Getty Images:** Astrid Stawiarz 7tl, Christopher Jue 165tr, Wundervisuals / E+ 124tr; **innocent drinks:** 190t; **Jaguar Land Rover Limited:** 187bl; **Joe & Sephs:** 101tr; **JustPark:** 30tr; **Mo Bros Grooming Co:** 90cr; **Pearson Education Ltd:** Clark Wiseman / Studio 8 226bl; **Premier Inn:** 235tr; **Rex Shutterstock:** Albanpix 256tr, Photofusion 73tl; **Shutterstock.com:** Arthimedes 45cl, asharkyu 212br, bibiphoto 211bl, bloomua 103bl, Candybox Images 284tr, chuyuss 148, Dmitry Chumich 98tl, dotshock 128br, Gajus 105br, Jacob Lund 182c, LDProd 122br, michaeljung 132bl, Monkey Business Images 91cl, 224tr, Nicholas Jackson 6cl, Nick Starichenko 88, scyther5 164tr, Sorbis 94cr, 255tr, Thitisan 144bl, Uber Images 77cl, Vitaly Titov & Maria Sidelnikova 62tl; **Snowdonia Cheese Company:** 175cr; **Solent News and Photo Agency:** Brighton Argus 6tr; **Toucan Wholefoods:** 61tl; **Tyrrells:** 157bl; **Whisk. com:** 29tl; **York Cocoa House:** 89tl, 89cr

Cover images: *Front:* **Alamy Stock Photo:** Ammentorp Photography, JOHN KELLERMAN; **Getty Images:** andresr, Andy Smith, Carlina Teteris, Hero Images, Michael Blann, Plume Creative, Squaredpixels; **Shutterstock.com:** alphaspirit, blvdone, ESB Essentials, Eugene Partyzan, mavo, Savanevich Viktar, Uber Images

All other images © Pearson Education

We are grateful to the following for permission to reproduce copyright material:

Figures

Figure 2.4.5 adapted from 'Net cash flow of Investments A and B' by Marty Schmidt, https://www.business-case-analysis.com, copyright © 2004-2017 Solution Matrix Ltd. Used by permission; Figure 2.4.9 adapted from the exam paper *Edexcel GCSE Business Studies, Business Communications, Business Studies and Economics. Unit 1 Introduction to Small Business. 5BS01/01,* 21 May 2014, p.3, https://revisionworld.com/gcse-revision/business-studies/business-studies-gcse-past-papers/edexcel-gcse-business-studies-past-papers, copyright © Edexcel; Figure 2.4.10 adapted from 'The 2015 market share of each leading car manufacturer in the UK from '2.6 million record UK sales' by Rob Gill, *Sun Motors,* 07/01/2016, copyright © News Syndication, 2016; Figure 2.4.13 from 'Average weekly earnings growth rate (total pay)' in *Labour Market Statistics time series dataset (LMS),* Table 3, October 2016, Office of National Statistics, https://www.ons. gov.uk/employmentandlabourmarket/peopleinwork/earningsandworkinghours/ timeseries/kac3/lms © Crown copyright 2016, licensed under the Open Government Licence v.3.0; and Figure 2.4.14 text from 'Tesco posts 28.3 per cent profits slump' by Zlata Rodionova, *The Independent,* 05/10/2016, copyright © The Independent, 2016, www.independent.co.uk.

Logo Marks

The Kitemark on page 25. KITEMARK and the BSI Kitemark device are reproduced with kind permission of The British Standards Institution. They are registered trademarks in the United Kingdom and in certain other countries; The CE Mark on page 225. The Regulation (EC) No 765/2008 of the European Parliament and of the Council of 9 July 2008 setting out the requirements for accreditation and market surveillance relating to the marketing of products and repealing Regulation (EEC) No 339/93; and Logo on page 225 from Investors in People, http://www. investorsinpeople.com. Reproduced with permission.

Tables

Table 1.1.1 after 'Estimated number of businesses in the UK private sector, start of 2000 to start of 2015' and 'Estimated number of businesses in the UK private sector and their associated employment and turnover, by size of business, start of 2015' in *Business Population Estimates for the UK and Regions 2015,* Tables A and B, pp.3, 15, October 2015, Department for Business, Innovation & Skills, https:// www.gov.uk/government/statistics/business-population-estimates-2015; Table 1.5.8 showing data from 'CPI: Consumer Prices Index' February 2017, https:// www.ons.gov.uk/economy/inflationandpriceindices/timeseries/d7g7/mm23, Office for National Statistics, and Table 2.4.12 from 'Age distribution of the UK population, 1974 to 2039 (projected)' in *Overview of the UK population: February 2016,* Table 3, February 2016, Office of National Statistics, http://www.ons.gov.uk/

peoplepopulationandcommunity/populationandmigration/populationestimates/ articles/overviewoftheukpopulation/february2016, © Crown copyright 2015, 2016, 2017, licensed under the Open Government Licence v3.0; and Table 2.2.1 'Share of ad spend by media type 2015' in *Advertising Forecast 2010-2021,* Strategy Analytics, https://www.strategyanalytics.com. Reproduced with permission.

Text

Case Study on page 9 from Friska, www.friskafood.com. Reproduced with permission of Griff Holland and Ed Brown, co-founders; Case Study on page 13 from 'Risk, Reward And Worst Case Scenarios: How Entrepreneurs Like Richard Branson And Tony Hsieh Call It' by Linda Cheung, http://www.forbes.com/ sites/alisoncoleman/2014/05/11/risk-reward-and-worst-case-scenarios-how-entrepreneurs-like-richard-branson-and-tony-hsieh-call-it/2/#3ffbb5f910e8, 11/05/2014. Reproduced with kind permission from the author; Extract on page 21 from The Childbase Partnership, http://www.childbasepartnership.com. Reproduced with permission; Case Study on page 26 adapted from Cultivate, http://www.cultivate.uk.com. Reproduced with permission; Case Study on page 29 about Nick Holzherr, Whisk, adapted from www.whisk.com. Reproduced with permission, nickholzherr.com; Case Study on page 30 adapted from JustPark Parking Ltd, www.justpark.com. Reproduced with permission; Case Study on page 61 adapted from Sally Eveleigh, Toucan Wholefoods & Café, http://www. toucanwholefoods.co.uk. Reproduced with permission; Case Study on page 62 adapted from Pompy's Cycles, http://www.pompyscycles.co.uk. Reproduced with permission; Case Study on page 65 adapted from Bake-Me-Happy, http://www. bakemehappy.co.uk. Reproduced by permission of Carly Roberts; Case Study on page 81 adapted from Ogborne Electrical Engineers, www.marineelectrics. net. Reproduced with permission of Marcus Ogborne; Case Study on page 89 adapted from York Cocoa House, www.yorkcocoahouse.co.uk. Reproduced with permission of Sophie Jewett; Case Study on page 90 adapted from Mo Bros Grooming Co., www.mobros.co.uk. Reproduced with permission; Extract on page 95 adapted from 'Become an entrepreneur with your own Coffee-Bike mobile coffee franchise', http://www.franchisedirect.co.uk/coffeefranchises/coffee-bike-franchise-11752/. Reproduced with permission from Coffee-Bike and Franchise Direct; Extract on page 100 adapted from 'UK online retail sales to reach £62.7bn in 2020 ' by Kate Ormrod, 17/09/2015, http://www.verdictretail.com, copyright © Verdict Retail, a trading name of Progressive Digital Media Ltd; Case Study on page 101 adapted from Joe&Seph's, www.joeandseph.co.uk. Reproduced with permission of Joe's Gourmet Foods; Case Study on page 104 adapted from TyresOnTheDrive.com, https://www.tyresonthedrive.com. Reproduced with permission; Case Study on page 105 adapted from Chez Liz Bar & Grill, Cornwall, Ontario, https://www.facebook.com/Chez-Liz-1113433632013827. Reproduced with permission; Case Study on page 118 adapted from Fareshare, www.fareshare. org.uk. Reproduced with permission; Extract on page 128 from 'Consumer Rights Act 2015', http://www.legislation.gov.uk/ukpga/2015/15/contents/enacted, and Extract on page 135 from *UK Labour Market: July 2016,* https://www.ons.gov.uk/ employmentandlabourmarket/peopleinwork/employmentandemployeetypes/ bulletins/uklabourmarket/july2016, July 2016, Office for National Statistics, © Crown copyright, licensed under the Open Government Licence v.3.0; Extract on page 149 from Co-op Food, www.co-operativefood.co.uk. Reproduced with permission; Case Study on page 157 adapted from Tyrells Crisps, https://www. tyrellscrisps.co.uk. Reproduced with permission; Extract on page 160 from *UK Overseas Trade Statistics June 2016,* https://www.gov.uk, 2016, Office for National Statistics, © Crown copyright, licensed under the Open Government Licence v.3.0; Case Study on page 175 adapted from Snowdonia Cheese Company Ltd, http:// www.snowdoniacheese.co.uk. Reproduced with permission; Case Study on page 176 adapted from Big Bobble Hats Ltd, http://www.bigbobblehats.co.uk. Reproduced with permission; Extract on page 188 from *Advertising Forecast 2010-2021,* Strategy Analytics, https://www.strategyanalytics.com. Reproduced with permission; Extract on page 189 from Barclaycard® 'Glide with Us'® 2008 TV advertisement. Reproduced with permission of Barclays Bank PLC; Case Study on page 207 from PhotoBox Ltd, www.photobox.com. Reproduced with permission; Extract on page 240 from 'The most profitable industries in The U.S.' ending 27/08/15, http:// www.forbes.com/sites/sageworks/2015/09/06/these-industries-generate-the-highest-profit-margins/#4fdc835964ac, copyright © Sageworks. Reproduced with permission; Extract on page 261 from 'The social economy: Unlocking value and productivity through social technologies' by Michael Chui, James Manyika, Jacques Bughin, Richard Dobbs, Charles Roxburgh, Hugo Sarrazin, Geoffrey Sands and Magdalena Westergren, *McKinsey Global Institute,* July 2012, http://www.mckinsey. com/industries/high-tech/our-insights/the-social-economy. Reproduced with permission; Extract on page 264 from 'Remote and Overseas Working', http:// www.cpni.gov.uk/advice/personnel-security1/remote-working/, Centre for the Protection of National Infrastructure © Crown copyright 2017; and Extract on page 267 from *The Female FTSE Board Report 2014: Crossing the Finish Line* by Professor Susan Vinnicombe OBE, Dr Elena Doldor, and Caroline Turner, Cranfield International Centre for Women Leaders, Cranfield School of Management, 2014, http://www.som.cranfield.ac.uk/som/dinamic-content/research/ftse/The%20 Female%20FTSE%20Board%20Report%202014.pdf. Reproduced with permission of the authors.